True Detection

TRUE DETECTION

Edited by Edia Connole, Paul J. Ennis, and Nicola Masciandaro

TRUE DETECTION

schismmsihcs.wordpress.com

ISBN-13: 978-0692277379
ISBN-10: 0692277374

Cover design by Caoimhe Doyle and Kathy Tynan.
Interior images by Kathy Tynan.

CONTENTS

IV. *It's Just One Story*

V. *And Closure–No, No, No*

NB: Throughout this volume, the abbreviation 'TD,' followed by numerals indicating season and episode, respectively, is used to refer to *True Detective*, written by Nic Pizzolatto and directed by Cary Joji Fukunaga (HBO, 2014):

TD, 1:1 - THE LONG BRIGHT DARK

TD, 1:2 - SEEING THINGS

TD, 1:3 - THE LOCKED ROOM

TD, 1:4 - WHO GOES THERE

TD, 1:5 - THE SECRET LIFE OF ALL FATE

TD, 1:6 - HAUNTED HOUSE

TD, 1:7 - AFTER YOU'VE GONE

TD, 1:8 - FORM AND VOID

Monster at the End: Pessimism's Locked Rooms and Impossible Crimes

Gary J. Shipley

> To realize that all your life, all your love, all your hate all your memory, all your pain, it was all the same thing. It was all the same dream. A dream that you had inside a locked room.
>
> – TD, 1:3[1]

Introduction

Anything can possess novelty for a short time, even the man who arrives to tell you there is none; but the trick is to stay when the novelty has worn out, or to never see it in the first place; the trick is to be in the locked room without being there, to be both alive and dead, to wonder how you got there while knowing there's nowhere else, that the locked room is the human world, and that any solution to your predicament can only disappoint: 'Faced with the insoluble, I breathe at last.'[2] At the adverse point of no return, there is only an empty detection: logic thrown into the abyss and spewed up intact, the mind broken up inside the impossible. If lassitude is allowed to prevail, it soon becomes its own motivation, and there is no longer anything outside it, and the locks are an irrelevance, for the occupant is now too weary to reach the door.

---

[1] This essay was previously published online by *Bright Lights Film Journal*, http://brightlightsfilm.com/monster-end-pessimisms-locked-rooms-impossible-crimes-true-detective/.

[2] E. M. Cioran, *The Trouble With Being Born*, trans. Richard Howard (New York: Arcade Publishing, 1998), 85.

The pessimist knows how every life is acted, knows the erased space behind their lives. He has acted to return, to forget he's acting, to disappear. And he disappears in a room: where he's the murder and the murderee, where his status, though inexplicable from without, is morbidly certain from within. Possible solutions to any locked-room mystery come under ten general headings,[3] all at work in *True Detective*, and all of them are self-defeating and ultimately defy the power of detection to arrive at a satisfactory conclusion. The end has already happened, and all Rustin Cohle and Marty Hart can do is arrange the bodies in a pattern that makes them look less like bodies, more like things that might have existed in bodies, if those bodies hadn't been born human.

1. ACCIDENT

> *Certain coincidences (orchestrated or otherwise) accumulate to induce a death that appears to imply a second agency in the room: Detection relies on there being cogent human reasons behind a crime. Pessimism spurns this methodology.*

The pessimist's arguments (or rather, his declarations, or rather, his suspirations) are regurgitations of sensation, and as such they are always imperfect replicas: they are the detective's hunch that always refuses to become mere words. Like the anxiety detection seeks to overcome, each of its disenchanted murmurs 'tries to find a justification for itself, and in order to do so seizes upon anything, the vilest pretexts, to which it clings once it has invented them.'[4] The accident cannot be allowed to exist: an unarticulated mantra underpinning the human world we made but cannot solve, to which pessimism is the solution, the solution to the accident, by its simply letting it be.

---

3 Though John Dickson Carr lists seven, with five sub-categories, in *The Three Coffins* (New York: Charter Books, 1935), 160-173, and Robert Adey lists a full twenty in *Locked-Room Murders* (Minneapolis: Crossover Press, 1991), 275, the ten I have chosen cover all possible solutions, if with less specificity in places.

4 Cioran, *Trouble With Being Born*, 84.

Pessimism like depression attends to the details, an attention grown so assiduous that it becomes itself a variety of pain. And again and again Hart remarks on Cohle's myopia, his blinders, his tunnel vision, but this ridiculed focus is Cohle's only retreat from the whole that would otherwise consume him. Without the blinders on he wouldn't move. He talks the grand non-scheme but needs to exist in the minutiae, in the possibility of a solution, even while accepting that the entire edifice of argumentation is little more than a comfort blanket, a groundless distraction. And he does this because suffering only comes from outside the focus, and he can't make it mean anything outside of itself, so he must remain inside it, in the locked room, but looking in as if from outside.

It is no coincidence, then, that Cohle and Hart's investigations mirror the chorology of the bayou, leading them back to the shallow, slow moving, boggy, ill-defined morass from where they started, to a place where it is hard to discern where the bodies of water start and end, the shoreline always penumbral, always contingent, always shifting. Although, it's not until the last episode that Cohle acknowledges the sunless and corrosive drag of the fact of things just happening: 'I could feel my definitions fading. And beneath that darkness there's another kind, and it was deeper, warm, like a substance.'[5]

Only a deeply shameful and ugly world would demand such intense levels of blindness of its inhabitants, would have clarity seek a cure, and would have that cure itself look like a process of clarification, while taking us further away from the initial revelation – only such a world would bother to guard itself so complexly. And Hart warns Cohle early on about what he sees as Cohle's tendency to bend narrative to support evidence, and how he prejudices himself this way. We're told how Cohle was nicknamed 'The Taxman'[6] on account of his ledger, and taxmen

---

[5] TD, 1:8.

[6] In Robert William Chambers' 'The Repairer of Reputations' (the first of four stories to deal with the greater or lesser side-effects of the mysteriously deranging play 'The King in Yellow,' which figures significantly in Season 1 of Pizzalatto's *True Detective*), Mr. Wilde also keeps a ledger, containing the names and debts of those whose reputations he has salvaged. In it the debts of ruined men and women are tallied and their repayments listed, and those reparations bring huge

make things add up, but it is Hart and not Cohle that realizes[7] that it's important to allow for the possibility that maybe it's just an aggregation of numbers, and that the design you seek is taking you away from the only thing worth seeing, the only thing praying naked that you see it, or naked enough to be seen. (And maybe this exercise in extrapolation you are reading is itself a contortion of narrative, leading me away from the unashamed and deliberate banality that is *True Detective*.)

When Hart is reunited with Beth, the under-aged prostitute he advised to seek a new life years earlier, she tells him that 'the universe forgives all.'[8] And they both laugh, not because they don't believe it, but because they feel themselves coming apart under its gaze, feel their own lightness once the grime of their existence has been expunged. Forgiveness accepts the sin and redeems the agent behind it, separating the two, pulling them apart. The forgiver performs an illusion, a trick: for in annihilating the sin it leaves nothing behind, the nothing we've chosen to inhabit. There is no such thing as forgiveness, there is only destruction and the illusion that, because it is nothing, remains intact. Analyzing the sigh just takes you further away from the contingency of it, not the contingency of the sigh itself, for it is integral to human life, but the contingency of the being from which it issues, the accident that you forget to become.

---

profits to Wilde, but ultimately they are profits that never get spent, because the order he reinstates is contrived outside his own workings and he is left with nothing. See Robert W. Chambers, *The King in Yellow* (Hertfordshire: Wordsworth Editions, 2010), 3-31.

[7] TD, 1:1.

[8] TD, 1:6.

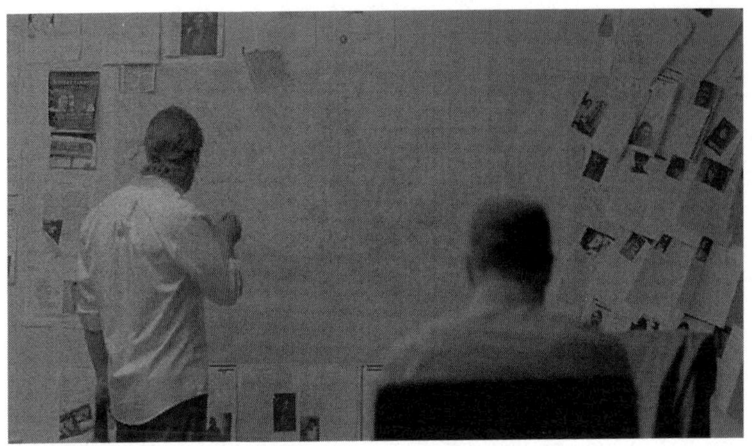

2. SUICIDE

> *What looks like murder is actually suicide: The agent of death is at all times within the room, the outside ineffectual. However, pessimism often distorts this solution by formulating an impossible crime not from the event of suicide, but from a suicide's nonoccurrence. The murder weapon flies up the chimney. The icicle melts. But these things happen before they are ever used. The dead keep themselves alive while seemingly lacking the means to do so.*

'Dying is a superiority few seek out,'[9] so although Cohle advocates us 'denying our programming' and 'opting out of a raw deal,' it comes with the defeatist caveat that he is not in a position to act on this judgment: 'I lack the constitution for suicide.'[10] This blatantly cognitivist and externalist[11] appraisal of his own ethical motivation makes his approbation for the escape

---

9 E. M. Cioran, *Drawn and Quartered*, trans. Richard Howard (New York: Arcade Publishing, 2012), 115.
10 TD, 1:1.
11 Schopenhauer, by way of contrast, believed that if something is truly willed it is necessarily done.

of suicide every bit *de dicto*, and with it 'fetishistic,'[12] attracted as it is by the reasons and not the thing itself. That he fails to act on these judgments allows the world outside the room back in, as he passively submits to its contingency. The problem, as we know, with externalist accounts of motivation, is the doubt they inevitably throw on the attendant judgments that remain impotent; and so we are forced to question the legitimacy of Cohle's judgments regarding suicide (and purveyors of pessimism that endure in general), judgments that look increasingly hollow as he throws himself into life off the back of them. The pessimist would seem to presage his own certain death-by-suicide, and yet he often, like Cohle, continues to live. His, then, is not the impossible murder, but the improbable circumvention of committing murder on himself. The incredulity lies not in how he was killed in an hermetically sealed chamber, but how he continues to survive in there, how the world gets in, for he does so by allowing the outside to dictate the potency of his beliefs. 'Then why . . . denigrate? Because to exist is to evaluate, to emit judgments, and because abstention, when it is not the effect of apathy or cowardice, requires an effort no one manages to make.'[13] If the room could act it would have the pessimist kill himself, putting all external motivations at the mercy of its foul flavoured interior.

But what does it mean to be a pessimist that persists? Cohle obviously views it not as reflecting some inner strength or nobility of character, but rather some inescapable weakness, a flaw in his makeup. However, it is problematical how this fits with the pessimist's account of life as an endurance test, especially the life of the pessimist, who must without the armour of his illusions feel every blow. It is weakness because though he claims to know death when he can't, his fear of this known yet unknown end outweighs the painful drudgery of staying where he is, and so he fears a 'death, which is more feared than any suffering.'[14] He's been institutionalized by life, attached to the person he's become, a person that despite the fact that such

---

[12] See Michael Smith's *The Moral Problem* (Oxford: Blackwell Publishers, 1994).

[13] Cioran, *Trouble With Being Born*, 51.

[14] Arthur Schopenhauer, *The World as Will and Representation*, trans. E. F. J. Payne, 2 vols. (New York: Dover Publications, 1969), II: 636.

abstractions are impervious to destruction he still fears nature would eradicate in death: 'In any case, the "denial" of death is given in the original complex, not only as it relates to the horror of annihilation, but insofar as it restores us to the power of nature, of which the universal ferment of life is the *repulsive* sign.'[15] In the Robert William Chambers story 'The Repairer of Reputations,'[16] suicide has recently been legalized and 'lethal chambers' have been installed in the streets of the city and elsewhere for the relief of those who wish to end their lives. But we are told that suicide rates do not increase as a result and that those sealed chambers remain largely unvisited, pedestrians looking on them as they do on death itself: the outsides of a void they do not imagine themselves seeing.

When Cohle interviews Charmaine,[17] a woman suspected of having murdered her infant children, he debunks the notion that the deaths were some aspect of their internal programming (the result of SIDS), and proceeds to elicit a full confession from the mother, the outside agency of her children's deaths. Munchausen's by proxy is the name of the condition he consoles her with, the affliction that allows him to assimilate some kind of motivational empathy with her. With the interview over, he warns her that her life in prison is likely to be one of unabated torment, ending with the words: 'If you get the opportunity, you should kill yourself.' Here Cohle is talking to himself, and it's him that wants her as his suicide by proxy. Although suicide on such a small scale could never achieve what a true pessimist suicide would seem to want to effect, as for 'the suicide, to be effectual, [it] must be that of the cosmos.'[18]

---

[15] Georges Bataille, *The Bataille Reader*, eds. Fred Botting & Scott Wilson (Oxford: Wiley-Blackwell, 1997), 242.

[16] In Robert W. Chambers, *The King in Yellow* (Hertfordshire: Wordsworth Editions, 2010), 3-31.

[17] TD, 1:6.

[18] Edgar Saltus, *The Philosophical Writings of Edgar Saltus: The Philosophy of Disenchantment & The Anatomy of Negation* (Baltimore: Underworld Amusements, 2014), 172.

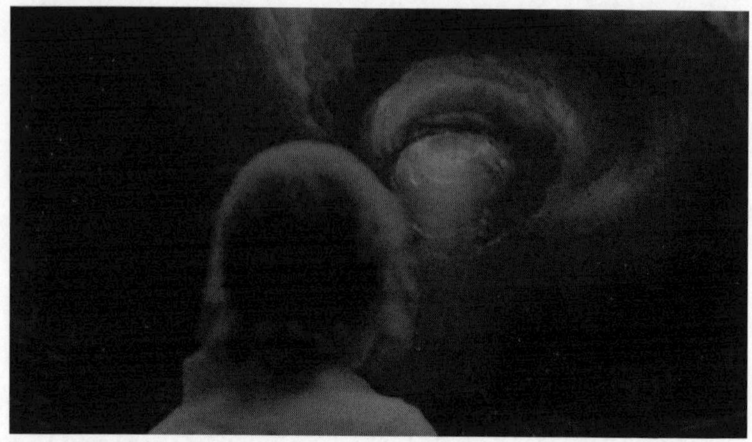

3. Remote Control

> *An automatic killing-device is hidden inside the room: The need for further outside agency is removed. The grander scheme of the murder investigation is forgotten – the whole outside the room is guilt and darkness – God and meaning are dispensed with, and all that is left is us living out our automated existence, each of us a mechanical device winding its way down to an un-owned death.*

Without God (or some proximal mystery) we cannot look at ourselves, and before long there is nothing to look and nothing to find – just an empty room with us still inside it: 'Unmaking, decreating, is the only task man may take upon himself, if he aspires, as everything suggests, to distinguish himself from the Creator.'[19] It is Cohle and Hart's task to unmake the mystery of a series of murders and disappearances, to actualize certain methods of detection that will then disassemble the case's alterity, its existence-outside-thought, and through this slow dismantling discredit its claim to an independent logic, a claim made off the back of a stylized inexplicability. The problem with pessimism, the challenge it sets itself, is that it can't unmake

[19] Cioran, *Trouble With Being Born*, 6.

without taking itself seriously, that same seriousness that rests at the core of the very anthropocentric structures it seeks to take apart, apart in such a way that they can never be reassembled. And while metaphysical and moral pessimism may appear to point to a wider, 'cosmic,' pessimism, (as Eugene Thacker suggests) the disharmony of these two perspectives belie such a pacific segue; for the former tells us that life is futile and loaded with suffering, that the self or the person is a lie, that morality is mere convenience, and that there is no way out, whereas the latter, 'a pessimism of the world-without-us' demands a much humbler rigor: 'the unhuman orientation of deep space and deep time, and all of this shadowed by [...] the impossibility of ever adequately accounting for one's relationship to thought.'[20] One tells us the work is done and we are doomed, and the Other, by its very retention of its otherness, tells us that the work can never be done. And while that same doom would seem to be implied in the futile struggle to understand what cannot be understood, this very impossibility smacks of the salvific, of the mysticism that the pessimist's weariness and defeatism debar. One appears to dismantle the otherness of everything except the self, while the Other retains the otherness of everything but – which is not to say that the cosmic pessimist is an advocate of the existence of persons, but just that his own ghost is not presumed to be congruent to the ghost of the universe.

This fortification of the cosmos's otherness, of its impossibility for us, is itself a form of possibility, and serves to elevate our suffering from the mundanity of known possibilities: its attendant 'anxiety is freedom's actuality as the possibility of possibility.'[21] And it is no hindrance that this 'possibility of possibility' is impossible to know. The distinction is savoured often by Pessoa: 'Let us always search for the impossible, since that is our destiny, and let us search for it by way of the useless, since no path goes by any other way, but let us rise to the consciousness that nothing we search for can be found, and that

---

[20] Eugene Thacker, 'Cosmic Pessimism,' *Continent* 2.2 (2012): 66–75, 68.

[21] Søren Kierkegaard, *The Concept of Anxiety*, eds. & trans. Reidar Thomte & Albert B. Anderson (Princeton: Princeton University Press, 1980), 42.

nothing along the way deserves a fond kiss or memory.'[22] Cosmic pessimism, then, far from being the pessimist's concluding abrogation, is instead his version of God, in whose presence he often falters and falls back on the useless, on the human life he knows to be vain, on the world he feels he has already conquered, even if that conquering was at his own expense.

When Cohle claims 'meaning is historical,'[23] he's enmeshed in the first of these types of pessimism (his personhood shunned, eradicated, and via it the world) from which he sees no way out; but later he wearies of this affliction of knowing: 'I don't wanna know anything anymore. Why should I live in history, eh?' concluding that ours 'is a world where nothing is solved.'[24] And his 'anxiety has here the same meaning as melancholy at a much later point, when freedom, having passed through the imperfect forms of its history, in the profoundest sense will come to itself.'[25] This coming to itself of freedom is the acceptance of the debt of the eternity it cannot know, and through this Cohle undergoes something of a Kierkegaardian recognition of that which though outside the influence of self is itself the constitutor of self. In fact, Hart had already alluded to this process with his recounting of the 'detective's curse': 'The solution was right under my nose, but I was paying attention to the wrong clues.'[26] The solution was in the room from the start, and the problem was not the otherness of the outside, but the attempt to bring it inside, when you should have left it where it was.

Cosmic pessimism is the refuge of the pessimist who still finds himself alive, the refuge of a futility he has not made his, the refuge of the mystery of his not knowing and the vanity of trying, and he finds that claiming this impossibility, the externally codified nature of his predicament, to be less taxing than any weariness of knowing. For to remain is not to make the world and its secrets yours via the self you have first established as other, but rather to make the self the potential agent of its own redemptive ignorance via the otherness of what's outside it. Hart

---

[22] Fernando Pessoa, *The Book of Disquiet*, trans. Richard Zenith (London: Penguin Classics, 2002), 206.

[23] TD, 1:2.

[24] TD, 1:5.

[25] Kierkegaard, *Concept of Anxiety*, 42-3.

[26] TD, 1:4.

diagnoses this condition in Cohle, tells him his denial lies in being 'incapable of admitting doubt,'[27] and so articulates how salvation lies not in the flimsy panoply of faith but in acknowledgement of what is not known, for Hart like Cioran knows that 'doubt is less intense, less consuming, than despair.'[28] And while, as Eugene Thacker explains, horror and our philosophical interest in the world around us may well be intertwined, both being concerned with 'the paradoxical thought of the unthinkable, in so far as it deals with this limit of thought . . . [and] in so far as it evokes the world-without-us as a limit,'[29] pessimism somewhat counter-intuitively becomes the antidote to this horror, and cosmic pessimism the antidote to Lovecraftian/Thackerian cosmic horror:[30] in the case of the pessimist the horror of unthinkability is transformed into a salve, a place of solace for thinking that cannot escape itself, a perspective smeared with the excrement of that which being must always become.

'We weary of thinking to arrive at a conclusion, because the more we think and analyze and discern, the less we arrive at a conclusion.'[31] The pessimist, then, is weary not only of his conclusions, but the thinking that got him there, and which could never get him anyplace else. And like the theologian whose thinking always leads him to God, the pessimist's thinking drags him always to nothing and no one, so that maybe it is *True Detective*'s evangelist preacher, Joel Theriot, who best encapsulates both their endgames: 'All my life I wanted to be near to God. The only nearness: silence.'[32]

---

[27] TD, 1:3.

[28] E.M. Cioran, *On the Heights of Despair*, trans. Ilinca Zarifopol-Johnston (Chicago: The University of Chicago Press, 1992), 37.

[29] Eugene Thacker, *In The Dust Of This Planet: Horror of Philosophy Vol. 1* (Winchester and Washington: Zero Books, 2011), 9.

[30] 'I would propose that horror be understood not as dealing with human fear in a human world (the world-for-us), but that horror be understood as being about the limits of the human as it confronts a world that is not just a World, and not just the Earth, but also a Planet (the world-without-us)' (Eugene Thacker, *After Life* [Chicago: The University of Chicago Press, 2010], 268).

[31] Pessoa, *The Book of Disquiet*, 206.

[32] TD, 1:6.

4. Impersonation or Illusion

> *A person, though already dead inside the room, is impersonated by someone outside it and so thought to be alive: Human life has become the impersonation of persons, extending into situations where the dead victim can itself be seen as the impersonation of the mind of the killer.*

The person, like any kind of illusion, forms like a hernia, so that what is inside comes to be seen as outside, and all this as the result of a weakness in the walls of the room, thereby allowing illusions to take on independent life outside their rightful jurisdiction. And in the same way that J.G. Ballard thought that fiction and reality had become reversed,[33] it is through this breach that the world outside the room becomes the illusion, and reality only that which remains inside. While discussing Chuang-Tzu, John Gray expresses his concurrence: 'There is no self and no awakening from the dream of self . . . We cannot be rid of illusions. Illusion is our natural condition.'[34] And as our natural

33 Solveig Nordlund, 'Interview with J.G. Ballard,' *Future Now / Framtiden Vari Gar* (1986), last modified May 20, 2011, https://www.youtube.com/watch?v=SS6MWpFX_No.
34 John Gray, *Straw Dogs: Thoughts on Humans and Other Animals* (London: Granta Books, 2002), 81.

condition we take exception to explanations that serve to rid us of those to which we've become (quite literally) attached, even when 'this self is fiction and confusion, anguish and the grave.'[35] But the illusion, as we see it, is at least something worth creating, something elaborate and mysterious, even if suffering is its price, even if what we come to resemble is less like this and more like those inside-out cats some nobody nails to the front door of a church in the middle of the night.

In the locked-room lecture, an artful build up to the ultimate dénouement in John Dickson Carr's *The Three Coffins*, Dr. Fell asks why it is we are 'dubious when we hear the explanation of the locked room?' and answers thus: 'Not in the least because we are incredulous, but simply because we are *disappointed.* And from that feeling it is only natural to take an unfair step farther, and call the whole business incredible or impossible or flatly ridiculous.'[36] Whether the illusion is performed in a detective story or in real life by an illusionist, 'we merely call the explanations disappointing. And the secret of both disappointments is the same – we expect too much.'[37] And as for who we are, we balk at being told of the underlying mechanisms that account for something we'd previously marveled at, as with the eliminative materialism of Thomas Metzinger, as he tries to explain how it is that phenomenal personhood can be experienced in a world in which there are no persons, and this is simply because 'the effect is so magical that we somehow expect the cause to be magical also. When we see that it isn't wizardry, we call it tomfoolery.'[38]

Although we sometimes hear of how dreams can reveal themselves as inexplicable reservoirs of truth and clear sight, as in Lovecraft's 'The Call of Cthulhu,' Cohle's recognition of dreams is rather more ambiguous than this seemingly uncomplicated reversal. For while there's the sense that within the dream of his life, recognized as such, there's some semblance of accuracy not afforded to others ('I don't sleep, I just dream,'[39]

35 Pessoa, *The Book of Disquiet*, 129.

36 John Dickson Carr, *The Three Coffins* (New York: Charter Books, 1935), 162.

37 Dickson Carr, *The Three Coffins*, 162.

38 Dickson Carr, *The Three Coffins*, 162.

39 TD, 1:1.

and yet residing inside the dream, the belief that he can somehow usurp the illusory: 'I thought I was mainlining the secret truth of the universe'),[40] thereby evoking the Pessoan notion of 'dreams without illusions,'[41] whereby 'only the eyes we use for dreaming truly see,'[42] dreams are also regarded as the source of our befuddlement: 'To realize that all your life, all your love, all your hate all your memory all your pain, it was all the same thing. It was all the same dream. A dream that you had inside a locked room. A dream about being a person . . . And like a lot of dreams, there's a monster at the end of it.'[43] And there is a monster, but as Cohle has stipulated, it will come at the end. So while, as in the Lovecraft story, dreamstates are regarded as possible conduits of revelation, they are also responsible for the Barmecidal conditions of human life in general, the former becoming like Metzinger's incorporation of lucid dreaming[44] into his materialist account of consciousness, wherein he allows for the possibility of us waking within the dream, so that maybe what we are is the point at which we wake up, and that we never truly wake is unimportant.

Gray, like numerous other Animalists,[45] tells us that personhood has no legitimate place in the essential constitution of human beings, and that what we've tended to call persons 'are only humans who have donned the mask that has been handed down in Europe over the past few generations, and taken it for their face.'[46] But the actuality is more complex and interesting than this picture suggests, and makes considerably more sense of the matrix of beliefs that go toward accounting for our identities. For what happened is that the mask became our face, like the

---

[40] TD, 1:2.

[41] Pessoa, *The Book of Disquiet*, 61.

[42] Pessoa, *The Book of Disquiet*, 111.

[43] TD, 1:3.

[44] Thomas Metzinger, *Being No One: The Self-Model Theory of Subjectivity* (Cambridge, MA: MIT Press, 2003), 634.

[45] Animalism is a philosophical position that equates you and me with human animals. See Eric T. Olson, *The Human Animal: Personal Identity Without Psychology* (Oxford: Oxford University Press, 1997), and David Mackie, 'Personal Identity And Dead People,' *Philosophical Studies* 95 (1999): 219-242.

[46] Gray, *Straw Dogs*, 58-59.

Hannya mask that cannot be removed in the film *Onibaba*,[47] consuming the insides through the farce of an outward presence. When in the film the mask is eventually broken and removed, the old woman's face is every bit as hideous as the mask. Impersonation leaves its mark, and to believe that the mask can remain no more than a mask indefinitely is no less naïve than taking it for a face to begin with. Cohle claims 'You can just let go,' and so somehow turn your back on this 'jerry rig of presumptions and dumb will.'[48] But isn't this just yet another instance of Cohle's proclivity for wishful thinking? Albeit one shared by Metzinger who likewise hints at just such an escape toward the end of *Being No One*, when he talks of possibly waking from the 'biological history' that imprisons us, and that while there may be 'no one whose illusion the conscious self could be, no one who is confusing herself with anything,' there nevertheless remains the theoretical possibility of 'a new dimension'[49] opening up of what it is selfhood could be, albeit a selfhood of the same nobody as before. But any talk of explanatory newness is ultimately void of consolation in virtue of its merely documenting the fog of oneiric myth in which we rely on hiding: 'It was shocking to have the foulest nightmares of secret myth cleared up in concrete terms whose stark, morbid hatefulness exceeded the boldest hints of ancient arid mediaeval mystics.'[50] And there is no clearer indication of this than the victims of the serial killer, who end their days as points of ingress to their killers' recesses, who have through their murderous offerings turned themselves inside out.

'A desperate sense of entitlement isn't it? Surely this is all for me . . . I'm so fucking important, right?'[51] but while pessimism says that this is not all for me, and is rather something to which I find myself comprehensively unsuited, all the fretting[52] and the disillusion smacks of disappointment, a

47 Kaneto Shindô, *Onibaba* (1964).

48 TD, 1:3.

49 Metzinger, *Being No One*, 634.

50 H.P. Lovecraft, 'The Whisperer in Darkness,' in *Necronomicon* (London: Gollancz, 2008), 337.

51 TD, 1:3.

52 TD, 1:3. Hart to Cohle: 'For a guy who sees no point in existence you sure fret about it an awful lot.'

disappointment grounded always in the error of expecting too much.[53]

5. Outside Looks Like Inside

> *Although the murder is committed outside the room, it appears to have been committed inside: The world comes to reflect the consciousness of the pessimist, the world emptied of meaning and substance. The serial killer looks outward to find his inside. Consciousness can never escape the outside, the outside in it from the start.*

'I have looked upon all that the universe has to hold of horror, and even the skies of spring and the flowers of summer must ever afterward be poison to me.'[54] The horror that we've come to accept as typically Lovecraftian is marked with a standardized construction: that of coming to know the unknown, of the outside coming in (replete with a taxonomy of gruesomely put together creatures and their alien modes of existence), where there should instead be ignorance, nothing, the void that cannot know us (or is otherwise ostensibly indifferent) and which we in turn cannot know. Lovecraft's pessimism results from his characters' dismantling of the Other, which is nothing less than the refuge of the unknown and the unknowable. Elsewhere is not a place but a thing, a thing that isn't me – and all the better for it. If we look at Heidegger's observation that Dasein's Being is essentially Being-with-others, that 'The Other can *be missing* only *in* and *for* a Being-with,'[55] from an extraterrestrial perspective, then we see that our aloneness on the cosmic scale is the not the same deficiency as it appears to be on the terrestrial level, and that in fact it becomes prerequisite to our sanity; and so, *pace* Cohle, it is not the case that we 'might as well be living

[53] The very reason Schopenhauer was disinclined to favour suicide.

[54] H.P. Lovecraft, 'The Call of Cthulhu' in *Necronomicon* (London: Gollancz, 2008), 225.

[55] Martin Heidegger, *Being and Time* (Oxford: Blackwell Publishers, 1997), 157.

on the fucking moon'[56] unless our concerns are good travelers, and they are not. Pessimism on earth is a rejection of the distractions that embody our humanness, a rejection that cannot escape its own concern; while on the moon it's you that's rejected and the concern that's absent, and there's not even any air left to make your pessimist's sigh. Just when you thought you'd undone all God's good work, he gives you something you cannot touch, much less dismantle. And he does this to save you from yourself, or so the story might go. Or as Tellenbach (as recounted by Feld) would have it: 'The melancholic needs to transcend himself, thus effecting a restructuration of personality that would help the self ascend out of Hell and regain the freedom of being.'[57]

We see the same hubris played out in Lovecraft's 'The Whisperer in Darkness,' in Albert N. Wilmarth's initial zeal at the prospect of visiting his remarkable correspondent, Akeley: 'To shake off the maddening and wearying limitations of time and space and natural law – to be linked with the vast outside – to come close to the knighted and abysmal secrets of the infinite and the ultimate – surely such a thing was worth the risk of one's life, soul, and sanity.'[58] But he soon finds out that his life, his soul and his sanity mean more to him than he thought, that what he experiences of the Other is very quickly too much. Similarly, when Cohle shows Hart the ritualistic snuff film in the storage unit, their mutual disgust and anxiety at having seen it is a palpitant despair, as there was something in the sickening possibilities that had left room for doubt, a way out, that now having witnessed they have irrevocably sealed shut.[59]

However much we work on making the chambers of our consciousness impermeable, filling any cracks we find with an ever-multiplying debris of words and ideas, the outside is always immanent and continuing to seep in. Hart eats out his girlfriend's arse and we cut to Cohle swilling mouthwash,[60] for the pessimist's curse is having to always carry the burden for

---

56 TD, 1:1.

57 Alina N. Feld, *Melancholy and the Otherness of God: A Study of the Hermeneutics of Depression* (Lanham, MD: Lexington Books, 2013), 185.

58 Lovecraft, 'The Whisperer in Darkness,' 326-7.

59 TD, 1:7. Which was of course Cohle's intention.

60 TD, 1:2.

those, and there are many, who remain unaware, to protect himself against the shit of life at large that the rest don't even seem to taste.

6. ANIMALS

> *The murder is perpetrated by an animal: Persons are clever animals cursed with an overdeveloped self-awareness. The animal escapes the locked room, but the lie of the person does not, and we are the lie. The scope of fabrication is limitless, and from these possibilities comes anxiety, which is not yet despair.*

In Section 4, the victim remained inside the room, while a visible manifestation of him walked about and was seen outside its walls. Once again we have the assumption of personhood where, as pessimism tells us, there is none. There was only ever the animal, an animal who escapes detection through leaving the room in a way human persons could not: the snake in Arthur Conan Doyle's 'The Speckled Band,' the orangutan in Edgar Alan Poe's 'Murders in the Rue Morgue.' *True Detective* has its green-eared spaghetti monster, its Cthulhu, in human form. The first victim Hart and Cohle encounter is herself made animal, a trophy in the most obvious way, the antlers, like the deer heads on the sheriff's wall, and posed as if in prayer, the crown of thorns, 'some Halloween shit,'[61] the killer showing himself through his kills, and what he shows is the animal that thinks, that is aware of itself to the point of having to become something else: the animal that suffers.

---

[61] TD, 1:1.

7. WOUNDED OR KILLED OUTSIDE, DIED INSIDE

> *No crime is committed inside the room, because the victim enters the room dead or dying: The lie that circumstances outside just being human must be the cause of the living death of the pessimist inside the locked room: the death of Cohle's daughter.*

It seems there has to be the earlier death of Cohle's daughter to explain away his pessimism, as if it couldn't happen in a life lived without significant trauma, as if it were some increasingly rampant disease of grief, as if life itself weren't trauma enough, as if Pessoa's head cold of the soul could actually be cured, instead of masked or force fed with illusions. And that the underlying cause is a child is apt, for it's the same sublimation that's at work when parents compulsively want more happiness for their children than it is reasonable to expect, why they are so concerned that they enjoy living while they are young enough, as if it was to serve as counterbalance to the misery to come, which of course it must. It's why children are often seen as never being as happy as they could be, because the weight needed is so great and we cannot rightly approximate this abstract antipode.

In a moment of maximal candour, Cohle makes the following admission: 'I think of my daughter now and what she was spared. Sometimes I feel grateful.'[62] But the source of this gratitude is a much deeper form of blackness than the grief he escapes through it. For in order to distract from the pain of his loss he doesn't, as we might expect, choose a series of lesser pains but a single much greater one. 'Spared [...] the sin of being a father,' Cohle adopts the demon of acedia-melancholy, receiving his poison from outside, taking on the unbearable physical weight of existence as supplement to his daughter's weightlessness, her irretrievable absence: 'The symbol of defilement is the most archaic of the symbols of evil and posits the evil of contagion and contamination, in other words, the evil of substance. It is the body that suffers evil from the outside. It is the most physical and objectified form of evil, one that is seen in its positivity and realism as an infectious power, literally a disease, and the external evil agency can extend to include demonology.'[63]

8. Presumed Dead but Killed Later

> *The victim is murdered by the first person to enter the room: The death of the world enters the previously sealed space, the eternity before birth. The murderer entering the same room over and over to perpetrate his crime, the imposition of the death of living on something that had before been spared its necessity. The crime of making actual what was only speculation.*

Cohle's somewhat discordant evocation of (ardent anti-pessimist) Nietzsche's theory of eternal return[64] begins to make more sense once we take account of the necessities engendered by his still being alive. 'You'll do this again,' he says. 'Time is a flat circle,' he says, 'an eternity where there is no time: [where] nothing can grow, nothing can become, nothing changes.' And he can live and face this future by having already done it, living 'like

---

[62] TD, 1:2.

[63] Feld, *Melancholy*, 36-7.

[64] See Friedrich Nietzsche, *The Will to Power* (New York: Vintage Books, 1967).

the future's behind you, like it's always been behind you.'[65] And so the machismo of his pessimism has some reward, as he rids himself of the architecture of fear, of dread, of possibility and its attendant anxieties, and so cauterizes everything that might never have happened with the fact, the irreversible injustice, of his being born. 'I know who I am,' he says 'after all these years, there's a . . . there's a victory in that,'[66] but it's a victory indistinguishable from defeat: it's the Nietzschean yes-sayer, the man who when forced to eat his own shit chooses to deceive himself that it tastes good. Having been made a victim in this way, and realizing his own powerlessness to alter it, what better solution than to imagine it had happened before, and will happen again, and that once born either amounts to the same thing. For what else is he to do with this life that is also death? 'with this day which never manages to end? When will the light stop shedding its beams, deadly to the memory of a night world anterior to all that was? How far away chaos, restful and calm, the chaos dating from before the terrible Creation, or sweeter still, the chaos of mental nothingness.'[67]

9. DOORS AND WINDOWS

> *The room has been sealed from the outside, but made to look like it was sealed from the inside: The case is always what the detectives see from outside it, not how it was from within. Pessimism has been perpetrated from outside, as a form of illness, a condition that was not chosen, as something internal that only the outside can unlock.*

To briefly expand on certain themes regarding metaphors of illness touched on in Section 7: The world, existence, human life, yourself, all should seem utterly inexplicable, unnecessary, absurd, burdensome, a solecism moulded from fecal matter, and where there is no breaking from the world and your being of it

[65] TD, 1:5.
[66] TD, 1:2.
[67] E.M. Cioran, *A Short History of Decay*, trans. Richard Howard (London: Penguin Books, 2010), 93.

we find only suffering and breathing, only the immanent cruelty of existence. 'We can live the way the others do and yet conceal a "no" greater than the world: that is melancholy's infinity . . .'[68] This afflicted sensing of the world is directly comparable both to Cohle's synaesthesia, which despite being an inbuilt inversion and rebuke of what are otherwise standardized human mechanisms for experiencing the world is also utterly ineffectual – a fundamental difference reduced to a banal sameness. Cohle can taste colours, see sounds, hear shapes, 'smell a psychosphere,'[69] but that they remain senses keeps him outside and distanced from his own experiences, looking on from without, though seemingly within.

10. Perpetrator Still In Room

> *The murderer never left the room, but leaves secretly later, after the door has been opened. The causing of death is not the end of the perpetrator's subterfuge: Similarly, death is not the end of the inherently illusory nature of human existence, for only if it continues, if the room is truly locked, can we bear the full weight of the pessimist's curse.*

'Death is not the end,' repeated over and over by Sam Tuttle's former maid, echoing like a warning, an alarm. Cohle's response is to say how the 'old lady was wrong . . . about death not being an end to it,'[70] and so we see him leaving pessimism behind, indulging in the (albeit tainted) sanguinity he abhors but cannot seem to resist. Before the narrative has initiated its consumption of Cohle's pessimism,[71] he'd claimed that 'nothing is ever over,'[72] and this is the response you'd expect from a true pessimist, because the pessimist does not expect things to get better, doesn't believe there's a way out of the room, so eternal life is not for him the gift it is for others, it is rather the icing on the curse,

[68] Cioran, *Short History of Decay*, 63.
[69] TD, 1:1.
[70] TD, 1:7.
[71] From TD, 1:4 onwards.
[72] TD, 1:3.

the crested seal on the horror of all horrors. 'Death is not the end,' is just too much weight to bear. When Dr. Fell speculates on the locked room occupant's final moments he imagines this: 'He tried to scream out, and he could not, for the blood was welling in his throat. And at that moment Charles Grimaud suddenly knew what he would never have believed possible, the breaking of the last and most shattering mirror-illusion in his bitter life . . . He knew he was dying . . . And stranger than any of his dreams, he was glad.'[73] That we end with our deaths is a realist's optimism, a form of salvation for anyone who's unpicked all the positive trappings of existence, so in the same place we find horror we also find reclamation, God, ourselves – and there's a reason it's the (substratal) dream of Buddha. In the words of St. Paul: 'I am persuaded that neither death . . . nor any affliction can separate me from what I find within me.'[74] This is the pessimist's nightmare, and one enacted unflinchingly by Julius Bahnsen,[75] a student of Schopenhauer who denuded his theories of the succour of ever dying out of this. Once again, the machismo of pessimism outreaches itself: a hard stance to maintain, the toughest way to live, and even he must have his rest someday, and that rest can only come when the pessimist is no longer there to witness it.

Without death there is no escape from the illusion, and the long con of consciousness has us forever, as in Leonid Andreyev's short story 'The Lie,' in which a lovelorn narrator waxes on the trials of eternity: 'a panther did I become in my stone cage. I walked and thought. I walked in one line right across my cage from corner to corner, and along one short line travelled my thoughts, so heavy that it seemed that my shoulders carried not a head, but a whole world. But it consisted of but one word . . . / "Lie!" that was the word.'[76] But perhaps the best example of what

---

73 Dickson Carr, *The Three Coffins*, 220.

74 Romans 8:38-39. Cf. Meister Eckhart, *Meister Eckhart: A Modern Translation*, trans. Raymond B. Blakney (New York: Harper Collins, 1942), 101.

75 See Julius Bahnsen, *Das Tragische als Weltgesetz und der Humor als ästhetische Gestalt des Metaphysischen* (Saarbruchen: VDM Verlag Dr. Müller, 2006).

76 Leonid Andreyev, 'The Lie,' in *The Little Angel* (Cambridge: Dedalus, 1989), 80.

it means to face the eternal fabrication of consciousness takes place in Philip K. Dick's *The Three Stigmata of Palmer Eldritch*, in which an enigmatic space traveller (the eponymous anti-hero), long presumed dead, returns (physically at least) with a drug, by the name of Chew-Z, offering its users immortality. As it transpires, Chew-Z-users enter an entirely different universe, one of Eldritch's creation, and one from which there appears to be no escape, at least not one you can ever be entirely sure of, such is the utter convincingness of this ersatz cosmos. Although Dick eventually offers his characters a likely reprieve, the way in which he does so is particularly revealing: first claiming that even if Eldritch is God, albeit a hostile one, then he could well be a lesser and inverted version of a greater, loving God, and secondly that the real unclosed world of dull actualities and unfathomed potentials still exists as a possibility, and so the hope of an outside remains. What is so nightmarish about this novel is that should Eldritch's plan prove successful his control would be complete, there would be no room for salvation, no Other, even in death. The reader's imaginative project would be at an end, the knots would be tied and Dick would have left his characters in hell, whether or not they ever come to realize it. On the penultimate page, Leo Bulero reflects on the predicament in which he finds himself: 'It's nothing more than faith in powers implanted in me from the start which I can – in the end – draw on and beat him with. So in a sense it isn't me; it's something in me that even that thing Palmer Eldritch can't reach and consume because since it's not me it's not mine to lose. I feel it growing. Withstanding the external, nonessential alterations, the arm, the eyes, the teeth – it's not touched by any of these three, the evil, negative trinity of alienation, blurred reality, and despair that Eldritch brought back with him from Proxima.'[77] And the 'something in' him that not even Palmer Eldritch can reach, that something that grows inside him but which is not him or his to lose, is the gap in what appeared to be a closed system. Bulero might see that void as the Christian God working through him, or as some positive attribute of his self, but having been gifted the possibility of a flaw in his seemingly exhaustive state of despair, a chink in the hermetically sealed and labyrinthine universe in

[77] Philip K. Dick, *The Three Stigmata of Palmer Eldritch* (London: Grafton, 1978), 203.

which he believed himself captive for an eternity, that condition of absence is enough, and no more should or can be said.

11. SECRET PASSAGES

> *The secret passage is, as Dr. Fell tells us in his lecture, a 'low trick' and an 'outrage.' An hermetically sealed room that has built into it a secret exit is a flagrant inconsistency: The conclusion of* True Detective *appears to perpetrate this very offence.*

'The willo-o'-the-wisps generated by our rotting lives are at least a light in our darkness.'[78] The allure of some apparitional light, a light from something not there, the stars of the light that Cohle tells us is winning, arrives as nothing more than due recognition of weakness. Having been reduced to 'a vague awareness in the dark,'[79] Cohle exits not to the black stars, for that time has passed, in 'Carcosa where black stars hang in the heavens,'[80] but to the fake light of what should not be there, a solution that time has disgraced. And so the conclusion of *True Detective* tells us that contrary to rational expectations, Cohle lives and that that living too must be contrary to rational thought, his continuance necessitating illusion. Cohle had once been turned to stone like Geneieve in Chambers' story 'The Mask,'[81] and like her he too returns to flesh, to feeling, to the abstractions of love, of the figment of the need of something finding itself forever dying in the dark.

What's obvious is empty, the solution of the secret passageway tells us this, so we can, if we choose, flatter the end of *True Detective* with knowingly exemplifying the more than human weight of pessimism, with how it necessarily debilitates our stories, but then after all maybe even the mention of flattery is unfair, and the realism is exemplary and baleful and perfectly

---

[78] Pessoa, *The Book of Disquiet*, 61.
[79] TD, 1:8.
[80] Robert William Chambers, *The Yellow Sign and Other Stories: The Complete Weird Tales of Robert W. Chambers* (Hayward, California: Chaosium, 2004), 9.
[81] See Chambers, *The Yellow Sign and Other Stories*.

intact: 'Life is like a story that is spoiled by an unsatisfactory resolution of preceding events.'[82]

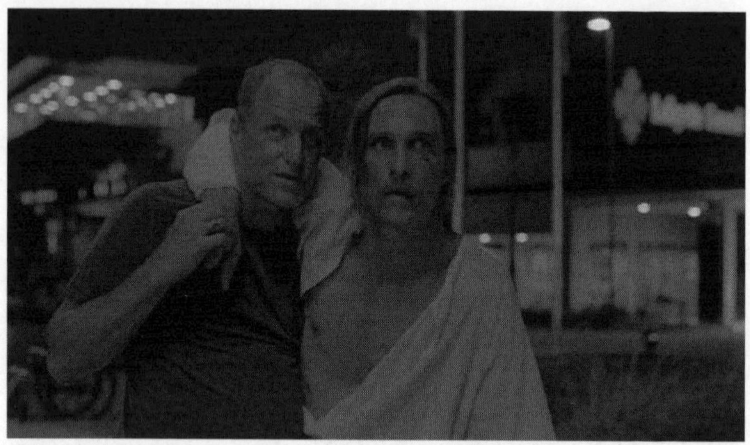

CONCLUSION

> Particles decay, molecules disintegrate, cells die, organisms perish, species become extinct, planets are destroyed and stars burn-out, galaxies explode . . . until the unfathomable thirst of the entire universe collapses into darkness and ruin. Death, glorious and harsh, sprawls vast beyond all suns, sheltered by the sharp flickerlip of flame and silence, cold mother of all gods, hers is the deep surrender. If we are to resent nothing—not even nothing—it is necessary that all resistance to death cease. We are made sick by our avidity to survive, and in our sickness is the thread that leads back and nowhere, because we belong to the end of the universe. The convulsion of dying stars is our syphilitic inheritance.[83]

[82] Thomas Ligotti, *The Conspiracy Against the Human Race* (Hippocampus Press, 2010), 113.
[83] Nick Land, *The Thirst for Annihilation* (London and New York: Routledge, 1992), 146.

We were warned that there would be a monster at the end, and the monster came and the monster was Hope. And as a monster it remains true to the definition: being at any one time 'categorically interstitial, categorically contradictory, incomplete, or formless.'[84] When asked if he still sees things (things he shouldn't see), Cohle replies: 'It never stops, not really. What happened in my head is not something that gets better.'[85] But was he really so immedicable? After all, don't we see him recover in those final minutes? Don't we get to see under the mask that Errol Childress tells him to remove?[86] So although Cohle undoubtedly undergoes some kind of heathenized kenosis, the realism remains intact, even intensifying, amounting to a meta-position, a pessimism about pessimism. For as Cioran tells us 'However disabused one may be, it is impossible to live without any hope at all. We always keep one, unwittingly, and this unconscious hope makes up for all the explicit others we have rejected, exhausted.'[87] And however much 'we dread readapting ourselves to Hope . . . betraying our disaster, betraying ourselves . . .'[88] we enact that perturbable orientation just in virtue of staying alive (or in being born, if Bahnsen is correct and death is not the extremity we were promised).

For all the posturing of the subjugator that's gone before, we remain inchoate little grubs, weaklings shivering in blackened rooms, deranged dogs slavering for the tiniest mote of light, in which we imagine some state of ataraxy lurks and waits for us, some end to being anything at all.

[84] Noël Carroll, *The Philosophy of Horror: or Paradoxes of the Heart* (London and New York: Routledge, 1990), 32.
[85] TD, 1:8.
[86] During the showdown at Carcosa in TD, 1:8.
[87] Cioran, *Trouble With Being Born*, 54.
[88] Cioran, *A Short History of Decay*, 69.

Contemplating the Crucifixion: Cohle and Divine Gloom

Edia Connole

1. True Detective, 'As I Am Trew Knyght'

Edgar Allan Poe (1809-1849) is generally credited with having written the first modern detective story. Within a few years of the establishment of England's Bow Street Runners, the world's first official police force, Poe presented the proto-detective, C. Auguste Dupin, over the course of three short stories: 'The Murders in the Rue Morgue' (1841), 'The Mystery of Marie Rogêt' (1842), and 'The Purloined Letter' (1844). As the only recurring character in these stories, the ideally cerebral and reclusive Dupin established a number of standards that have more or less been observed by Poe's successors in the genre: the detective who works by deductive method, the less astute sidekick, and the detective as atypical or anomalous mastermind.[1]

While Poe may have established the genre, he did not invent the story of detection, many of the elements of which can be seen in the earliest of literary works. In Sophocles's *Oedipus Rex* (ca. 430 B.C.), for example, Oedipus can be read as 'a detective as gifted and dogged as Holmes himself, out to investigate one crime,

---

[1] John T. Irwin uses the term '*analytic detective fiction*' to distinguish the genre established by Poe in the Dupin stories of the 1840s from stories whose main character is a detective but whose main concern is not analysis but adventure—tales whose true genre, Irwin suggests, is not detective fiction but the quest romance (typified for the latter by the work of Raymond Chandler, and by extension, then, the hard-boiled detective genre, as discussed below). See John T. Irwin, *The Mystery to a Solution: Poe, Borges, and the Analytic Detective Story* (London: The John Hopkins University Press, 1996), 1-2. Cf. Raymond Chandler, 'The Simple Art of Murder,' *Raymond Chandler: Later Novels and Other Writings*, ed. Frank MacShane (New York: The Library of America, 1995), 977-992.

the murder of King Laius.'[2] The essential components of the detective story's 'mechanical form' were detected in the high-art of ancient tragedy by W.H. Auden who, in his 1948 essay 'The Guilty Vicarage,' drew a distinct line between the latter and the non-art of detective fiction, conceding comparisons between the two, by calling attention to three shared elements: concealment ('the innocent seem guilty and the guilty seem innocent'), manifestation ('the real guilt is brought to consciousness'), and peripeteia (the 'reversal from apparent guilt to innocence,' and vice versa).[3] Accordingly, while Poe can be said to have established the genre of detective fiction, many of the standards he set for this genre find their origins in earlier literary works. Further, the genre that followed from Poe's stories—British, or classic, detective fiction—developed its own conventions. It is not inconsequential, as Thomas Leitch has noted, that 'Dupin, unlike his successor Sherlock Holmes, spawned no imitators and no immediate legacy.'[4]

The first major departure from the conventions established by Poe occurred in the 1930s and 1940s when prohibition, gangsterism, and the Great Depression gave rise to the distinctly American genre of hard-boiled detective fiction.[5] Delivering

---

2 Max Byrd, 'The Detective Detected: From Sophocles to Ross MacDonald,' *The Yale Review* 64 (1974): 73. Cf. Sophocles, *The Three Theban Plays: Antigone, Oedipus the King, Oedipus at Colonus*, trans. Robert Fagles (London: Penguin Books, 1982). See also Martin Priestman, *Detective Fiction and Literature: The Figure on the Carpet* (Basingstoke: Palgrave Macmillan, 1990), 23, and E. M. Beekman, 'Raymond Chandler & an American Genre,' *Massachusetts Review* 14 (1973): 149-173, for just two more instances of this claim in a potentially long list of examples. As Beekman was already noting here in the early 1970s, 'Several historians of the genre have asserted that Sophocles' Oedipus was the first detective' (169).

3 W.H. Auden, 'The Guilty Vicarage' (1948), *The Dyer's Hands and Other Essays* (London: Faber, 1962), 146-158. This essay has been reprinted several times, most notably in *Detective Fiction: A Collection of Critical Essays* ed. Robin W. Winks (Woodstock, Vermont: Foul Play Press, 1988), 15-24.

4 Thomas Leitch, *Crime Films* (Cambridge: Cambridge University Press, 2002), 19.

5 As noted previously, in *Mystery to a Solution* Irwin disagrees with this proposition insofar as he suggests that hard-boiled detective fiction does not belong to the genre of detection but to the quest romance (1-4). Irwin

decidedly American heroes and villains, 'imbued with the disenchantment peculiar to postwar American writing,' the hard-boiled detective novel replaced the atypical mastermind of Poe-esque descent with a more candid, common and cynical individual, who was nevertheless very sharp-edged.[6] The hard-boiled school as a whole was construed as an accurate portrayal of American life, capturing the look and feel of the 'mean streets,' in a nation 'populated by real criminals and real policemen.'[7]

In many respects, the aesthetic that characterizes the genre was inherited from pulp magazines. Thrashy 'hack' literature targeted readers with a limited education who 'did not want uplift or information [but escapism, and] . . . to kill time with a good read.'[8] Pulp fiction needed to seize and hold its readers attention from beginning to end, a task that put to the test English detection's gratuitous literary effects. Pandering to the constraints

---

is no doubt not alone in this view, but some, such as Andrew Pepper, in his study of 'The "Hard-boiled" Genre' in *Companion to Crime Fiction*, ed. Charles J. Rzepka (Chichester: Wiley-Blackwell, 2010), argue that 'hard-boiled crime [fiction] does not constitute a distinctive genre or [even] sub-genre, at least insofar as it has its own readily identifiable set of codes and conventions that all hard-boiled crime novels readily adhere or depart from' (142). In denying a separate status of genre or sub-genre to hard-boiled literature Pepper suggests it should be logically classified as a 'mode' of (analytic) detective fiction. As John Frow notes in his study *Genre* (London and New York: Routledge, 2005), modes emerge from existing genres and are not separate units rather their real nature is one of modification and extension of the original genre (65).

[6] George Grella, 'The Hard-Boiled Detective Novel,' in *Detective Fiction*, 105. Cf. 'Detective Novel, Crime Fiction,' in *International Encyclopedia of Men and Masculinities*, eds. Michael Flood, Judith Kegan Gardiner, Bob Pease et al. (London: Routledge, 2007): 'Hardboiled fiction can be read as a reaction against [the analytic or "armchair"] version of the detective. Due in part to social transformation at the turn of the twentieth century, the upper-class gentility of the analytic detective story became by the late 1920s and 1930s increasingly inadequate for resolving contemporary manhood's contradictions. "Masculinity" emerged now as the radical antithesis of "femininity," as a quality cleansed of any soft or feminine taint' (134).

[7] David Lehman, *The Perfect Murder: A Study in Detection* (New York: MacMillan, 1989), 136; Grella, 'The Hard-Boiled Detective Novel,' 105.

[8] Frank MacShane, *The Life of Raymond Chandler* (New York: Penguin Books, 1976), 44.

imposed by the contemporary American reader, hard-boiled pulp writers exchanged 'the static calm, the intricate puzzle, and the ingenious deductions' for 'rapid action, colloquial language, emotional impact, and the violence that pervades American fiction.'[9] As Frederic Jameson has claimed, the result of this formal change 'is that the detective no longer inhabits the atmosphere of pure thought, of puzzle-solving and the resolution of a given set of elements.'[10] Further, in Raymond Chandler's assessment, unlike English detection, which was concerned 'with the upper classes, the week-end house party and the vicar's rose garden,' hard-boiled pulp writers 'gave [murder] back to the people who commit it for reasons, not just to provide a corpse; and with the means at hand, not hand wrought dueling pistols, curare and tropical fish.'[11]

In his passionate partisanship of proletarian realism within the genre, announced with deafening directness in 'The Simple Art of Murder' (1944), Chandler defended the hard-boiled stories of Dashiell Hammett, and by extension his own work, by arguing against the 'badly scarred champions' of classic or formal analytic detection (typified at this time 'by the same incomprehensible [Golden Age] trick of how somebody stabbed Mrs. Pottington Postlethwaite III with the solid platinum poignard just as she flatted on the top note of the Bell Song from *Lakme* in the presence of fifteen ill-assorted guests').[12] 'Fiction in any form,' Chandler announced in the first line, 'has always intended to be realistic.'[13] In opposition to the 'burlesque' quality of contemporary analytic narratives, Chandler championed the gritty realism of Hammett, who 'took murder out of the Venetian vase and dropped it in the alley.'[14] The revolutionary debunking of the language and material of fiction exhibited in the pulps can probably be traced back to Walt Whitman, but as Chandler noted, it was Hammett who was the first to apply this 'spare, frugal and hardboiled' style to the

[9] Grella, 'The Hard-Boiled Detective Novel,' 104.
[10] Frederic Jameson, 'On Raymond Chandler,' *The Critical Response To Raymond Chandler*, ed. J.K. Van Dover (Connecticut: Greenwood Press, 1995), 84.
[11] Chandler, 'The Simple Art of Murder,' 988-89.
[12] Ibid., 986.
[13] Ibid., 977.
[14] Ibid., 987.

genre of detection: 'He wrote at first (and almost to the end) for people with a sharp, aggressive attitude to life. They were not afraid of the seamy side of things; they lived there. Violence did not dismay them; it was right down their street.'[15]

Like Hammett before him, Chandler used the pulps as an apprenticeship, eventually graduating and moving on to write 'real' fiction in the form of the hard-boiled detective novel: 'The thing is to squeeze every last drop out of the medium you have learned to use. The aim is not essentially different from the aim of Greek tragedy, but we are dealing with a public that is only semiliterate and we have to make an art out of a language they can understand.'[16] Chandler's aim from the beginning, then, was to use the popular form of hard-boiled detective fiction as a medium through which to impress some markedly subtler notions, in particular, the theme of human misery; a theme that runs right to the core of what Philip Durham, in his introduction to Chandler's *Killer in the Rain* (1964), calls 'serious' literature.[17] From the perishable pages of the pulps emerged a form of detective fiction that took on its distinctive shape with emphasis on a certain atmospherics and characterization,[18] in part because of its vision

[15] Chandler, 'The Simple Art of Murder,' 987.

[16] Raymond Chandler, *Selected Letters of Raymond Chandler* ed. Frank MacShane (New York: Columbia University Press, 1981), 173.

[17] Raymond Chandler, *Killer in the Rain* (New York: Pocket Books, 1965), xii.

[18] For the sake of brevity here, my choice of phrasing risks rendering dubitable the facts of this statement. As Irwin notes in *The Mystery to a Solution,* it is an emphasis on atmospherics and characterization (full stop, not on a 'certain atmospherics and characterization,') that distinguishes hard-boiled from analytic detective fiction. The emphasis in the hard-boiled genre 'is on the detective's character and his adventures, with the revelation of a hidden truth simply serving as a device to illuminate the former and motivate the latter. But in the analytic detective story the situation is different. As a character Dupin is as thin as the paper he is printed on, and his adventures amount to little more than reading newspaper accounts of crime and talking with the prefect of police and the narrator in the privacy of his apartment' (1). That said, my statement remains correct insofar as the hard-boiled genre's emphasis on atmospherics and characterization is always and inevitably an emphasis on a 'certain' atmospherics and characterization arising from the fact that everything within the genre is subordinated to action and realism. Recalling the almost twenty year period surrounding the genre's

of the nature of evil. As Peter J. Rabinowitz has claimed, this vision necessitated any number of structural changes within the genre, but none more pertinent than the disengagement of the hero, the reasons for which become evident if we contrast the vision of evil presented in the Chandlerian novel to that presented in classic analytic detection, exemplified by Agatha Christie.[19]

For Christie, evil emerges from the sick minds of unhinged individuals, and is preserved by deceit (puncturable by logic) rather than raw power. The task for Christie's detective is thus relatively easy and resolution of the crime (and the novel) takes place through a deductive process of speculative reasoning that the text's initial disorder empowers. Following the same thread

---

establishment and leading up to the Second World War Chandler offered an explanation for this: 'Possibly it was the smell of fear which the stories managed to generate. Their characters lived in a world gone wrong, a world in which, long before the atom bomb, civilization had created the machinery for its own destruction and was learning to use it with all the moronic delight of a gangster trying out his first machine-gun. The law was something to be manipulated for profit and power. The streets were dark with something more than night.' See Chandler, 'Introduction to "The Simple Art of Murder",' in *Later Novels and Other Writings,* 1016. As Peter J. Rabinowitz notes in 'Chandler Comes To Harlem: Racial Politics in the Thrillers of Chester Himes,' *The Sleuth and Scholar: Origins, Evolution, and Trends in Detective Fiction,* eds. Barbara A. Rader and Howard G. Zettler (New York: Greenwood Press, 1988), the 'existential' loneliness that is a characteristic trait of the detective across the hard-boiled genre 'follows more or less inevitably' from a 'worldview' accrued at a time when the resolution of crime and eradication of evil seemed impossible (20). And as Beekman notes further in 'Chandler & an American Genre,' it was this very impossibility of solving crime(s) that gave rise to the necessarily 'bleak' and 'gloomy' atmospherics: 'the autumnal mood, of weariness and futility' (166). From a strictly methodological point of view, the lack of resolution surrounding the mysteries arising from this new criminal milieu necessitated the ingenuity of the puzzle become secondary. With this pushed back, the writer had to depend a great deal more on atmospherics and characterization, which quite naturally tend towards notes of dissatisfaction and negative romanticism. Cf. Paul J. Ennis, 'The Atmospherics of Consciousness,' in this volume.

[19] Peter J. Rabinowitz, 'Chandler Comes To Harlem: Racial Politics in the Thrillers of Chester Himes,' in *The Sleuth and Scholar: Origins, Evolution, and Trends in Detective Fiction,* eds. Barbara A. Rader and Howard G. Zettler (New York: Greenwood Press, 1988), 19-20.

back to its origin in Chandler, however, leads not to the pith of one perverted individual, but to a complex web of political relationships in which the detective becomes ever more entangled. Resolution of the crime (and the novel) becomes nigh impossible, because even insofar as the sources of certain evils can be deciphered, they are so deeply embedded in political and societal structures that it would take nothing short of total social transformation to uproot them.[20] Hence, where Christie's Poirot, in the manner of Poe, brings 'inductive light to moral darkness,' Chandler's Marlowe 'cannot cheat his vision,' his 'corrupt universe can house no justice or, inversely, justice would be an embarrassing intruder.'[21] It is no coincidence, then, as Rabinowitz claims, that while Poirot is characterized by his arrogance, Marlowe is characterized by his unremitting gloom.

While most literary detectives are notably detached, the specific kind of gloom or self-encircled sorrow that characterizes Philip Marlowe is different in kind from the sort of isolation that characterizes Hercule Poirot. Marlowe's isolation, which 'is neither a character "trait" nor a psychological eccentricity,' stems directly from his creator's vision of evil.[22] That is because for a novel to succeed as detective fiction it must offer at least some sort of resolution, and since that resolution cannot come for Chandler, as it does for Christie, 'in the eradication of evil and the restoration of the initial peaceful order,' given that from Chandler's perspective 'that order was not *interrupted* by evil, but was itself the very source of evil,' it must come from somewhere else. As Rabinowitz says, 'some other kind of affirmation is required.'[23]

It is generally agreed that in Chandler's novels this affirmation comes in the form of a katabatic journey of personal discovery.[24] This journey, which is 'ultimately, both a quest for healing and closure and a quest, albeit unconscious, for self-

---

[20] Rabinowitz, 'Chandler Comes To Harlem,' 20.

[21] Beekman, 'Chandler & an American Genre,' 164.

[22] Rabinowitz, 'Chandler Comes To Harlem,' 20.

[23] Ibid., 20.

[24] Ibid. Rabinowitz does not discuss katabasis but the same anabatic impetus (of return) is implicit in what he terms 'personal discovery.' Cf. Rawson, 'To Hell with Ya,' 291-303.

knowledge,' follows the path that led Oedipus to Colonus.[25] That is to say, like the first sleuth in this tradition, Marlowe discovers the essential truth was within him all along, at the same time as he comes to accept his complicity in the crime. This also leads to an acknowledgement that, in following the various lines of investigation, he has been fouled by the web in which he has become entangled. Thus, echoing Oedipus' oracular plea to Theseus, not to touch 'a man stained to the core of his existence,' Marlowe mutters at the end of *The Big Sleep,* 'Me, I was part of the nastiness now.'[26] With acceptance of complicity comes responsibility and the kind of affirmation or resolution with which the hard-boiled genre is endowed. In confronting a world absurd in its cosmology and corrupt in its morality, Marlowe choses to maintain his principles, principles which, though they cannot take on any meaning in terms of effect, gain an aesthetic quality through their portrayal of a purely autonomous self-generated integrity.[27] This kind of affirmation, emerging from the gloomy labour of 'forever rolling the stone uphill,' is concomitant with the disengagement of Chandler's hero, with Marlowe's profound estrangement from people, who can betray you, in place of principles which cannot.[28]

Chandler's introduction of mythic and legendary elements into his novels is widely acknowledged. Marlowe's connection to the stone-rolling Sisyphus is but one lesser-discussed example of how the author wrapped his protagonist in a mythic and legendary

---

[25] On katabasis in hard-boiled detection fiction, see Eric Rawson, 'To Hell with Ya: *Katabasis* in Hard-Boiled Detective Fiction,' *The Journal of Popular Culture* 4 (2009): 291-303; 302. Cf. Rachel Falconer, *Hell in Contemporary Literature: Western Descent Narratives since 1945* (Edinburgh: Edinburgh University Press, 2005). Rawson does not mention Oedipus but the same general katabatic/anabatic principles apply. Cf. Rabinowitz, 'Chandler Comes To Harlem,' 20, which draws on Denis Porter's discussion of Oedipus in *The Pursuit of Crime: Art and Ideology* (New Haven: Yale University Press, 1981).

[26] Sophocles, 'Oedipus at Colonus,' in *The Three Theban Plays,* 352. Chandler, *The Big Sleep* (New York: Pocket Books, 1950), 214, quoted in Rabinowitz, 'Chandler Comes to Harlem,' 20.

[27] Rabinowitz, 'Chandler Comes To Harlem,' 20-21.

[28] R. W. Flint, 'A Cato of the Cruelties,' in *Critical Response To Raymond Chandler,* 328-330. Cf. Albert Camus, *The Myth of Sisyphus,* trans. Justin O'Brien (London: Penguin Books, 2000).

Fig. 1 John Everett Millais, *The Knight Errant*, 1870.

aura before placing his perpetually pointless struggle within an equally asinine environment. The most popular and widely accepted reading of Marlowe mirrors the merging of early Irish *echtrai* and *immram* tales with Christian themes, and then French romance, to produce chivalric grail stories.[29] In this reading—of drama, proficiently apprised by the high modernists directly prior to the heyday of the pulps—classical katabasis merged with the grail quest to produce the knightly attitude that would become the principle characteristic of the hard-boiled detective.

What the knight-errant retains in attitude from Sisyphus is the sufficiency of the quest itself rather than the successful conclusion. And insofar as seeking individual integrity is a sufficient quest, and finding it a sufficient end, he subsists in self-encircled sorrow—one of God's lonely men.[30] The opening lines of Chandler's *The Big Sleep* (1939) condense at once the long-lost, distant, already nostalgic quality of the quest and its significance for the detective. Looking up at a stained-glass panel which reproduces an 1870 painting by John Everett Millais entitled *The Knight Errant,* Marlowe (our narrator) says:

> Over the entrance doors, which would have let in a troop of Indian elephants, there was a broad stained-glass panel showing a knight in dark armor rescuing a lady who was tied to a tree and didn't have any clothes on but some very long and convenient hair. The knight had pushed the visor of his helmet back to be sociable, and he was fiddling with knots on the ropes that tied the lady to the tree and not getting anywhere. I stood there and thought that if I lived in this house, I would sooner or

[29] See for instance Rawson, 'To Hell with Ya,' 296. Rawson suggests here that these tales are Celtic, but *echtrai* ('adventures') and *immram* (adventures that take place at sea, traditionally) are specifically Irish, the eight century archetypes being *Echtrai Chonnlai* and *Immram Brain*. See Kim Mc Cone, *Echtrai Chonnlai and the Beginnings of Vernacular Narrative Writing in Ireland: A Critical Edition with Introduction, Notes, Bibliography and Vocabulary*, Maynooth Medieval Irish Texts (Maynooth: Department of Old and Middle Irish, National University of Ireland Maynooth, Maynooth, 2000), 11-47; Seamus Mac Mathuna, *Immram Brain: Bran's Journey to the Land of Women* (Tubingen: Max Niemeyer Verlag, 1985), 1-27.

[30] *Taxi Driver*, directed by Martin Scorsese (1976; Culver City, California: Sony Pictures Home Entertainment, 2007), DVD.

> later have to climb up there and help him. He didn't seem to be really trying.[31]

When exhibited at the Royal Academy in 1870, Millais's painting was accompanied by a text of his own invention which, like his *Knight Errant*, drew heavily on Arthurian legend as laid out in Sir Thomas Malory's *Le Morte D'Arthur*, the first modern English edition of which appeared in the preceding years (1868). Malory's 300,000 word history of King Arthur and his knights, originally published in abridged form by William Caxton in 1485, is England's most enduring epic and the source of such ubiquitous Arthurian concepts as Camelot, the Round Table and the Holy Grail. A medieval masterpiece, deemed by John Ruskin to be on par with 'the Old and New Testaments,' it has exerted a profound influence, one that extends far beyond readers of the book.[32] But for readers of this book, such as Lord Tennyson, T.E. Lawrence, C.S. Lewis, and one must venture, *all* of the Pre-Raphaelites and of course Chandler himself, it has always assumed a place of special importance. Indeed, rather tellingly, Chandler's Marlowe was originally called Philip Mallory.[33]

What the detective inherits from the fictional fifth-century world of the *Morte D'Arthur* is Malory's conception of chivalry, the most complete and authentic record of which is found in the Oath which 'all the knights . . . of the Table Round . . . every yere were . . . sworn at the high feast of Pentecost':

> never to do outrageousity nor murder, and always to flee treason; also, by no mean to be cruel, but to give mercy unto him that asketh mercy, upon pain of forfeiture of their worship and lordship of King Arthur for evermore; and always to do ladies, damosels, and gentlewomen succour, upon pain of death. Also, that no man take no

---

[31] Raymond Chandler, *The Big Sleep* (Los Angeles, California: Indo-European Publishing, 2011), 1.

[32] Ruskin is quoted in *The Cambridge Companion to the Pre-Raphaelites*, ed. Elizabeth Prettlejohn (New York: Cambridge University Press, 2012), 72.

[33] See, for instance, Marlowe's literary debut in 'Black Mailer's Don't Shoot,' in *Black Mask* 16 (December, 1933): 8-3, reprinted in *Five Murderers* (New York: Avon Books, 1944), 70-101.

> battles in a wrongful quarrel for no law, ne for no world's goods.[34]

The Pentecostal Oath can be read as a set of ethical imperatives devised to regulate the behavior of adventurous knights-errant, at the same time as it outlines a design for meting out justice, so that the king, in this case Arthur, maintains effective governance. In their charge to keep these decrees, chivalrous (derived from the French *chevalier*, or 'horsemen') Round Table knights function as quasi-policemen, preventing and investigating crimes, rescuing victims or those in potential distress and, unlike present-day policemen, administering summary, even capital, punishment.

More broadly, it would be wrong to assume that such medieval police-like action was simply a social phenomenon, the sole charge of the knightly class, just as it would be wrong to assume that there was only one (Oath, or) code of chivalry with which all knights complied. In English culture alone, in the fifteenth century in which Sir. Thomas Malory was writing, there were at least three competing views of knighthood, each with different social and political orientations and, correlatively, with different principle loyalties (to family, to God, and to king [and career]), each with its own distinct code of ethics. As Beverly Kennedy attests, these three views produced three types of knight in Malory's text: the Heroic knight, the True knight, and the Worshipful knight.[35]

Rather than reading the *Morte D'Arthur* as a sort of *summa* of medieval chivalry, then (which is more than justified by the fact that we find therein examples of every conceivable kind of knightly excellency recorded in the literature of the previous five centuries), Kennedy argues that most of Malory's text is devoted to developing a three-tiered typology based on the social, ethical and political views perpetuated at that time by the three customary sources for a code of chivalry: feudal, religious, and courtly.

---

[34] Namely, the Roundtable Oath, otherwise known as the Pentecostal Oath (Thomas Malory, *Sir Thomas Malory: Morte D'Arthur*, ed. Janet Cowen, 2 Vols. [London: Penguin Books], I: 115-116).

[35] Beverly Kennedy, *Knighthood in the Morte Darthur* (Suffolk and New York: D.S. Brewer, 1992).

The first of these sources is rooted historically in the feudal and military past and views knighthood as the privilege of the aristocratic class, deems a knight to be *good* or chivalrous if he displays boldness and prowess in battle, and is unfailingly loyal to his liege lord (who will generally be his kinsman). The knight that emerges from this source has the longest literary history, reaching back to Beowulf, and beyond, to the heroic ideal celebrated in Homer's *Iliad*.[36]

The second of these sources is rooted historically in the crusades and regards knighthood as a 'High Order' ordained by God, and deems a knight to be chivalrous if, in addition to the feudal virtues of boldness, prowess, and loyalty, he has the religious virtues of piety, chastity, and humility, and serves God before all, even before his liege lord (as demonstrated *par excellence* in Balian's response to Tiberias when asked to erroneously take rule of Jerusalem [the so-called 'Kingdom of Heaven']): 'No . . . It will be a kingdom of conscience or it will be nothing').[37] The knight that emerges from this source has the shortest (and, not surprisingly, least popular) literary history, but one that was circulated widely in the first treatises on knighthood written by Ramon Llull, amongst others, in the thirteenth century.[38]

The third of these sources is rooted historically in the court culture of the late Middle Ages and views knighthood to be an honor bestowed by the king, and so deems a knight to be chivalrous if, in addition to the feudal virtues of boldness, prowess, and loyalty, he has the virtues and accomplishments necessary to a career at court: demonstrating courtesy, and competency in courtly pastimes, as well as prudence and justice in matters of royal governance. The knight that emerges from this source is well represented in the French prose romances, and in some of the later medieval treatises on knighthood that extol a more modern, rationalist outlook.[39]

---

[36] Kennedy, *Knighthood,* 56-98.

[37] *Kingdom of Heaven*, directed by Ridley Scott (2005; Los Angeles, CA: 20th Century Fox, 2005), DVD.

[38] Kennedy, *Knighthood,* 56-98. Cf. Ramon Llull, *The Book of the Order of Chivalry or Knighthood* (William Caxton Edition, 1484), http://www.rgle.org.uk/Llull_B_C.htm.

[39] Kennedy, *Knighthood,* 56-98.

From these sources emerge, foremost, the 'worshipful knight,' embodying the (courtly and feudal) political view of knighthood conveyed in the Pentecostal Oath. This view of knighthood is the most prominent in Malory's text because it is the view of King Arthur and most of his fellowship. These knights are called 'worshipful' because the qualities admired and cultivated by them are those of men who always treat ladies with respect, and who will risk their lives, and repress even their strongest natural desires, to win 'great worship.' To the extent that this can and almost always does lead to the neglect of their Christian duties, they typically adopt a more modern, rationalist and cynical view that discounts the need for religious virtues, but trusts instead in man's own rationality and strength whether in courtly pastimes or trial-by-battle.

It is in stark contrast that we find the 'heroic knight,' embodying the older (militaristic and more feudal) social view that knighthood is the privilege of the aristocracy and should be exercised principally in the interest of family. These knights are called 'heroic' because the qualities cultivated and admired by them are those of men who expect to spend most of their lives fighting. They typically adopt a fatalist view according to which God determines all things—a recurrent theme in their trial-by-battle.

It is in less austere simplicity that we find the 'true knight,' embodying the ethical (religious and feudal) view that knighthood was ordained by God and should be exercised principally in the interest of Him and the Holy Roman Emperor. These knights are called 'true' because the qualities cultivated and admired by them are those of men who, unrelenting in helping the defenseless, are totally committed to the idea that their swords were given to them to do 'trew justyce.' They typically adopt a mystical and providentialist view according to which God is imminent in His creation and, though they believe He metes out the verdict in trial-by-battle, they are not fatalists: rather, in assuming a knight must have the grace of God to be advantageous in arms, they adopt the late medieval view that a man's fate is made by him and God acting in concert.[40]

---

[40] Kennedy, *Knighthood,* 56-98. Cf. Hadewijch of Brabant, 'Man must so keep himself pure from sin among all vicissitudes that he will seek his growth and work, according to the manner prescribed by reason, above

Of these three types, it is the true knight that interests us here. The true knight is Malory's most complex ethical type because it novelly incorporates principles from all three of the customary sources for a code of chivalry. The knight that emerges from these sources to supremely embody the composite ideal type feudal-religious-courtly in the *Morte D'Arthur* is Sir. Lancelot du Lac, who will go on to provide the outline for the archetypal hard-boiled detective: a man insolent because of his ethics ('true'), cynical because of his rationalist outlook ('worshipful'), but a man of honor who will go to certain death because all death is certain ('heroic'); a man who is called 'trew' because his holiness, eschewing religious fanaticism, consists in right action.

As a type, Lancelot stems from the religious-feudal ideal described in Ramon Llull's *Book of the Order of Chivalry*. The designation 'trew' derives from Lull's description therein of the 'vrai' or 'veray' knight, in order to distinguish him, on the one hand, from the purely feudal heroic type, and on the other, from the courtly-feudal worshipful knight.[41] As in Bernard of Clairvaux's view, Lull believed the 'veray' knight was a soldier of Christ, given a sword to chastise the wicked and bring glory to the good.[42] Beyond this, there are, as Kennedy notes, very few 'individualizing strokes' in Malory's portrait of Lancelot as the religious-feudal type; rather, he emerges in the composite ideal form of feudal-religious-courtly 'trew knyght' by comparison and contrast with other characters.[43]

In exploring each of the elements that comprise his composite ideal type in turn, Malory begins with the most fundamental feudal virtue of heroism by comparing Lancelot to Gawain in this aspect's most flattering context, the battlefield, specifically that of Arthur's Roman Campaign. In the fourteenth-century alliterative poem which is Malory's source for this

---

all things. And so God will work all things for him and with him, and with God will *fulfill all justice* (Matt. 3:15) and will desire that, in himself and in all of us, God may accomplish the just works of his nature,' in 'Letters,' *Hadewijch: The Complete Works* (Mahwah, N.J.: Paulist Press, 1980), 74.

[41] Kennedy, *Knighthood,* 87-88.

[42] St. Bernard is quoted in Max J. Ellul, *The Sword and the Green Cross* (Bloomington, IN: Author House, 2011), 82.

[43] Kennedy, *Knighthood,* 101.

Campaign, Arthur and his nephew Gawain are the central characters. In Malory's version, however, Lancelot plays an equally prominent role as co-captain to Arthur's chief soldier and statesman, Sir Cador of Cornwall. During the battle, Lancelot displays great boldness and prowess by choosing to face rather than flee an ambush of 60,000 Romans. In a report to the king, Sir Cador praises the 'knyghthode of Sir Lancelot,' saying 'hit were mervayle to telle.'[44] Whereupon the king decides to keep the knight by his side for the ensuing fray against Lucius. During this fight, Lancelot performs a feat with which not even Gawain could compete when he fearlessly rides into the midst of the Emperor's bodyguard, knocking him from his horse, killing a Saracen king, and riding away again with 'the banner of Rome' in his possession. While, as Kennedy notes, Malory himself clearly disapproves of such reckless behavior, Lancelot's knighthood—'his strength and skill in horsemanship and the use of arms, as well as sufficient courage and loyalty to spur a man to use his prowess even in the face of death'—emerges unequalled, displaying a 'greatness of spirit' that writers on chivalry called 'noblesse de courage,' and the philosophers and scholastics termed magnanimity (*Magnanimitas*).[45]

Magnanimity, as it is understood here, has little to do with the meaning we attribute to it in a contemporary context. It was first outlined by Aristotle in the *Nicomachean Ethics* where, in a discussion of virtues, it is defined as 'ambition' or, given the preceding conversation on 'magnificence,' as the simultaneous 'love [and worthiness] of honor'; thus hinting at both its cognitive and conative elements.[46] For Descartes, magnanimity is the highest virtue, it is 'the virtue of justified self-esteem that causes a person's self-esteem to be as great as it may legitimately be.'[47] For Thomas Aquinas also, it is similarly described as 'a stretching forth of the mind to [do] great things.'[48] So simple and direct a

---

44 Malory is quoted in Kennedy, *Knighthood,* 103.
45 Kennedy, *Knighthood,* 103-108.
46 Aristotle, Ethica Nicomachea, Bk. IV: Ch.2-5, in *The Basic Works of Aristotle,* ed. Richard McKeon (New York: The Modern Library, 2001), 989-997; 995.
47 Descartes is quoted in Lilli Alanen, *Descartes's Concept of Mind* (Harvard: Harvard University Press, 2003), 251.
48 St. Thomas Aquinas, *Summa Theologica,* II-II, Q. 129, Art. 1.

concept, it would seem, that medieval scholars such as Alexander Murray have concluded that the best modern English translation would simply be 'thinking big.'[49] Within the militaristic context of Arthur's Roman Campaign both Lancelot and Gawain exhibit aspects of magnanimity and thus establish themselves as fundamentally 'Heroic knights,' but it is Lancelot who, through his prowess, comparatively emerges one step further toward Malory's composite ideal type. Lancelot's magnanimity incorporates the religious-ethical nuance assigned to it by Aquinas.

Following Aristotle, Aquinas would agree with Descartes that magnanimity is dependent on nobility of birth, but insofar as this virtue was taken up and extolled in treatises on knighthood, one must also assume that, unlike the former philosopher, he would concur with the latter that a good education could correct such birth defects. And further, insofar as Descartes construed magnanimity as a *generosite*—which is to say, 'both a passion and a virtue, [and thus, the very] passion for virtue'—that it consists, on the one hand, 'in the knowledge that nothing is truly one's own but the free disposition of one's volitions,' and on the other, 'in the firm and constant resolution to use [these volitions] well, that is, never to lack the will to undertake and carry out what one judges to be best.'[50] In fact, this is implicit in Aquinas's discussion of mediocrity, which he opposes qua 'pusillanimity' or 'smallness of soul' to magnanimity: the pusillanimous man shrinks from great things in ignorance of his qualifications, i.e. that he was made in the image and likeness of God (Gen. 1:27).[51] But where the philosopher would conclude that magnanimity or prowess consists in having a good will and in this sense always being committed to doing one's best, for the scholastic it necessarily follows that doing one's best is living in imitation of Christ, whereby the noble knight ought to 'think big' by undertaking the greatest task of all, not just figuratively but literally taking up the cross of Christ, his passion thus becoming Christ's passion and dereliction, 'wholly destitute of all repose,' and his errancy, nothing less than a sign of this holiness, this sanctity.[52]

---

[49] Murray is quoted in Kennedy, *Knighthood,* 108.
[50] Descartes is quoted in Alanen, *Concept of Mind,* 252.
[51] St. Thomas Aquinas, *Summa Theologica,* II-II, Q. 133, Art. 2.
[52] Hadewijch, 'Letters,' in *The Complete Works,* 81.

While many young would-be noble knights were convinced by this Thomist argument, many more were not, and it was for these that the first treatises on knighthood were written—a fact made plain in Caxton's Epilogue to Llull's *Book of the Order of Chivalry,* which laments the fact that 'that Order [which] was previously practiced according to the instructions [therein] . . . more recently has fallen into neglect.' 'O ye Knights of England,' Caxton asks, 'where is now the practice of noble chivalry that was used in those days? What do you do now but go to the public baths and play dice?'[53] Emphasizing the necessity of cultivating Christian virtues in order to be a 'trewly' noble knight, such treatises assured their readers that the 'maist noble man of curage' needed not only the Heroic virtues of 'force' and 'leautee,' but the theological and cardinal Christian virtues of 'fayth,' 'gude hope,' 'cheritee,' and 'justyce,' 'temperance,' and 'prudence,' respectively.[54]

In comparing the actions of Malory's Gawain and his Lancelot in light of this discussion, and within the context of the Roman Campaign, there would seem to be little difference, both emerge chivalrous by the standards of Heroic knighthood: displaying boldness, prowess, and loyalty to their lord. As Kennedy suggests, it is only in the degree of recklessness that each knight exhibits that we can spy a difference.[55] This difference derives directly from the religious-ethical nuance assigned to prowess qua temperance ('Master yourself as you ought, for the sake of God's purest sublimity') and prudence ('Listen gladly to good counsel in matters of virtue').[56]

Gawain's reckless actions appear to be entirely spontaneous and without consideration. He beheads the emperor's aide at one stage, simply because he is angry, and goes off in search of adventure in enemy territory at an other, presumably because he is bored. As Kennedy notes, one cannot even accuse him of vanity, 'so little does he seem to think about what he is doing.'[57] Lancelot, on the other hand, takes counsel with his co-captain before deciding to fight rather than flee the Roman ambush, and the

53 Llull, *Order of Chivalry,* 'Caxton's Epilogue.'
54 Llull, *Order of Chivalry,* Ch. VII.
55 Kennedy, *Knighthood,* 108-109.
56 Hadewijch, 'Letters,' in *The Complete Works,* 81.
57 Kennedy, *Knighthood,* 109.

nobility of his action on this occasion is heightened by its premeditation. For, as the latter essays, there is something far nobler about acts of bravery undertaken with forethought, and to take counsel first and then face certain death, as Lancelot and his companions did, may be as close as possible to combining the virtues of prudence and courage in the way that Ramon Llull would have the 'trewly' noble knight do.[58] By simple comparison with Gawain, then, who proves weak of heart and childish in his behavior, too quickly angered and bored, thus lacking moderation in his activities, Malory's Lancelot emerges not only 'heroic' but a 'true knight,' tempering even his most reckless exploits as though he were in the presence of Christ, 'who is truth itself.'[59]

It is, of course, this very same Christ-like virtue that will prove to be Malory's greatest obstacle in his endeavor to posit Lancelot as the composite ideal type of the 'trew knyght.' So utterly devoted is he to the High Order of knighthood, so unshakably determined to give himself wholly over to its religious-feudal ideal, according to which he is God's knight and King Arthur's, that he is resolved never to marry. But as Kennedy suggests, 'Malory had to be radically selective in dealing with his source, the French prose *Lancelot*, in order to derive from it this portrait of an idealistic and ascetically inclined young man . . . [for even] those who had never read the French romances, and therefore would have known little or nothing of the details of the affair, would have thought of Lancelot primarily as Guinevere's lover.'[60] Lancelot's affair with his liege lord's wife is the source of his only vice as an otherwise perfect specimen of true knighthood. But then again, we are the behest of this author to believe that Malory would not have chosen to make Lancelot perfect even if he was at liberty to do so.[61]

---

[58] Cf. Kennedy on Sir. Gilbert Hay in *Knighthood,* 109.

[59] Hadewijch, 'Letters,' in *The Complete Works,* 81: 'You are too weak of heart and too childish in all your behavior. You are too quickly saddened and you lack moderation in your activity. . . . Always be joyous among your companions and let all their suffering be yours . . . . Watch over all your words as if they were spoken in the presence of Christ who is truth itself.'

[60] Kennedy, *Knighthood,* 110.

[61] Kennedy, *Knighthood,* 94.

What is betrayed in Llull's treatise on the 'trewly' noble knight is its religious-ascetic bias, it fails to mention love in either its courtly or marital contexts, at the same time as it makes the protection of all women an essential element of the knight's office. On the contrary, in the courtly literature of the thirteenth century, central to the idealization of heterosexual love expressed, was the idea that to love a lady was to make a better knight, that a knight was made better by that love. Kennedy contends that the basis for this idealization may be understood in terms of rebellion, against the asceticism of the Church, on the one hand, and the aristocratic practice of contracting loveless marriages, on the other.[62] Pointing to the same phenomenon, Scott Wilson remarks,

> In an age and class when marriages of dynastic convenience were still the primary and most accepted mode of sexual union, a certain developing notion of love became invested with intense value. In thousands of stories, legends, myths and poems that were produced and reproduced, people were ready to die for love. This is at a time when 'romantic' love is beginning to be represented as the highest ideal of human happiness, and most subversively as the basis of the transcendent union of marriage.[63]

As both Kennedy and Wilson go on to suggest, ever since romantic love succeeded family negotiation as the basis for marriage in the West, the experience has been that this passion 'invested with a value worthy of death' does not survive the prolonged intimacy of the contract.[64] Needless to say, there was no way of knowing this in the thirteenth century: 'At that time, if a knight loved a woman passionately . . . and had vowed to be her servant in love as long as he lived, the lady in question was most unlikely to be his wife, or ever to be able to become his wife.'[65]

Things had changed considerably by the fifteenth century, certainly in the fictional if not in the real world in which Malory

---

62 Kennedy, *Knighthood,* 87-88.

63 Scott Wilson, *Elizabethan Subjectivity and Sonnet Sequences* (Unpublished Thesis, PhD: The University of Wales, 1990), 27.

64 Wilson, *Elizabethan Subjectivity,* 27. Cf. Kennedy, *Knighthood,* 87-89.

65 Kennedy, *Knighthood,* 89.

was writing. Here, we witness a literary synthesis of Christian marriage and courtly love in both French and English romances. As Kennedy attests, what enabled this synthesis was one common principle and one common virtue: *trouthe*. This was true love, in principle, because it was truly chosen by both parties and, in virtue, because it was true unto death.[66]

This literary synthesis, which led to marriage being viewed as the ideal consummation of courtly love between a knight and his lady, also made it possible for him to be a 'true knight' according to the religious-feudal ideal inaugurated in Llull's treatise. The knight could now be both a lover of Christ, and a lover in life, the composite ideal type of feudal-religious-courtly 'trew knyght,' but only within the bonds of holy wedlock, which presents an obvious obstacle for Malory with regard to Lancelot. It is not one that he shies away from, however. On the contrary, he overcomes it, and the result is a transformation of the knight's character, so complete, that Eugène Vinaver would praise him for having succeeded 'in concealing from us the essential [persona] of the French prose *Lancelot*.'[67]

Malory's passage on 'the month of May' is the author's most eminent extolment of the transcendental virtues of courtly love. It serves as a prelude to his compression of Chrétien's *Knight of the Cart*, which relays the story of the queen's abduction and valiant rescue by Lancelot. It is clearly intended to justify events in the five episodes that follow, in which Lancelot and his queen pursue their love, only narrowly escaping detection:

> But nowdays men can nat love seven night but they must have all their desires: that love may not endure by reason, for where they be soon accorded and hasty heat, soon it cooleth. Right so fareth love nowadays, soon hot soon cold: This is no stability. But the old love was not so: men and women could love together seven years, and no licours lusts were between them, and then was love, truth and faithfulness: and lo, in like wise was used love in King Arthur's days.[68]

[66] Kennedy, *Knighthood,* 90.

[67] Vinaver is quoted in Kennedy, *Knighthood,* 111.

[68] Malory, *Le Morte D'Arthur,* Bk. XVIII, Ch. XXV.

This passage, in which Malory speaks of true love, of an honorable love devoid of intemperance and tempestuous passions that, 'soon hot soon cold,' demand immediate satisfaction, has been situated in the circulation of such intriguing works as Chaucer and Bocaccio's versions of *Troilus and Creseyde* and Boethius's treatment of the dynamics of cosmic love in *The Consolation of Philosophy*. But it more properly belongs to the mystical tradition which fuses love for God with chivalric wisdom, such as we find in the thirteenth-century Flemish mystic, Hadewijch, for example, whose letters at once recall what Malory saw as the transcendental virtues of courtly love:

> But nowadays Love is very often impeded, and her law violated by acts of injustice. For no one wishes continually to renounce his emotional attractions for the honor of Love. All wish to hate and love at their pleasure, and to quarrel and to be reconciled in accordance with their whims, not in accordance with the justice of brotherly love.[69]

In Hadewijch's writing all begins with a dynamic concept of love (*minne*) through which union with God on earth is imaged as a courtly relationship. In place of the worshipful knight's service to the lady, the mystic places the soul's service to God. In her poems, Hadewijch sees herself as a knight-errant riding down roads and courting adventure in fine garments which, 'as acts, / Performed with new ardor,' are 'best adorned, / With blazons of nobility, to the honor of high Love.'[70] But such Love is not easy, as Malory intended, and it is here that the distance between the beloved and the lover, that is, the distance experienced by Hadewijch between the soul and God, is perfectly imaged in the unattainability of the lover in courtly love, 'a high Love,' befitting the 'High Order' of knighthood.

That the transcendental virtues of such Love be deemed 'brotherly' and yet demand chastity (to 'renounce emotional attraction') is recapitulated in the *Morte D'Arthur*, on the one hand, through Malory's portrayal of Lancelot as the queen's lover in the manner that any knightly retainer was a lover to his lord, in

[69] Hadewijch, 'Letters,' in *The Complete Works*, 71.
[70] Poems in Stanzas 9, II. 31-40, in *The Complete Works*, 150.

what John F. Benton, adopting Aquinas' terminology, would call 'the love of friendship,'[71] and on the other, through a series of speeches and scenarios which serve to suggest that the knight's chastity is a function of his piety. The most notable of these is the Chapel Perilous episode, in which Lancelot meets a 'fair damosel' beyond the chapel who asks him to kiss her 'but once,' to which the knight responds 'Nay, that God me forbid.'[72] When he then learns that the damsel is a sorceress and that his chaste refusal has saved his life, he gives praise to 'Jesu' for preserving him from her 'subtle crafts.'

In Kennedy's explanation of this scene, which, following Benton, departs from all previous interpretations that see Lancelot's refusal to kiss the damsel as proof of his loyalty to Guinevere, she suggests it should be read instead as a consequence of his devotion to chastity, 'a devotion so radical that it can be compared to that which caused some virtuous young people to be burned at the stake as suspected Cathars in the late twelfth century.'[73] Dubbed 'a sort of pulp nonfiction for the prurient,' the seditiousness of this heresy hinged upon the question of good and evil, and the Cathar's heterodoxy in this regard, that is, their irreducible bone of contention regarding the role and power of evil in human life.[74] As one historian notes (and I quote him at length here because of the lyricism of the content):

> For the Cathars, the world was not the handiwork of a good god. It was wholly the creation of a force of darkness, immanent in all things. Matter was corrupt, therefore irrelevant to salvation. Little if any attention had to be paid to elaborate systems set up to bully people into obeying the man with the sharpest sword, the fattest wallet, or the biggest stick of incense. Worldly authority was a fraud, and worldly authority based on some divine sanction, such as the Church claimed, was outright hypocrisy.

---

[71] Benton is quoted in Kennedy, *Knighthood,* 112.

[72] Malory, *Le Morte D'Arthur,* Bk. VI, Ch. XV. Cf. Kennedy, *Knighthood,* 115.

[73] Kennedy, *Knighthood,* 115.

[74] Stephen O'Shea, *The Perfect Heresy: The Life and Death of the Cathars* (London: Profile Books, 2001), 7.

> The god deserving of Cathar worship was a god of light, who ruled the invisible, the ethereal, the spiritual domain; this god, unconcerned with the material, simply didn't care if you got into bed before getting married, had a Jew or Muslim for a friend, treated men and women as equals, or did anything else contrary to the teachings of the medieval Church. It was up to the individual (man or woman) to decide whether he or she was willing to renounce the material for a life of self-denial. If not, one would keep returning to this world - that is, be reincarnated - until ready to embrace a life sufficiently spotless to allow accession, to death, to the same blissful state one had experienced as an angel prior to having been tempted out of heaven at the beginning of time. To be saved, then, meant becoming a saint. To be damned was to live, again and again, on this corrupt Earth. Hell was here, not in some horrific afterlife dreamed up by Rome to scare people out of their wits.[75]

Whether deserving or not, in aligning Lancelot vis-à-vis the cause of his devotion to chastity with this band of Christian pacifists who, embracing tolerance and poverty, believed that human consciousness was a mistake and that the only corrective to that mistake is to shut down reproduction by embracing what Thomas Ligotti calls the Cathars' 'dual ultimatum of sexual abstinence or sodomy,' Kennedy firmly establishes Malory's composite ideal type of 'trew knyght' within a fellowship of pessimists, nihilists, and anti-natalists who, stemming from Job ('I go about in gloom, without any sunshine' [30:28]), and reaching down to the present day, 'want to go from the womb straight to the grave' (10:18).[76]

Far from unorthodox, this move actually reinforces the feudal-religious (mystical and providential) and courtly (rationalist) view proper to the composite ideal type of knight Malory intended and Lancelot represented. As Ligotti notes, that 'the mistake of consciousness or the corrective of shutting down the assembly line of reproduction . . . is exclusive to philosophy' is

75 O'Shea, *The Perfect Heresy*, 10-11.
76 Thomas Ligotti, *The Conspiracy Against the Human Race* (New York: Hippocampus Press, 2011), 22.

a falsity.[77] The Buddhists have long maintained that the highest aspiration of man should be the rooting out of his soul or self viz. atman, and while Christians are often shocked by this nihilism, they think nothing of it when the Saint says 'I am crucified with Christ, yet not I but Christ liveth in me' (Gal. 2:20). The very 'flower of chivalry,' Lancelot, as Malory's composite ideal type of 'trew knyght,' must put on the whole armor of God and court high Love in a land *where the light itself is darkness* (Job 10:22).

2. 'FROM THE TOURNAMENT TO THE ROUND-UP!'

According to George Grella, drawing on the observations of D. H. Lawrence in relation to the heroes of James Fenrimore Cooper, the chivalric romance is not the only tradition from which the hard-boiled detective emerged.[78] In championing the struggle of the individual against a corrupt society, the pulps had ostensibly created a new hero, but accordingly this 'new' hero was merely an 'avatar of that prototypical American hero, Natty Bumppo, also called Leatherstocking, Hawkeye, Deerslayer, and Pathfinder.'[79] Characters in the image of Cooper's Leatherstocking had proliferated through the phenomenon of the dime novel, the tradition of boy's adventure magazines that the pulps grew out of. Grella argues that, as urban existence encroached on the American wilderness, the frontier hero evolved in both role and character into the hard-boiled detective typified by Marlowe. In 'preferring his own instinctive justice to the often tarnished justice of civilization,' Marlowe is the man, who, like Leatherstocking before him, 'turns his back on white society. A man who keeps his moral integrity hard and intact. An isolate, almost selfless, stoic, enduring man, who lives by death, by killing, but is pure white.'[80] Both archetypes possess pronounced physical ability and a keen sense of morality that 'exacts personal sacrifice,' are thus isolated

---

[77] Ligotti, *Conspiracy*, 21.
[78] Grella, 'The Hard-Boiled Detective Novel,' 106.
[79] Grella, 'The Hard-Boiled Detective Novel,' 106.
[80] D.H. Lawrence, *Studies in Classic American Literature* (New York: The Viking Press, 1961), 62-63.

from relationships, and labour outside the established social code.[81]

Fig. 2 Frank E. Schoonover, *My Canoe Is All My Good*, 1933.

[81] Grella, 'The Hard-Boiled Detective Novel,' 109.

For instance, just as Marlowe's code exacts personal sacrifice in the area of love, because the prospective suitor is deemed 'corrupt, a bitch or a murderess, too evil to deserve [his] compassion,' in *The Deerslayer* (1840), the continent Leatherstocking must remain celibate because his prospective suitor is 'stained by past coquetries.'[82] As with the knight-errant, then, it would seem that what Marlowe and the frontier hero share, in particular, is a kind of self-encircled sorrow or gloom. Indeed, just as Leatherstocking is known as 'the lonely man of the forests,' embodying the 'antithesis between nature and [culture], between freedom and law,' Marlowe is known as the lonely man of the city, the man who must walk down these 'mean streets' alone; at odds with the law (he deems 'incompetent'), incomparably valiant towards women but denied personal relationships because of his principles, he is the quintessential hero of a negative romanticism nursed in the dime novel and nurtured in the pulps.[83] But whether this negative romanticism, which forms the dominant mode of American literature from Nathaniel Hawthorne, Edgar Allan Poe, and Herman Melville down to contemporary writers like Ligotti and Cormac McCarthy, that power of darkness and gloom which Mark Twain could not laugh away, and which had our proto-detective 'be enamored of the night for her own sake,' and which, anything but passive, sees Chandler's protagonist in the lineage of Leatherstocking raging against the recalcitrance of existence with all the quixotic energy of Bartleby's 'I would prefer not to,' is truly distinct from Malory's

---

[82] Grella, 'The Hard-Boiled Detective Novel,' 109. Henry Nash Smith, *Virgin Land: The American West as Symbol and Myth* (Cambridge, MA: Harvard University Press, 1950), 67. Cf. James Fenrimore Cooper, *The Deerslayer* (New York: Washington Square Press, 1967), 152-155, and Gilmore, 'Cooper and the Western,' 63.

[83] Grella, 'The Hard-Boiled Detective Novel,' 106. Smith, *Virgin Land,* 60. Raymond Chandler, 'The Simple Art of Murder,' 992. Cf. Philip Durham, *Down These Mean Streets a Man Must Go: Raymond Chandler's Knight* (North Carolina: University of North Carolina Press, 1963). Chandler, *The Long Goodbye* (New York: Vintage Books, 1992), 48. On the third decree of the Pentescostal Oath, regarding valiancy towards women and its hold over the knight-errant, see for instance Felicia Ackerman, '"Always to do ladies, damosels, and gentlewomen succor": Women and the Chivalric Code in Malory's *Morte Darthur*,' in *Midwest Studies in Philosophy* 26 (2002): 1-12.

world, and not simply one and the same 'shop-soiled Galahad' speaking, remains unclear.[84]

In attending to the prevailing stereotypes of frontier life at the turn of the twentieth century, distilled in illustrated articles and through stories published in the popular press, and typical of the imagery that sought to perpetuate the myth of the West—e.g. Percy Ivory's *Knight Errant of the Plains,* which was published on the cover of *Harper's Weekly* in 1909—Kirsten H. Powell has noted how, in searching for their vocabulary, American artists and writers turned to the terminology of medieval England.[85] Western frontiersmen were frequently equated with knights not only in paintings but in written accounts. In a 1901 article published in *Scribener's*, entitled 'A Section Hand on the Union Pacific Railway,' for example, the narrator, on passing through Nebraska, recounts:

> That evening, in a village inn, while the rain poured without, I sat cheek by jowl with a Knight Templar who had just returned from a convention of his order in Denver. It was not the meeting that inspired him; it was

[84] Poe says this of Dupin in 'The Murders in the Rue Morgue,' 106-107. As has been noted in a study of 'Holmes as a Copy,' that Dupin and his narrator close the shutters of their house during the day and only go out at night, thus emphasizing their physical withdrawal from society, is nicely reflected in the case of Sherlock Holmes whose 'withdrawal and gloominess lead to a cocaine addiction; when Holmes isn't on a case he withdraws from ordinary life as well as society.' See Edward Bailey and Philip Powell, *The Practical Writer with Readings* (Boston: Thomson Wadsworth, 2008), 123. For Bartleby's repeated use of this phrase see Herman Melville, *Bartleby the Scrivener* (London: Hesperous Classics, 2007). The term 'shop-soiled Galahad' is Chandler's own, see *The High Window* (New York: Vintage Books, 1992), 109. I'm referring to Lancelot here, of course, who emerges very much a shop-soiled Galahad in Malory's *Morte D'Arthur,* punctuated in Kennedy's typology. For the most part, my remarks in this sentence have been inspired by, and are an albeit contemporary compression of observations made by Beekman in 'Chandler & an American Genre,' 164-166.

[85] Kirsten H. Powell, 'Cowboy Knights and Prairie Madonnas American Illustrations of the Plains and Pre-Raphaelite Art,' in *Great Plains Quarterly* 5 (Winter 1985): 39-52.

Fig. 3 P.V.E. Ivory, *Knight Errant of the Plains*, 1909.

> the mountains. Raised on the prairie, he had never seen hills before, and the sight of the earth rising from a plain until it touched high heaven was like giving his mind the sense of a new dimension.[87]

In adding that the band of 'knights errant and ladies fair' proceeded to climb Pike's Peak, the author compares their 'steep ascent of heaven' with that of a 'struggling saints.' Asking why this imagery of England's remote past was applied to the American experience of the West, Powell suggests one explanation may stem from the difficulty of defining heroes in a democratic structure based on equality. In seeking to distinguish special individuals from the general populous, artists and writers turned to the hierarchical structure of the English monarchy, so that Buck Taylor became 'King' of the cowboys, Deadwood Dick, the 'Black Prince,' and more recently, John Wayne, the 'Duke.' However, as Powell goes on to essay, this line of figurative descent, from 'the heroes of Anglo-Saxon history to the cowboys of the plains,' had already been firmly established in Owen Wister's 1895 text 'The Evolution of the Cow-Puncher.'[88] In this text, Wister—who would go on to write *The Virginian* (1902) and with that crystalize the Western genre into the recognizably formulaic form we know today—argued that 'in personal daring and in skill as to the horse, the knight and the cowboy are nothing but the same Saxon of different environments.'[89]

The cowboy, who coincided with technological innovations which led simultaneously to the settlement of the West and to the proliferation of its myth through the first profitable means of mass production and distribution of literature in the U.S., namely, the Beadle dime novels in 1860, was a direct descendent of

87 Quoted in Powell, 'Cowboy Knights and Prairie Madonnas,' 42.

88 Powell, 'Cowboy Knights and Prairie Madonnas,' 42. Wister's text was originally published in *Harper's Magazine*. See Owen Wister, 'The Evolution of the Cow-Puncher,' reprinted in *Owen Wister's West: Selected Articles*, ed. Robert Murray Davis (Albuquerque: University of Mexico Press, 1987), 33-53.

89 Wister, 'Evolution of the Cow-Puncher,' 34. See Owen Wister, *The Virginian* (London: Macmillan, 1902). It is a widely acknowledged fact that Wister consolidated the stereotype of the cowboy in this book. See for instance James K. Folsom's classic study of *The American Western Novel* (New Haven: College and University Press, 1966), 107.

Leatherstocking; embodying many of the contrasting qualities of his character, but harmonizing them where they had before remained in conflict. As Christina Bold has stated in her book *Selling the Wild West,* this cowboy character was anything but 'new' to literature, like Leatherstocking before him, he had high morals, fought evil and underwent some sort of rite of passage, but though romantic to a certain degree was far more realistic in his attitudes than Cooper's protagonist.[90] While using the West as a setting, Cooper was still working with the conventions of the historical romance, it was not until writers like Wister and Frederic Remington transcribed the details of their diurnal lives into literature, whether fictionalized or not, that Leatherstocking evolved into the cowboy and the Western became a stand-alone genre with its own specific formula, generally credited to *The Virginian.*

Fig. 4 Frederic Remington, *The Last Cavalier*, 1895.

[90] Christina Bold, *Selling the Wild West: Popular Western Fiction, 1860 to 1960* (Bloomington: Indiana University Press, 1987), 65 and 42, respectively.

In Wister's book, as well as in his 1895 essay, he likens the cowboy to a slumbering Saxon who has suffered at the hands of impoverished writers: not since the deaths of Hawthorne, Longfellow and Cooper, who he holds in the same company and esteem as the chronicler of King Arthur, has it been acknowledged, of whom, beneath 'the dirt and stains,' the cowboy is 'the direct lineal offspring.'[91] Suggesting that 'no hoof in Sir Thomas Mallory' has shaken 'the crumbling plains with quadruped sound more valiant than the galloping that has echoed from the Rio Grande to the Big Horn Mountains,' he then draws a direct line of descent from Leatherstocking to Lancelot.[92] This is punctuated by Remington's illustrations, which accompanied the text's original publication. In *The Last Cavalier,* for example, a phantasmic procession of knights of Old England flank the cowboy as he rides on horseback, thus linking the cow-puncher to his Arthurian ancestors. Powell notes how Wister's and Remington's impressions provided the ground for other artists and writers to apply their assumptions about medieval adventure and knight-errantry to the western experience.[93] The particular value of her study lies in showing how, beneath the popular equation of the West with Camelot, there is at least one specific source for the general parallels between the chivalrous depictions of medieval art and literature and the American vocabulary of hero-worship, namely, the Pre-Raphaelite Brotherhood.[94]

The influence of the Brotherhood's art on the American imagination at the turn of the twentieth century was distilled through the writings and illustrations of Howard Pyle. Elaborating on the Brotherhood's subject matter and style, Pyle was not only one of the most famous American illustrators at this time, but a very influential teacher whose students (e.g. Frank Schoonover and Newell Convers Wyeth) would go on to illustrate the pages of the pulps after the dime novel, thus distilling into the hard-boiled

---

91 Wister, 'Evolution of the Cow-Puncher,' 34 and 35-36. Wister, *The Virginian,* 119.

92 Wister, 'Evolution of the Cow-Puncher,' 36-37.

93 Powell, 'Cowboy Knights and Prairie Madonnas,' 42.

94 Ibid., 42-52.

genre the codified image of the true detective as a direct descendent of the *trew knyght-errant*.[95]

3. 'LITTLE PRIEST,' . . . 'I COMMEND YOU TO THE MYSTICAL BODY OF CHRIST'

Season 1 of *True Detective*, the HBO series authored by Nic Pizzolatto, is at once heir to the pulps, those 'literate comic strips,' and to the genre that marks their development and acceptance as serious 'works of art.'[96] While the puzzle inherited from Poe remains, *True Detective* places emphasis on atmospherics and characterization, deemed the 'saving grace' of this development.[97]

Fig. 5 Nic Pizzolatto, 'The Long Bright Dark,' *True Detective*.

In keeping with the rebellion in crime fiction initiated by Hammett, Pizzolatto's heroes are men not far removed from the criminal elements they combat. Organized crime pervades Season

95 See for instance Howard Pyle, *The Story of King Arthur and his Knights* (New York: Charles Scribener's Sons, 1909), and *N.C. Wyeth: The Collected Paintings, Illustrations and Murals*, eds. Douglas Allen and Douglas Allen Jr. (New York: Wings Books, 1996).
96 Beekman, 'Chandler & an American Genre,' 152; Auden, 'The Guilty Vicarage,' 147, quoted in Beekman, 149.
97 Beekman, 'Chandler & an American Genre,' 151.

1 of *True Detective,* not in order to disclose some quotidian familiarity with guns and violence, but to show how the law and its agents of social justice are either incapable of solving certain crimes because of the orthodoxy of their methods, or unwilling to for reasons of political prosperity.[98] In this 'world gone wrong,' where 'nothing grows in the right direction,' the miscreant is no longer an idiosyncratic glitch in the system, but a faceless cog in a larger whole or 'sprawl' which exercises violence with a ruthless neutrality.[99]

One of the show's opening and in many ways most definitive scenes is codified with imagery of medieval knight-errantry.[100] Here, the detective Rust Cohle, arguably Pizzolatto's principle protagonist, tends to a naked (albeit, dead) damsel tied to a tree. As in Millais' painting, the tree can be identified in this instance both with the female gender—its twigs traditionally used in flagellation, either as a religious discipline or for sexual gratification—and with the figure of Christ whose crucifixion bore the particular curse of hanging on a tree, a tangible specimen of the more general curse He bore for humanity.[101] As we read in Melito of Sardis: 'He who hung the earth is hanging. He who fixed the heavens in place has been fixed in place. He who laid the foundations of the universe has been laid on a tree.'[102] In Cohle's

---

[98] See for instance TD, 1:4 and TD, 1:8 respectively.

[99] Chandler, 'Introduction to "The Simple Art,"' 1016; TD, 1:7.

[100] TD, 1:1.

[101] The tree is of course also the source of the first curse, see Genesis 3:14-19. Cf. Galatians 3:13: 'Christ hath redeemed us from the curse of the Law, having become a curse for us - for it is written, "CURSED IS EVERYONE WHO HANGS ON A TREE."' See also Acts 5:30, 10:39, 13:29 and Peter 2:24, all of which make reference to Christ's having been crucified on a tree. Most of the time in the New Testament one will find that the noun *stauros* ('stake') and the verb *stauroo* ('crucify') are used in connection with Christ's death, thus designating a 'pole' or a 'cross.' There is a logical cross reference to be found in Deuteronomy 21:23, to which Paul was referring. This passage pertains to the Torah's prescribed form of punishment by stoning as being followed-up with the person's body being hung on a tree; which, for the Jews, had become a metaphor for apostasy, which is exactly how they viewed Christ.

[102] Melito of Sardis, *On Pascha,* trans. Alistair Stewert-Skyes (Crestwood, NY: St. Vladimir's Seminary Press, 2001), 64, quoted in Nicola Masciandaro, 'Introduction - *In Caliginem,*' *Sorrow of Being*

proximity to the tree in this scene, the scene of the original crime—'the profane *contrapasso* of divine creation'—to which he will return many times, we are shown in the juxtaposition of feminine and Christlike qualities what type of knight our protagonist will be—a juxtaposition which reached an apogee in the medieval opinion that, as Hildegard of Bingen wrote, 'man signifies the divinity of the Son of God, and woman his humanity.'[103]

The human vulnerability of Jesus, played-out from the twelfth century in the writings of holy women, and in increasingly realistic depictions of the crucifixion—intensifying in the kind of grotesque hyperrealism we find in this *True Detective* scene: the effects of scourging, beating and crowning with thorns—led, in the fifteenth century to the appearance of a specific 'Man of Sorrows' image in art. This image was accompanied by the production of meditative texts, which were intended to stir the imagination to the point of empathetic identification with such severe physical torments, through the proliferation of lyrics of complaint or lament.

Within a contemporary context, fitting that of *True Detective*, such lyrics can be found in the work of Nicola Masciandaro. In Masciandaro's *Sorrow of Being*, for example, we read that Christ's suffering is said to be shared with the whole of creation, through the 'general coincidence of repetition and compassion that marks Christianity,' so that even the 'sun hid its face so as not to see him when he was crucified. It retracted its light back into itself so as to die with him,' veiling its 'gleaming head in gloom.'[104]

(unpublished manuscript), 27. See also, Nicola Masciandaro, 'Paradisical Pessimism: On the Crucifixion Darkness and the Cosmic Materiality of Sorrow,' in *Qui Parle: Critical Humanities and Social Sciences* 23 (2014).

103 Masciandaro, 'Introduction - *In Caliginem*,' 27. Hildegard of Bingen is quoted in Brian C. Vander Veen, *The* Vitae *of Bodleian Library MS Douce* (Unpublished Thesis, PhD: University of Nottingham, 2007), 84. As Vander Veen observes, 'whereas men expressed Christ *qua* God through the intellectual activity of preaching and teaching, holy women could express Christ *qua* man through their very physical identification with his suffering humanity . . . [because] the fleshly humanity whose suffering redeemed the world was female flesh' (84).

104 Masciandaro, 'Introduction - *In Caliginem*,' 23. *Saint Ephrem's Commentary on Tatian's Diatessaron: An English Translation of Chester Beatty Syriac MS 709*, trans. Carmel McCarty (New York: Oxford

Drawing on historical and mystical accounts of persons such as Pseudo-Dionysius who claimed to have witnessed this divine gloom, accounts whose 'representational point or *punctum*' is 'at once lost on and proven in the expended explanation of it,' Masciandaro proffers through a material lesson antipodal to much contemporary thinking that this gloom is not the image of a cosmos crying, but 'of tears that are materially at the heart of its being made.' 'From this perspective,' he says, 'the Creator's death is invisibly identical with the gaze that brings the universe into being.'[105]

This divine gloom, which is in the end, then, 'nothing more than the simple knowing and feeling of being itself,' is one of the defining characteristics of Sir Thomas Malory's Lancelot, Chandler's Marlowe, and Pizzolatto's Cohle, knights whose duty to their liege lord is tempered with devotion to God.[106] Like the self-darkening sun on the day of the crucifixion, such knights, following Mathew 16:24, deny themselves and take up Christ's cross, 'sorrowing without sorrow, refusing evil without refusing its fact.'[107]

University Press, 1996), 319, quoted in Masciandaro, 'Introduction - *In Caliginem*,' 23. Virgil, *Georgics*, trans. Peter Fallon (Oxford: Oxford University Press, 2006), no pagination, quoted in Masciandaro, 'Introduction - *In Caliginem*,' 22.

[105] Masciandaro, 'Introduction - *In Caliginem*,'25, 26 and 27 respectively.

[106] Ibid., 34.

[107] Ibid., 23 (for the discussion of Mathew 16:24) and 34, respectively. As Rust Cohle would note in TD 1:7—thus mirroring Pope Leo I's reflections on the crucifixion darkness in relation to a world that owed this witness to its creator—'[We] have a debt.' Cf. Masciandaro, 'Introduction - *In Caliginem*,' 25.

CODA

Q. Is life a battle?
MEHER BABA: Yes, it is a battle, and if rightly fought, would bring infinite *anand* (bliss).
Q. Why should life be a battle?
MEHER BABA: Necessarily, otherwise existence would be a drag.[108]

[108] Meher Baba, October 11, 1933, London, to a woman visitor, http://www.meherbabadnyana.net/life_eternal/Book_One/Morality.htm. I am indebted to Nicola Masciandaro, as always, for this and various other bits of chivalric wisdom littered throughout this essay.

I Am Not Supposed To Be Here: Birth and Mystical Detection

Nicola Masciandaro

> Take off your mask . . . Here! Here! We're here! . . . It's so good to see you all, I didn't expect you . . . What are you doing here? Nothing . . . I am not supposed to be here . . . Don't ever change . . . Let's get out from under this roof. Good idea . . . I shouldn't even fuckin' be here.
>
> – TD, 1:8

True detection lies in being extra circumspect about birth, life's originary and seemingly unerasable crime. 'If attachment is an evil,' says Cioran, 'we must look for its cause in the scandal of birth, for to be born is to be attached. Detachment then should apply itself to getting rid of the traces of this scandal, the most serious and intolerable of all.'[1] The mystery of birth is the ur-object of detection in that the impossible fact that I am me, even more than there being something rather than nothing, is an absolute disproportion or asymmetry which is per force unaccountable to empirical understanding and unassimilable to reason, as reflected in Albert Einstein's statement, 'There is something essential about the Now which is just outside the realm of science.'[2] Being living proof that the truth about reality cannot be positively known, birth is the negative ground upon

---

[1] E. M. Cioran, *The Trouble with Being Born*, trans. Richard Howard (New York: Seaver Books, 1976), 19. This essay was previously published online: *Black Sun Lit*, http://blacksunlit.com/2014/05/i-am-not-supposed-to-be-here-birth-and-mystical-detection-by-nicola-masciandaro.

[2] See Paul Davies, *About Time: Einstein's Unfinished Revolution* (New York: Simon & Schuster, 1995), 77.

which detection trues itself, restoring knowledge to the mystical process of nihilation and aphairesis. As Pseudo-Dionysius says, 'If only we lacked sight and knowledge so as to see, so as to know, unseeing and unknowing, that which lies beyond all vision and knowledge . . . We would be like sculptors who set out to carve a statue. They remove every obstacle to the pure view of the hidden image, and simply by this act of clearing aside (*aphaeresis*) they show up the beauty which is hidden.'[3] Detecting or uncovering truth is a negative matter of seeing through falsehoods, cancelling zeros, naughting lies. As Sherlock Holmes observes, 'When you have eliminated the impossible, whatever remains, however improbable, must be the truth.'[4] Due to the knower's monstrously unmasterable complicity with birth, according to which all murder mirrors my own coming-to-be, detection is authentically true only insofar as it sees into evil's specular abyss, fearlessly following a path into the radically immanent correlative identities of innocence and victimhood, investigator and criminal.[5] Birth's wrongness limns the speculative threshold of science and the real. 'The hellishly real impossibility that you are you is the true stupidity according to which the absolute is alone knowable.'[6] Or as Meillassoux says, in terms that figurally evoke the circumspection of birth, 'We now know the location of this narrow passage through which thought is able to exit from itself—it is through facticity, and through facticity alone, that we are able to make our way towards the absolute.'[7] Likewise, to sense my essential wrongness is both to see the impossibility of

---

[3] Pseudo-Dionysius, *Mystical Theology*, 1025B, in *Complete Works*, trans. Colm Luibheid (New York: Paulist Press, 1987), 138.

[4] Sir Arthur Conan Doyle, *A Study in Scarlet and The Sign of Four* (New York: D. Appleton, 1902), 69.

[5] 'Whoever fights with monsters should see to it that he does not become one himself. And when you stare for a long time into an abyss, the abyss stares back into you' (Friedrich Nietzsche, *Beyond Good and Evil*, eds. Rolf-Peter Horstmann and Judith Norman [Cambridge: Cambridge University Press, 2002], 69).

[6] Nicola Masciandaro, 'Absolute Secrecy: On the Infinity of Individuation,' in *Speculation, Heresy, and Gnosis in Contemporary Philosophy of Religion: The Enigmatic Absolute*, eds. Joshua Ramey & Matthew Harr Farris (Burlington, VT: Ashgate, 2014), forthcoming.

[7] Quentin Meillassoux, *After Finitude: An Essay on the Necessity of Contingency*, trans. Ray Brassier (London: Continuum, 2008), 63.

absolute knowledge and an absolute knowing in its own right. If I knew everything about everything, possessed perfect science of the universe and all of its processes, what could possibly answer the question, why am I me? And were I to know the answer to this question, what else could I possibly not know? The negativity of birth is solid evidence, the first clue that truth lies in the fact that I am not me, that the real trouble with being born is that one was not, that *we are things that labor under the illusion of having a self.*[8]

Such is the pessimal frame within which *True Detective* saves the significance of detection from forensic positivism and restores its essential negativity to the immanent cosmic and existential horizon, that is, to the diurnal hell that is 'you.' Beyond its own necessarily imperfect narrative representation, the show presents—at least for anyone who is not so far gone into identification as to insist upon fictional solutions to the problem of themselves—the imperative to practice true detection in the sense of mystically solving the mystery of birth and working out one's own salvation with fear and trembling (Phillippians 2:12) in the name of the personally terrifying principle that there is no one in need of saving. Silently implying that life ought to be lived like a crime drama in which the detective investigates birth instead of death, *True Detective* is hardly incompatible with mystical or superessential nihilism and the traditional meaning of mortal birth as the spiritual opportunity for the eternal birth which saves one from hell and/or further thrownness.[9] As Meher Baba states in his 43rd birthday message,

> The incident of birth is common to all life on earth. Unlike other living creatures which are born insignificantly, live an involuntary life and die an uncertain death, the physical birth of human beings connotes an important and, *if they are extra circumspect about it*, perhaps a final stage of their evolutionary progress. Here onward, they no longer are

[8] TD, 1:1.

[9] 'None of us is the ground of her own existence. Instead we are thrown in the world and this thrownness [*Geworfenheit*] is something that cannot be undone' (Daniel O. Dahlstrom, *The Heidegger Dictionary* [New York: Bloomsbury, 2013], 212).

> automatons but masters of their destiny which they can shape and mold according to will. And this means that human beings, having passed through all the travails of lower evolutionary processes, should insist upon the reward thereof, which is 'Spiritual Birth' in this very life, and not rest content with a promise in the hereafter.[10]

We all fit a certain category . . . and any of those types could be a good detective, and any of those types could be an incompetent shitheel.[11] Seeing the worldly, human event of oneself as neither for this life nor for another, this doctrine gives birth back to the always-new domain of immanent will and saves it from the self-dramatizing and auto-celebratory passivity of the subject who decides to dwell in paradoxically egoistical epiphenomenality, predicating itself upon irresponsibility for the fact of its own being. As Julius Evola posits at the end of *Ride the Tiger*,

> If one can allow one's mind to dwell on a bold hypothesis . . . once the idea of *Geworfenheit* is rejected, once it is conceived that living here and now in this world has a sense, because it is always the effect of a choice and a will, one might even believe that one's own realization of the possibilities I have indicated—far more concealed and less imaginable in other situations that might be more desirable from the merely human point of view, from the point of view of the 'person'—is the ultimate rationale and significance of a choice made by a 'being' that wanted to measure itself against a difficult challenge: that of living in a world contrary to that consistent with is nature.[12]

---

[10] Lord Meher, 1788, http://www.lordmeher.org, italics mine.

[11] TD, 1:1.

[12] Julius Evola, *Ride the Tiger: A Survival Manual for the Aristocrats of the Soul*, trans. Joscelyn Godwin & Constance Fontana (Rochester, VT: Inner Traditions, 2003), 227. Cf. 'The whole of evolution, in fact, is an evolution from unconscious divinity to conscious divinity, in which God Himself, essentially eternal and unchangeable, assumes an infinite variety of forms, enjoys an infinite variety of experiences and transcends

It's all one ghetto, man, giant gutter in outer space . . . Well, then what do you got the cross for in your apartment? That's a form of meditation. How's that? I contemplate the moment in the garden, the idea of allowing your own crucifixion.[13] My aim in what follows, therefore, is to detect how this deathly natal sorrow, the perfect sorrow of being which precedes and exceeds my feeling of it, is neither melancholy nor pessimism, but a true sign of an absolutely optimal worst.

†

The intuition that one should not be here, that there is something inexplicably wrong or wrongly inexplicable about being, oneself, in this universe—whatever universe this is—is not to be taken lightly. The simple fact that I am capable of this intuition is astonishing and lends it a peculiar kind of unquestionable authority, as worthy of being believed as my being here. *You want to hear this or not?*[14] That being is a sorrow, that this entity is strangely equipped and bound to grope around the most dark cell of itself is really something. A need for escape vaster and more confining than all prisons. A vector of adventure killing and

---

an infinite variety of self-imposed limitations. Evolution from the standpoint of the Creator is a divine sport, in which the Unconditioned tests the infinitude of His absolute knowledge, power and bliss in the midst of all conditions. But evolution from the standpoint of the creature, with his limited knowledge, limited power, limited capacity for enjoying bliss, is an epic of alternating rest and struggle, joy and sorrow, love and hate, until, in the perfected man, God balances the pairs of opposites and transcends duality. Then creature and Creator recognise themselves as one; changelessness is established in the midst of change, eternity is experienced in the midst of time. God knows Himself as God, unchangeable in essence, infinite in manifestation, ever experiencing the supreme bliss of Self-realisation in continually fresh awareness of Himself by Himself. This realisation must and does take place only in the midst of life, for it is only in the midst of life that limitation can be experienced and transcended, and that subsequent freedom from limitation can be enjoyed' (Meher Baba, *Discourses*, 6th ed., 3 vols. [San Francisco: Sufism Reoriented, 1967], III.12).

[13] TD, 1:1.

[14] TD, 1:1.

outliving every quest. From the start, let us once and for all never confuse this intuition of essential wrongness with there being anything the matter, that is, with evil as we like to think about it. Let us sever and silence in advance all traces of its relation to *worry* and right now cease forever to fall into the trap of considering the problem of birth, of coming to be, to have anything whatsoever to do with the issue of death. *Not at first, but right there in the last instant. It's an unmistakable relief.*[15] Worry is the way of the lifetime actor, the diurnal identitarian liar, who, in the self-interest and pseudo-life of being someone, dramatizes existence and in doing so blindly *goes along with it*, never failing to show up for the show, even after it is too late (to not show up). Not that anyone is entirely deprived of the illumination of this wrongness, it being also the proper light in which everyone assumes the mask and hallucinates escape. *It was all the same dream, a dream that you had inside a locked room, a dream about being a person and like a lot of dreams there's a monster at the end of it.*[16] How do you like living with yourself? As Levinas states, 'Escape is the need to get out of oneself, that is, to break that most radical and unalterably binding of chains, the fact that the I [*moi*] is oneself [*soi-même*] . . . In escape the I flees itself, not in opposition to the infinity of what it is not or of what it will not become, but rather due to the very fact that it is or that it becomes.'[17] *He's gonna come for you, he is worse than anybody.*[18]

The horror of this binding—the horror of the *this*—is only superficially that it is a horror to me, a horror of me as victim of my own being. That is the level dramatized in Lovecraft's *The Outsider* in which you both abhor and hold to yourself as most prized possession within a hideously unknowable and unownable cosmos: 'Such a lot the gods gave to me—to me, the dazed, the disappointed, the barren, the broken. And yet I am strangely content, and cling desperately to those sere memories, when my mind momentarily threatens to reach beyond to *the other*. I know not where I was born, save that the castle was infinitely old

[15] TD, 1:3.
[16] TD, 1:3.
[17] Emmanuel Levinas, *On Escape*, trans. Bettina Bergo (Stanford: Stanford University Press, 2003), 55.
[18] TD, 1:8.

and infinitely horrible.'[19] For under this too-familiar being-in-the-world level of horror lurks the greater horror still of a more universal binding, a more terrible cosmic complicity, one according to which hiding within the given, my cowardly acceptance of its fraud as my own, is simply no longer possible. Here is where the need to escape, to get out of myself, as no longer conceivably *my* need, is already so close to being something universally free from myself, that to entertain it is too dangerous, too threatening to escape per se and the singular sense it holds to me, to me. Here is the threshold of a greater—neither human nor inhuman—internal outdoors, the boundary of the limitless unlocked prison whereupon almost everyone really plans to stay inside, where you keep planning *your*—or worse *our*—escape via designs perforce designed to prevent you from actually escaping! Being oneself is easy. Anyone can do that. Now your lot, your precious little fate, so safely guarded by the personal spectre of your eventual non-being, is all yours. Go ahead, cling to it, all you want. Stay in hell. *Hail Mary, full of grace, the Lord is with thee.*[20] The stronger you do the clearer I see the deeper oceanic death which this clinging fears, that decollative drowning into being *neither oneself nor someone else.*[21] Not birth nor death do you really fear, but the birth and/or vanishing found in the death of death, a living death and undying life born from the *death of birth.* 'It is no longer I who live . . .' (Galatians 2:20).

What if the I is not, never becomes, is *not* oneself? *Can you, uh, tell us anything about that?*[22] How that silently wrecks your palatial prison. How that destroys, exposes as always already eroded, your standing in the world! As Cioran explains in *The Temptation to Exist*, 'Even more than the style, the very rhythm of our life is based on the *good standing* of rebellion. Loath to admit a universal identity, we posit individuation, heterogeneity as a primordial phenomenon.'[23] What kind of sick creature is this? Someone who celebrates his birthday all the while counting

[19] H. P. Lovecraft, 'The Outsider,' http://www.hplovecraft.com.
[20] TD, 1:2.
[21] Pseudo-Dionysius, *Mystical Theology*, 1.3, 1001A.
[22] TD, 1:2.
[23] E. M. Cioran, *The Temptation to Exist*, trans. Richard Howard (Chicago: University of Chicago Press, 1968), 42.

on death to save him from never having been and/or being forever, from the unborn abyss of eternity! Simply not to be such a creature is reason enough to affirm, over and against whatever this essential wrongness of being consists of, the purer fact *that* I feel it as an index of a self-destroying and self-fulfilling universal truth, to see it for what it is, namely, a real and direct sign of the fact that I am never who I think I am. *Put your hands on your head right now.*[24] One way or another, I am universal. I was not born and will never die. This is the only sane conclusion, the only true solution not absolutely intolerable to itself, the only one that speaks with the self's own absoluteness: 'the essence of my self arises from this—that nothing will be able to replace it: the feeling of my fundamental improbability situates me in the world where I remain as though foreign to it, absolutely foreign.'[25]

Even if there is no escape, or no one here to escape, or if the only escape lies in realizing either, knowing this feeling is really something else. *Other times I thought I was mainlining the secret truth of the universe.*[26] Now at least I start at last to actually grasp existence, to know more than intellectually what I've known all along, that 'Existence is the unheard of, *what cannot happen.*'[27] The inescapable freedom of being a thing that should not be is a supervenient truth according to which escape is eternally accomplished—divinely or nihilistically it does not matter—on the basis of its necessarily being an escape from itself, an escape from escape. Escape escapes escape. Salvation is the sheer non-existence of anyone in need of saving. So the need to break out of oneself is really real only for someone who somehow already has. Whether or not anyone ever breaks out, I am outta here! The rest is escap*ism* or false appropriation of freedom in the interest of further binding. See how everyone, the whole world, destroys this freedom with plans for escape. Why not stop? Why not rest in the self-evident openness wherein the cosmic prison walls are the innermost boundary of paradise? *No numbers on this place—fire must've happened a long time ago.*[28]

---

[24] TD, 1:5.

[25] Georges Bataille, *Inner Experience*, trans. Leslie Anne Boldt (Albany: State University of New York Press, 1988), 69

[26] TD, 1:2.

[27] Cioran, *The Temptation to Exist*, 218.

[28] TD, 1:2.

Why not cease your infantile clamoring for justice and just—for once in your life—*be* just? 'The just man,' says Eckhart, 'serves neither God nor creatures, for he is free, . . . and the closer he is to freedom . . . the more he is freedom itself. Whatever is created, is not free. . . . There is something that transcends the created being of the soul, not in contact with created things . . . not even an angel has it . . . It is akin to the nature of deity, it is one in itself, and has naught in common with anything.'[29]

That I see the wrongness of my being, that I know it, is enough wrong for me. 'Sufficient unto the day is the evil thereof' (Matt. 6:34). *Tell me what you see. Ligature marks on her wrists, ankles, and knees. Multiple shallow stab wounds to the abdomen. Hemorrhaging around throat, lividity at the shoulders, thighs, and torso. She'd been on her back a while before he moved her.*[30] That I sigh with secret indifferent sorrow is a cosmically sufficient secret. 'My secret to myself, my secret to myself, woe is me' (Isaiah 24:16). Flying faster than Satan, this sigh passes the widest sphere, surpassing God. 'For my essential being is above God, taking God as the origin of creatures. For in that essence of God in which God is above being and distinction, there I was myself and knew myself so as to make this man. Therefore I am my own cause according to my essence, which is eternal, and not according to my becoming, which is temporal.'[31] *Her body is a paraphilic love map.*[32] Birth, whose negativity is instant evidence that one is not one's body, that 'a body came into the world, but it wasn't you,'[33] is my negative bond of love with the absolute. 'O blissful Estrangement from God,' says Mechthild of Magdeburg, 'how lovingly am I connected with you!'[34] How else that I have these blind antennae, these weirdly haptic polymelic phantom limbs, which grasp the endless beginningless chain of my binding, touching its matter and

---

[29] Meister Eckhart, *The Complete Mystical Works*, trans. Maurice O' C. Walshe (New York: Crossroad Publishing, 2009), Sermon 17.
[30] TD, 1:1.
[31] Eckhart, *Complete Mystical Works*, Sermon 87.
[32] TD, 1:1.
[33] Vernon Howard, *Your Power of Natural Knowing* (New Life Foundation, 1995), 164.
[34] Mechthild of Magdeburg, *The Flowing Light of the Godhead*, trans. Frank Tobin (New York: Paulist Press, 1998), 4.12.

feeling its form? How else do I sense the infinite verticality of my self-foreignness, this otherness more myself than me, according to which birth, insofar as the event or its world can be blamed for establishing my miscarried belief in its happening as my own, is unmistakably death? Simply accept as proof of this the fact that it is actually happening. Close your eyes and see the invisible hands that tied you to the tree of life with a binding that reveals the difference between yourself and the tree by blinding you to it, blinds you to the difference by binding you to it. *The hubris it must take to yank a soul out of non-existence.*[35] The hands are your own.

Coda: 'My soul is chaos, how can it *be* at all? There is everything in me: search and you will find out . . . in me anything is possible, for I am he who at the supreme moment, in front of absolute nothingness, will laugh.'[36]

[35] TD, 1:2.

[36] E. M. Cioran, *On the Heights of Despair*, trans. Ilinca Zarifopol-Johnston (Chicago: University of Chicago Press, 1992), 86.

THE LABOUR OF THE PESSIMIST: DETECTING EXPIRATION'S ARTIFICE

Fintan Neylan

A detective cannot but see the worst in people. From the carnage of the murder scene to the mind of the serial killer, even when convincing himself that it is not in the human character to do such horror, he still must bear, analyse and act on evidence that is directly to the contrary. Always coming up against the worst, it is no surprise that a detective would hold a pessimistic outlook; indeed it seems to be intrinsically bound up with the nature of detection. For the pessimistic is an opening that most of us dare not peer into, and yet we find ourselves still drawn. In this essay, I wish to show that pessimism is a disposition which has the dynamics of re-evaluation at its core, a rethinking of who 'we' are.[1] Though it undermines reasons to affirm life, it does not do so out of any dark fascination with the absence of meaning. Rather it is because this re-evaluation inherent in pessimism inevitably leads to unsettling the vision of how we are constituted; it leads to a vision which affords us no return to a previous—usually brighter—way of thinking.

Given its re-evaluative impulse, we may say the pessimistic view opens up new vistas to possibilities, yet does not stop upon reaching them. Unhalting and always assuming the worst of

[1] In terms of the specific type of pessimism I shall be advancing, I take as my starting point Emil Cioran. While Cioran never explicitly phrases his thoughts in terms of elaborating a re-evalution, one can clearly see, in his *A Short History of Decay*, a calling out for a change in how conscious beings see themselves: '[there is] no salvation so long as we still conform to our being. Something must disappear from our *composition*, some deadly spring dry up; hence there is only one way out: *to abolish the soul*, its aspirations and abysses' (Emil Cioran, *A Short History of Decay* [Harmondsworth: Penguin Books, 2010], 127]).

them, it pushes ever further to deeper negative superlatives, to ever bleaker leads. To be pessimistic is to be a vector, always cutting away at the given topsoil and detecting evidence—all of which further reveals the distant time of arbitrary evolutionary programming and cosmic errancy.

***

'People: so goddamn frail they'd rather put a coin in a wishing well than buy dinner.'[2] Exclaimed by the weary Cohle of 2012, this statement stands beside his more memorable characterisations of people as not unique somebodies but each a nobody, or as an aggregate of sentient meat.[3] Though it lacks the serrated edge possessed by his other pronouncements on humanity's capacity for self-delusion, it is far more telling of his views on people.[4] From his sneering one could easily conclude we are dealing with a pessimistic misanthrope, i.e., one who thinks that when it comes to endeavours of the living, the whole is worse than the sum of its parts; recall that Cohle urges us to 'deny our programming' so as to 'walk hand in hand into extinction.'[5] More generally, it is tempting to think misanthropy as a consequence of pessimism. Yet Cohle's activities throughout the series show precisely the contrary: while he has deep misgivings about how humans view themselves, and—far more dangerously—how some humans tell others to regard themselves, it is not from a hatred of people that he recommends the self-endangerment of the human species. It is rather from a recognition of the arbitrariness of the cosmos, of the cruelty that

---

[2] TD, 1:3.

[3] TD, 1:1. On these points of Rust's philosophical views, there is clear reference to the work of Thomas Ligotti, to the point of homage; according to Ligotti, 'the worst possible thing we could know—worse than knowing of our descent from a mass of microorganisms—is that we are nobodies not somebodies, puppets not people' (Thomas Ligotti, *The Conspiracy Against the Human Race* [New York: Hippocampus Press, 2010], 109).

[4] For example, see his monologue regarding people's belief in religion: 'What's it say about life, hmm? You've got to get together, tell yourself stories that violate every law of the universe just to get through the god damn day? What's that say about your reality, Marty?' (TD, 1:3).

[5] TD, 1:1.

humans undergo such arbitrary suffering, and the perversity that humans are told that their suffering is necessary.

That a self-professed pessimist should care about others' suffering might seem at first glance to be paradoxical, but there is ample evidence of his interaction with the denizens of the bayou displaying a curious type of empathy—one devoid of sentiment, but an empathy nonetheless.[6] For Cohle's actions show on a practical level how pessimism is not a criticism, but rather a resignation to what humans are: frail beings. This is a resignation to people possessing a tendency to delude themselves, of them having a yin for fairy tales. Time and time again we are shown how he loathes the image of what people believe they are, but is quite accepting of what they actually are—especially when he encounters a person who cannot deny their status as frail, suffering being with misplaced hope. In resigning himself to this, he cannot rightly judge humans for what is in large part due to their programming—and he certainly has no grounds to hate them.[7]

Even though pessimism does not necessarily entail misanthropy as a consequence, it still may be asked what in fact are the consequences of pessimism. This paper will investigate such outcomes and show how, underlying the discussions of the human in *True Detective*, there can be detected a far wider philosophical thesis on pessimism. In particular, it will show how the re-evaluative dynamic of pessimism is ontological in character, and that not only does the pessimistic involve implicit knowledge of this ontological status, but that it relies upon it in order to re-evaluate the human.

---

[6] For example, despite the fact Cohle adheres to a strict anti-natalism, he reaches out consistently to and forms relationships with those who have lost their children: a father whose son was apparently drowned, in episode six, and, more notably, the bar owner for whom Cohle works. As if to set this into relief, the only thing we are told about the latter character is that he owns the bar and that he lost his son. See TD, 1:6 and 1:7.

[7] A key example is that of the scene with Theriot late in the series, the preacher of the sermon in episode three. One might imagine Cohle would smugly critique the disillusioned preacher. Yet precisely the opposite occurs: in Theriot's struggling with his own limits, Cohle is at his most understanding. See TD, 1:6.

1. DETECTING THE FRAIL

To grasp this re-evaluative capacity of pessimism on an ontological level, what is first required is a detection of the frail and the chaotic, beginning with how they are manifest in the human. Our starting point lies in the intuition that the components of individual life are trussed by the weakest of threads, that it could all come apart at a moment's notice. In itself, this is unexceptional, for the philosophical exploration of death is nothing new. But while death has a long, celebrated history of analysis, when life's termination is viewed in terms of frailty, a very different story emerges. While death is venerated, human frailty is a crack which people have for centuries tried to paper over. Just like death, nothing will exempt humans from it; unlike death, the thought that nothing about us is free from extinction serves as a far more difficult basis on which to build notions of transcendence. Those who tell that we exist any differently are usually operating from an ulterior motive, seeking to transform the ever-present possibility of our death into a religious unit of currency, either by valorizing or embellishing it with hints of destiny. Even in secular guises we are told of stories where we humans occasionally transcended our usual non-fate; be it through heroism and sacrifice of life we may live on in history, that something of us will survive, that in death we each may give ourselves meaning. Yet from a stray shard of shrapnel on the battlefield to the near-comical suffocation on a poorly chewed crust, no death is any more glorious than the last and each is as accidental as the next.

Frailty is however only one side of this issue, for what is frail is always subject to what has been called chaos. The dominant philosophical schools have long recognised this pairing, but only so that it could banish them both in a single stroke.[8] Indeed, both

[8] Discussions on this are a variant on systems which privilege immutability, at the implicit expense of material world of change, and thus stretch back to at least the Platonic theory of the forms. Plato saw the world as divided in two: on one hand there is the material world, which is subject to change, and, in his eyes, decay; on the other hand, there is the world of perfect, unchanging and eternal entities—what he called the forms. See especially Book 5 in Plato, *The Republic* (Harmondsworth: Penguin Books, 2007). Referred to as the

are reduced to that which is to be overcome. In the picture of a cosmos governed by immutable structures, that which is frail is portrayed as that which is most subject to the influences of chaos and, by implication, may be torn apart at any given moment. Here frailty is not even a state in-itself, being subordinated to the status of the mere border between real existence and the indeterminate non-existence of chaos. It becomes the surface of being, wedged beside that which is and is not. [9] Thus it occupies an ambiguous position: things which are admitted as frail are granted the capacity for destabilisation, a determinacy which is at best only indefinite.

At work in this peripheralisation is an intense fear of chaos, one which is always present at the edges of every celebration of the cosmos's eternal ordering. For if frailty is the fringes of order, then it is always bordering on and prey to chaos, deception, and indeterminacy. Each human's philosophical quest is framed thus as an escape from this, a pilgrimage involving the recovery of order. In this claim that we follow the great chain of being, moving towards ever greater ontological degrees, there is at the same time a claim that we can attain a greater ontological distance from chaos.[10] This move serves a double-edged purpose: by explicitly stating that chaos can be shut out, there is implicit

---

'metaphysics of presence,' this tendency to advance immutability is given its best known critique by Derrida in 'Ousia and Grammē: Note on a Note from *Being and Time*,' in *Margins of Philosophy* (Chicago: Chicago University Press, 1982).

[9] A notable exception here is Deleuze and Guattari, for whom the surface has a positive association; in fact, they formulate it in terms of their key metaphysical term 'assemblage,' stating '[t]he surface of stratification is a machinic assemblage distinct from the strata' (Deleuze and Guattari, *A Thousand Plateaus* [London: Continuum, 2004], 45).

[10] While not mentioned in the works of Plato, the phrase 'great chain of being,' the metaphysical structure undergirding the sensible order of the cosmos, is most closely associated with Platonism. It receives its clearest expression in Neoplatonism, which establishes a hierarchy of existence with matter being the lowest and what is known as 'the One,' highest being, existing so far above that it is unknowable to humans. Indeed sensible matter is regarded as technically not on the scale of being but as a mere surface reflection of the lowest Forms of being on 'Prime Matter'—i.e., pure evil. See Plotinus, *The Enneads* (London: Penguin, 1991), 98.

the idea that one's frailty may be eluded, or dispensed with altogether. Putting it differently, the idea that we can flee from chaos, that we can transcend it, in turn is a driving out of the idea that we are frail beings. Our frailty is accidental and exorcisable, be it through a recognition that who we are is not a body but an immortal soul, or a subject on a quest to discover the conditions for which it itself is responsible.

To see that frailty generally finds itself banished in some way or another, one need only look at those who form a periphery to the *True Detective* story, i.e., both the bayou itself and those who live there. The environment we are presented with, that of South Louisiana, is one choked with industrialisation and pipelines. Those who live there are but exiles; victims such as the woman with incessant headaches and damaged from a lifetime of chemical exposure.[11] The setting is a place where the decrepitude of human ordering cannot be hidden: far more than the destructive sweep of hurricanes, unknown forces creep out from beneath the jungle and slowly tear it all apart. In short, frailty is on full show here. Given what they have been told by preachers and authority figures, the inhabitants pray desperately, hope insatiably—all in sheer desperation.[12] They cannot escape the fact they are frail, yet as long as they are given a basis to believe frailty can be overcome, they will do anything. This is not a place where hope fled; it is a place where hope could never take root. It is with these people and environs that the real horror is sourced.

This despair provides an interesting counterpoint to Cohle's intellectual route: buttressed by a pessimistic outlook, such withering of life can be easily rationalized and hopelessness coped with ('it's all one ghetto, man').[13] But what happens to

---

[11] TD, 1:2.

[12] For example, see Theriot's sermon: 'Your sorrows pin you to this place. They divide you from what your heart knows' (TD, 1:3). As noted above, Theriot is an interesting character in the programme, for he promulgates the vision of religious authority figures, but he himself falls prey to their mendacious activities. He represents the frail being *par excellence,* for by 2002 he is reduced to be like those of his earlier audience, but with the crucial difference that he cannot accept the message he once proselytized, for he knows it is an empty vision. See TD, 1:7.

[13] TD, 1:1.

those without arguments? Poverty stricken, occupants of the bayou find that their frailty can be manipulated, their weakness shaped, because one—say, a Tuttle—could take advantage to convert people's hopelessness into idolation, convince them they are other than they really are; that they are not just a step away from chaos.[14] Cohle's actions throughout the series, rather than being motivated by misanthropy, suggest a motivation to challenge those who either try to disguise or manipulate this frailty of humans for their own benefit. But if we keep this covering tendency in mind, in some ways Cohle comes up against not just corrupt politicians and monstrous church leaders, but an entire philosophical history which has taken its task as that of sweeping frailty away.

2. Rediscovery of Chaos

In large part, 20th-century continental philosophy attempted to define itself against this history whose composition lay in the narratives and images of fortifying thought against chaos. It had varying success, either by substituting its own amended histories (e.g. Heidegger), or as a critique of 'the One' (e.g., in post-war French thought).[15] Common to both strands is a critique of order through discerning a tendency of electing an entity as ontologically superior to all others, and which then functions in

[14] The Tuttle family forms, as close as there could be, the antagonist of the series. Yet even the cult they form, which abducted the women and children, is not impervious and cannot stop its own decay: as Nic Pizzolatto has pointed out, it was subject to far larger and more unknown forces 'existing on a local level' (Nic Pizzolatto, interviewed by Alan Sepinwall, *HitFix*, 10 March 2014, http://www.hitfix.com/whats-alan-watching/true-detective-creator-nic-pizzolatto-looks-back-on-season-1/single-page).

[15] Heidegger claimed that what had been 'forgotten' in the history of philosophy was the thought of 'being,' and in certain works he read historical philosophy text around instances of this 'forgetting.' Thus the history of philosophy as a history of denial. See Heidegger, *Introduction to Metaphysics* (New Haven: Yale University Press, 2000). For an excellent collection of these ideas as they were developed in post-war French thought, see *The Continental Philosophy Reader*, eds. R. Kearney and R. Rainwater (London: Routledge, 1996).

thought as an unshakable foundation upon which the whole edifice rests. Simply put, what was to be critiqued was the idea that there could be a non-frail entity.[16] While seeming to be an arbitrary yet harmless abstract tendency of thought, such a recurring commitment to a postulated 'highest being' invariably ended up with the same function. Regardless of what it was referred to, be it God or subject, it was always seen as that which was eternally responsible for ordering all around it, the gift against chaos and frailty.[17]

It is curious that, simultaneous with such philosophical critiques of order, there came renewed discoveries about chaos by the scientific community.[18] No longer negatively phrased as the region of deception and darkness, chaos began to receive a positive formulation. Its meaning shifted from being that which could undo creation to being the very progenitor of creation itself.[19] In the traditional picture, whatever orders does so by

---

[16] Indeed, one might be even tempted to think that 20th-century continental philosophy at times resembled a witch-hunt where a standard criticism of one philosopher against his or her contemporaries was to accuse their critique of the 'highest entity' as leaving the back door open for an election of another 'highest entity' in a clandestine way. An example in point would be Badiou's *Deleuze: The Clamor of Being* (Minneapolis: University of Minnesota Press, 1999).

[17] This critique is most prominently associated with Martin Heidegger. Though he shifted his philosophical vocabulary somewhat regularly, the critique of the 'highest being' is continuous across nearly all of his writings, be it identified as a 'highest being' in his early writings, or as the 'ontotheological constitution of metaphysics' in his later texts. See Heidegger, *Identity and Difference* (Chicago: University of Chicago Press, 2002), 42-75.

[18] I say 'renewed' because many such phenomena which manifest the existence of chaotic, non-linear dynamics were in fact registered by lone scientists throughout the ages. Prigogine and Stengers, agreeing with Serres, go so far as to state the Lucretian clinamen was not the product of a naïve metaphysics introduced without any good reason, but in fact constitutes some of the earliest evidence of an attempt to explain the chaotic dynamics of turbulence, which the Roman physicists would have observed in water (Ilya Prigogine and Isabelle Stengers, *Order out of Chaos* [London: Flamingo, 1984], 141).

[19] One might be tempted to think such processes as being exotic in occurrence, but, as Prigogine and Stengers point out they are in fact in abundance around us. A case in point is the Rayleigh–Bénard

acting on chaotic, unformed matter to create the simplest of beings, those with only a very basic structure. Structures of complexity were seen to arise as one achieved greater distances from chaos. But rather than the idea that structure arises solely from order, what began to emerge was the opposite: complex structure and coherence were found to be not because of an eternally ordering 'highest being,' but rather to emerge in the most chaotic of systems.[20] The discovery was shocking: one need not have order (in the traditional ontological sense) to possess structure. From this point in the sciences, the relationship between chaos and what exists in a stable sense became far murkier: chaos can directly produce either simplicity or complexity, rather than it only manifesting the simplest link on the great chain of being. That chaos can account for that which is, entails the possibility that anything that is, is equally subject to chaos.

***

It would seem that, with such an account of chaos, we are able to advance the thesis that frailty is universal, for if everything is equally subject to chaos, then it also possible that everything is equally frail. However, this chaos which was uncovered by the sciences can only allow us to assert the existence of an *empirical* frailty. Put differently, empirical chaos of the sciences permits the statement that, as far as we know, everything *seems* frail. This is not enough to square with Cohle's later views, for, as we shall see, he thinks everything is frail—that everything must be able to end.

---

convection effect, which emerges when one heats up certain liquids, e.g., coffee: one might think that by introducing such an extreme level of energy, the turbulence of convection would prevent any structure forming; however, '[t]he convection motion produced actually consists of the complex spatial organisation of the system. Millions of molecules move coherently, forming hexagonal convection cells of a characteristic size' (Prigogine and Stengers, *Order out of Chaos*, 142).

[20] For an account of the structure that has been discovered to be inherent in chaos, see Ian Stewart, *Does God Play Dice?: The New Mathematics of Chaos* (Harmondsworth: Penguin, 1997).

Over the next section we shall see that what Cohle develops, especially in the 2012 timeline, is what we may call a general positive ontology of the frail. How his views match up with both the philosophical and speculative thesis which states there is no entity which is not frail, that there is nothing which cannot just end. That is, how frailty is not something extrinsic to existence, but is fundamentally coded into it. Given this connection between frailty and chaos, and the critiques of order, it appears that a new ontology is demanded. We put the task as such: what would an ontology based on the frail look like? Pessimism is well suited to this task, for while it detects frailty in humans, it also recognises that frailty is not solely of the human.

3. ONTOLOGIES OF THE FRAIL

The twentieth century's critique of ontological order combined with the discovery of empirical chaos was not without its metaphysical ramifications. Indeed, it heralded a completely changed meaning of how the cosmos could be seen. To these ambiguous metaphysical problems, philosophy found itself able to muster two responses, each advancing rival positions on ontology: either from the idea that 1) the universe is ultimately a mystery to human thought (finitism); or, more recently, 2) that the universe is undergirded by a somewhat horrifying power, one which humans can know (the speculative position).[21] In addressing them, both responses had to reckon with the fact that not only were past certainties no longer viable, but, far more radically, if this is a frail world, then, as Cohle says, '[t]his is a world where nothing is solved.'[22]

---

[21] Regarding the term 'finitism,' I take its position as being all but the name of what Meillassoux has called 'strong correlationism.' I take statements of finitism as those which are, to use Meillassoux's words, 'expressions of an aspiration towards an absoluteness which would no longer retain anything metaphysical, and which one is generally careful to designate by another name. This is a piety that has been evacuated of content, and that is now celebrated for its own sake by a thinking that has given up trying to substantiate it' (Meillassoux, *After Finitude*, trans. Ray Brassier [London: Continuum, 2008], 48).

[22] TD, 1:5.

FINITISM AND THE MYSTERY

While finitism and speculation address this unsolvability, they break on its characterisation by holding differing positions on what it is we know about the world—or, rather, what thought thinks, when it thinks about the world. Confronted with metaphysical problems, the finitist admits that there may be a 'solution,' that metaphysical issues may be solved, but, owing to their belief that human thought is incapable of knowing them, such a solution will forever elude us.[23] Due to our thought being 'finite,' humans are incapable of recognising a solution as such—much in the same way that Hart claims that, in being hit by the 'detective's curse,' he could not recognise the solution right under his nose.[24] Finitists hold that anything that can be known about the world is always knowledge from the perspective of the human subject—even if we wish to talk of a time without the human. For them, metaphysical problems are unsolvable because we humans cannot solve them: they are not problems in themselves, but products of our incapacities. A finitist will back away from a statement asserting positively that the cosmos is frail, or at best will add the caveat 'as far as we know . . .' As such, finitists see humanity's philosophical position phrased as dealing with a mystery, for a mystery is a situation where there is a solution, but which the detective has insufficient understanding

[23] This move regarding the acquiescence of thought to actually solve metaphysical problems is well represented in twentieth century philosophy, especially with regards to Heidegger and Wittgenstein, and more recently in John McDowell's 'Quietism'; these can all be traced, albeit not neatly, to Kant. Having advanced his thesis that all information is subject mediated, even if it is information pertaining to a time before subjects, Kant declares that we must reconceive ontological and metaphysical problems: 'the proud name of an ontology, which presumes to offer synthetic a priori cognitions of things in general in a systematic doctrine (e.g., the principle of causality), must give way to the modest one of a mere analytic of the pure understanding' (Kant, *Critique of Pure Reason* [Cambridge: Cambridge University Press], 1998], A247/B303). For the link between this thesis and Heidegger and Wittengenstein, see Meillassoux's account of weak and strong correlationism in *After Finitude*, ch. 2. For Quietism, see John McDowell, *Mind and World* (Cambridge, MA: Harvard University Press), 1996.

[24] TD, 1:5.

or evidence to solve the case; it is a consequence of the fact that 'we shall never know one way or the other!' Philosophically, a mystery is not ontological but transcendental. The unsolvability of the world as a 'mystery' is understood as a universe whose ultimate operations eludes our capacities for knowledge.[25]

SPECULATION AND HORROR

Though the ideas finitism and its formulation of unsolvability as a mystery comprise the first response to twentieth century, we shall see that it jars with Cohle's worldview; rather, it will become clear that we must align him with the second response, that of speculation. The speculative approach is embodied in the earlier positive thesis that all entities are frail, that each and every one could simply not be, but aims to give it an ontological footing. Its starting point is to agree with the finitist's claim that we cannot know the true reason behind things. But instead of claiming that this is due to an incapacity to know on our part, the speculative thinker claims we cannot know the reason, because there in fact *is no reason*. That there is no reason for anything to be, entails that there is no necessity.[26] Not only that, but everything is ultimately contingent: not just everything in the cosmos, but the cosmos itself could just perish. Even though this in itself is a somewhat remarkable position to hold, the speculative does not halt there. For, having established the absence of the necessary reasons in the world, the next stage is comprised of the seemingly strange

[25] Given finitism's hemming in of thought's capacity, the question remains then of what there is left for thought to do. Here Meillassoux's criticism is at its most withering, because in 'forbidding reason any claim to the absolute, the end of metaphysics has taken the form of an exacerbated return of the religious . . . Once the absolute has become unthinkable, even atheism, which also targets God's inexistence in the manner of an absolute, is reduced to a mere belief, and hence to a religion, albeit of the nihilist kind' (Meillassoux, *After Finitude*, 46-47).

[26] Astute readers will recognise that I draw here on what Meillassoux has called 'unreason,' the thesis that it is not a lack of knowledge on our part that we cannot find metaphysical reasons for things, but a lack of facts to be found in reality regarding its necessity. He defines unreason as such: 'the ultimate absence of reason . . . [which] is an absolute property and not the mark of the finitude of our knowledge' (*After Finitude*, 53).

claim of contemporary speculative philosophy: in holding that contingency is a universal and necessary attribute of all possible entities, then not only can one claim that everything can just end, but also the somewhat startling point that another world may just as arbitrarily be brought forward. For absolute contingency means that anything is possible, that with the knowledge of an unlimited capacity for destruction, there is also a knowledge of a near unlimited capacity for creation, one without knowing what the capacity will bring forth. What is known through speculation is very little, but it is enough for Cohle to exclaim 'Fuck, I don't want to know anything anymore.'[27]

The name of this capacity is chaos, but in an ontological, absolute guise; one whose horror is best summed up by Meillassoux:

> If we look through the aperture which we have opened up onto the absolute, what we see there is a rather menacing power—something insensible, and capable of destroying both things and worlds, of bringing forth monstrous absurdities, yet also of never doing anything, of realizing every dream, but also every nightmare.[28]

Given that the pessimist speculates on the worst, he in some ways reaches this realisation performatively. That the labour of the pessimist detects this is made clear by Cohle in the pivotal scene in episode five, where he elaborates the possible non-existence of everything in the following extraordinary speculative statement: 'In eternity, where there is no time, nothing can grow. Nothing can become. Nothing changes. So death created time to grow the things that it would kill.'[29]

Cohle knows the worst, and in telling us aligns himself to the speculative, for this knowledge of 'Death' is a certainty on which a finitist will remain agnostic. That which is created—that which is—must be able to not be: a condition of any existing entity is the possibility of its not-being. It is not just the contingency found in an empirical chaos which we discover via

[27] TD, 1:5.
[28] Meillassoux, *After Finitude*, 64.
[29] TD, 1:5.

the sciences in the universe. For Cohle goes farther because what he expresses is a mirror image to Meillassoux's hyperchaos, a capacity, an artifice of 'menacing power'—what Cohle phrases as 'Death'—which creates without metaphysically underwriting that which is created.[30] That nothing is ever solved, that there is no closure, is not because there is an inherent mystery (due to our limitations), but is rather due to the structure of chaos being practically unlimited in its capacity to destroy and create. Cohle is not even particularly shocked that he thinks this: for a pessimist confronted with the questions posed by an arbitrary world, that the cosmos is primed to ontologically re-evaluate itself in the worst way possible is but an unsurprising answer.

Thus the speculative response transforms the 'Mystery,' which claimed that we would never know, into the horror of a universe which cannot ever be solved. When Cohle denies closure, going so far as to say that 'nothing is ever over' it relates directly to the unsolvability of the cosmos.[31] No world can ever be truly closed, none can ever come to an end, because the unsolving power of Death may reopen any case without need of any reason.[32] For each and every world, chaos is only a step away; not only that, but something far worse may take its place. The horror lies in that we can have positive knowledge of this, of a cosmos which possesses capacity to undo all other empirical knowledge. What has been discovered in speculation is re-evaluation in an ontological sense, of a power which can undo the world itself.

***

[30] Hyper-Chaos is Meillassoux's term for his absolute: 'Our absolute, in effect, is nothing other than an extreme form of chaos, a *hyper-Chaos*, for which nothing is or would seem to be, impossible, not even the unthinkable' (Meillassoux, *After Finitude*, 64).

[31] TD, 1:3.

[32] One may ask here whether we have not broken one of our own rules, for have we not made what Cohle calls Death a necessary entity? At this point we may turn to Meillassoux's own argument for hyper-chaos as absolute. Quite simply, he argues that one can have an absolute without having an absolute entity. See *After Finitude*, 60.

It should be made clear at this point that we have attained two distinct conceptions of chaos: an empirical conception and ontological one. In both, there is established a structure to chaos, both in its empirical and ontological senses, a notion which has since been registered by recent philosophy.[33] At the same time we also have attained an empirical frailty and ontological frailty. Whereas the former only allowed us a restricted notion of frailty, albeit a concrete one, we now possess frailty in an absolute, universal form: i.e., for anything to exist, it must be frail.

4. No Expectations

What then does it mean to know that everything is frail? As I mentioned in the opening, to be pessimistic is be re-evaluative: given the knowledge one has, one assumes the worst possibility entailed. Ontological knowledge of frailty makes clear the extent of possible re-evaluation: for the character of this frailty is one which demands that everything is subject to re-evaluation, even existence itself. When taken together, pessimism opens up two avenues for thought: 1) the re-evaluation of empirical existence (including the re-evaluation of the human); and 2) the always possible ontological re-evaluation brought by what Cohle calls 'Death.'

Thought through the optics of the empirical, and in particular the human, to get to 'the worst' requires the relinquishing of previous notions of self and refusing as illusory the possibilities which were previously open. In Cohle's terms this comes forth as accepting the hard neurobiological account of

---

[33] The distinction between the two philosophical forms of chaos is found in how Meillassoux, on the one hand, and Deleuze on the other, elaborate the concept. The already mentioned ontological chaos of Meillassoux (what he calls 'Hyperchaos'), is derived from an a priori argument; for Deleuze, it is explicitly designated as part of the empirical: 'The intense world of differences, in which we find the reason behind qualities and the being of the sensible, is precisely the object of a superior empiricism. This empiricism teaches us a strange 'reason,' that of the multiple, chaos and difference (nomadic distributions, crowned anarchies)' (Deleuze, *Difference and Repetition*, trans. Paul Patton [London: Athlone Press, 1994], 57).

what makes up a human.[34] But in getting to the worst, one also uncovers other possibilities, not contained in the previous image of oneself and world, which are not ruled out and in fact are equally possible. Given the on-going neurological revolution that Cohle performatively embodies, we may well accept the worst possibility, i.e., considering ourselves as meat-bags deterministically controlled by a slew of chemicals of varying complexity, but nothing stops us from seeing the advantageous possibilities in conceiving ourselves as being sentient meat.[35] But even for those who might imagine this as a disaster, one might benefit from an ontological windfall of a pessimist reaching the worst. The pessimist, just like an archaeologist, may end up uncovering more possibilities than he intended to find, or like the detective uncovering surprising new leads.

The thought of ontological re-evaluation may seem initially terrifying, for it means that nothing in existence is any more protected from annihilation. In getting to this worst, we return to Cohle, a person who has not only has no expectations on people, but none on life in general. While this may seem an initially bleak, stifling outcome, I want to conclude by showing that the ramifications this has on formulating a non-misanthropic pessimism, and the idea that pessimism opens new possibilities. What, then, is this worst on which Cohle ruminates? In his own words, he is quite clear about 'the secret and terrible fate of all life': any change in life is not possible.[36] Yet one might object that, given everything else we have seen, surely this edict now seems like something of an anomaly? Surely radical contingency of frailty means that change is always possible, that there is room

[34] For example, Cohle's point that 'as sentient meat, however illusory our identities are, we craft those identities by making value judgments. Everybody judges, all the time. Now, you got a problem with that, you're living wrong' (TD, 1:8).

[35] For example, if you find yourself having enraged someone, trying to immediately calm them down might indeed be out of the question, despite your best efforts. One could ascribe a 'folk psychological' reason for this, i.e., that they are angry with you, but far more likely is the fact that you have triggered a massive shift in their hormonal and neurophysical constitution, and that, until such a time as when they have passed from that material state, calming them might be a fool's errand.

[36] TD, 1:5.

for hope and affirmation of life? Put simply, if there is in fact hope, what grounds does Cohle have to be pessimistic? To see Cohle's point we must recall however that this secret and terrible fate has a specific cause, that we cannot remember our past lives, and because we cannot remember, we cannot change them.[37] This is a curious statement, as he is not claiming that it is a strict deterministic system, one where change does not exist, but one where if there was recollection, there would be the power to change. We reach the key juncture of this somewhat paradoxical point: for this is in fact change, but a very specific form of it, one which must be admitted is extremely restricted. For what is proposed here is not a change of your situation, but a change of 'you.' For the pessimist, recognising frailty means recognising re-evaluation—but not just any re-evaluation, as to be pessimistic demands a re-evaluative stance of who 'you' are. This can be contrasted with the change optimism promises, those suspect possibilities which give one hope and cause to affirm life. The promised possibilities of optimism demand nothing of you. It claims its life changing possibilities (for which we are told to hold out) can arise while you yourself remain the same. But it is never the case that new possibilities arise for you; rather it is that the 'you' must first change to open new possibilities. All affirmation of life relies on falling into what Cohle calls a life trap: '[a] certainty that things will be different, that you'll move to another city and meet the people that'll be the friends for the rest of your life, that you'll fall in love and be fulfilled.'[38] That is, that there will be change, that things will be different for 'you.' Cohle philosophy thus calls not for hope, not for anyone to fall into the 'ontological fallacy of expecting a light at the end of the tunnel,' one through which the illusion of 'you' may be delivered intact.[39] Pessimism knows such possibilities are not tenable and in fact are restrictive. Indeed, as a somebody, 'you' cannot remember and are barred from enact this change of 'your' life; but as a

---

[37] Cohle's full quote runs as follows: 'When you can't remember your lives, you can't change your lives, and that is the terrible and the secret fate of all life. You're trapped by that nightmare you keep waking up into' (TD, 1:5).

[38] TD, 1:3.

[39] Ibid.

nobody, change is not proscribed, for there is no 'you' or 'I' to be remembered and thus to be subject to this terrible fate.

****

As we have seen, the status of everything as frail is not at all grounds for optimism, for a simple reason: optimism is what is offered to those who despair in the face of their frailty. Confronted with the ontological significance of frailty, we may be dragged in two different ways: either optimistically (to the despot) or pessimistically (to impersonal chaos). Optimism possesses this danger and menace because it has a history of colluding with the despotic and the authoritarian. One need only look at those who tell us that the future is bright: generally it is the wealthy and the powerful, whose eyes are conveniently blinded to rampant inequality. So driven is Cohle to eradicate them, that he exposes his own philosophical tensions: for in lamenting to Hart at the end of the series that they 'didn't get them all,' that they could not close the case, Hart responds by reminding 'we ain't going to. This isn't that kind of world.'[40] This is a world which is unsolvable by nature, and no matter what we do, we cannot escape it.

Given this inescapability, to recognise frailty is to resign oneself to the necessity that you cannot change things, but in doing so, one already intuits the re-evaluative impulse of what 'you' are. Put simply, you cannot change anything, except 'you.'[41]

---

[40] TD, 1:8. Pizzolatto expands on this, pointing out that, '[t]his isn't the kind of world where you mop up everything. We discharged our duty, but of course there are levels and wheels and historical contexts to what happened that we'll never be able to touch' (Nic Pizzolatto, interviewed by Alan Sepinwall, *HitFix*). What should be noted here is that such contexts can be known, but not 'touched,' i.e., effected in any way.

[41] Malabou has gone even further on this point, claiming that material changes in our constitution force such relinquishments of identity: e.g., both large trauma to the brain and the process of ageing forces the person to lose their identity, becoming an 'ontological refugee': 'In the end it may be that for each one of us, ageing arises all of a sudden, in an instant, like a trauma, and that it suddenly transforms us, without warning, into an unknown subject. A subject who no longer has a childhood and whose fate is to live a worn-out future' (Malabou,

This recognition does not trigger just a single shift: every re-evaluation undertaken will draw possibilities which will require further re-evaluations. There is no possibility which does not demand re-evaluation and there is no true re-evaluation which does not yield new possibilities. Rather than placing an expectation on life to change, or offer new possibilities, expectation should be first on oneself to change one's self. Due to this there is in fact a speculative labour to reach the worst, which the rest of us may be grateful for, because rarely is the worst upturned as the sole possibility.

***

People are frail, and generally given to fascisms. Even the most suspicious of us is only possessed by fragile parts, parts which may be snatched up by exploitative forces which drag us along a line and suspends our critical faculties. Accepting the worst, Cohle is acutely aware of this: he knows himself as being no better than anyone else, for he is certain there is no reason to think otherwise. He knows that people can be led to do terrible things if one gives them hope that they may elude their frail existence. Equally susceptible to fairy tales which cover over ontological fragility, we can all just as easily end up in a horror story.

To recognise frailty is to recognise not only that humans are, by and large, empirically programmed, but also that, ontologically, this is not ultimately deterministic and may collapse into thanatopic chaos. Pessimism puts these senses into sharp relief, and also makes clear the connection between them: what underpins the empirically re-evaluative capacity is a far greater capacity—death—knowledge of which renders even the most apparently stratified as a frail circumstance. This is not to celebrate the pessimistic as having some sort of a priori privilege. Pessimism is a vector, which may indeed destroy us, but it also may open us up to new possibilities. Against the suspect messianic hopes of optimism, being pessimistic from time to time allows you to reassess what you are, and apprehend the new possibilities opened thereof. It forces us to shift expectations

---

Ontology of the Accident, trans. Carolyn Shread [Cambridge: Polity, 2012], 59).

away from life, and onto expecting a change from each of our selves alone. Coming to this recognition, saying that he knows who (and what) 'he' is, Cohle announces that 'there's a victory in that.'[42] On this point and this point alone, though precious few of us can bear to stay that way, I still think it the case that for most of us it helps to be pessimistic from time to time.

Indeed, nothing helps us better to guard against those who would partake in the sinister affirmation of life.

[42] TD, 1:2.

The Atmospherics of Consciousness

Paul J. Ennis

True Detective is many things: it is a reflection on contemporary masculinity, an odd-couple show, a traditional murder mystery, and much more besides. In many ways it is quite a conservative show in terms of narrative execution. We begin with a body, we find clues (about our characters and our case), relationships strain, we find our killer, and then we confront him. Our heroes are even transformed by the experience. And yet something happens in the show, quite early on, that ensured one group of people stood up and paid strict attention: a central character, one Rustin 'Rust' Cohle, explicated his worldview in blunt philosophical terms. Philosophers may have had their interest piqued, but a niche band of contemporary pessimists were witnessing something else entirely. Their specific, fringe perspective was now being aired to casual viewers of a HBO show.

As the show's creator, writer, and executive producer Nic Pizzolatto has admitted, Rust's monologue in the car in the opening episode is essentially inspired by Thomas Ligotti's *The Conspiracy against the Human Race*.[1] It is precisely Ligotti's use of contemporary perspectives – for example neuroscientific

---

[1] TD, 1:1. Michael Calia, 'Writer Nic Pizzolatto on Thomas Ligotti and the Weird Secrets of "True Detective,"' *The Wall Street Journal* (February 2, 2014), http://blogs.wsj.com/speakeasy/2014/02/02/writer-nic-pizzolatto-on-thomas-ligotti-and-the-weird-secrets-of-true-detective/. See Thomas Ligotti, *The Conspiracy against the Human Race* (New York: Hippocampus Press, 2011). This is, it must be noted, an unusual work since it exists somewhere between philosophical tract and meditation on the art of horror fiction. It is a little too blunt (and interesting) to be labelled academic philosophy, but also a little too broad to be just about horror fiction.

insights – that helps make Rust sound here like a very twenty-first century take on the *noir* detective.[2] He is not simply world-weary in the old-fashioned sense. He knows that there are good reasons to consider life meaningless. It really might be the case, these being reasonable (and well-informed) claims, that selves do not exist or that religion is a linguistic virus.[3] Beneath these scientific insights lies something closer to disposition. In other words, Rust, human as he is, tends to read in a certain direction and we can learn more about it by looking at the primary source material for this aspect of his character.

Ligotti posits that the tragedy of human existence is intimately bound up with the emergence of consciousness, which he considers the 'parent of all horrors.'[4] This theme crops up explicitly in Rust's monologue in episode one and it is fairly clear that Rust's claims that 'nature created an aspect of nature separate from itself' or that 'we are creatures that should not exist by natural law' are loose correlates of claims made by Ligotti that consciousness is 'something which should not be' and 'that cannot and should not exist by natural law.'[5] The rest of Rust's points are, more or less, a synthesis of Ligotti's blend of pessimist philosophers with the most weight placed on Peter Wessel Zapffe (who dominants the opening pages of *The Conspiracy against the Human Race*).[6] Ligotti's broad

---

[2] I have in mind here the specifically American take on film noir featuring hardboiled detectives. See Jon Tuska, *Dark Cinema: American Film Noir Cultural Perspective* (Westport: Greenword Press, 1984) or James Naremore, *More Than A Night: Film Noir in its Contexts* (Berkeley: University of California Press, 1998).

[3] TD, 1:3. To support the first thesis Ligotti relies on the pioneering neurophilosophy of Thomas Metzinger. See Thomas Metzinger, *Being No One: The Self-Model Theory of Subjectivity* (Massachusetts: MIT Press, 2003) and discussed in Ligotti, *Conspiracy*, 105-113. Rust's brief reference to religion as a linguistic virus at the revivalist tent in TD, 1:3 is surely based on the theory of memes in Richard Dawkins, *The Selfish Gene* (New York: Oxford University Press, 1976).

[4] Ligotti, *Conspiracy*, 15.

[5] TD, 1:1. Ligotti, *Conspiracy*, 16 and 111 respectively.

[6] Ligotti, *Conspiracy*, 22-32. Zapffe is certainly obscure and there is very little of his work in translation. Ligotti relies heavily on Peter Wessel Zapffe, 'The Last Messiah,' trans. Sigmund Kvaløy and Peter Reed, in *Wisdom in the Open Air: The Norwegian Roots of Deep Ecology*, eds.

conclusions are that humans are too aware for their good, that they believe they are selves when they are not, and that they should willfully stop pro-creating.[7] There is no more road to travel beyond these kinds of views. They seem to suggest suicide as the proper response to such knowledge. Rust blames his programming for his failure to do this, but such an explanation is not necessary as Ligotti reminds us:

> Simply because someone has reached the conclusion that the amount of suffering in this world is enough that anyone would be better off never having been born does not mean by force of logic or sincerity he must kill himself. It only means he has concluded that the amount of suffering in this world is enough that anyone would be better off having never been born.[8]

Ligotti's contribution to the pessimist tradition, beyond his masterful talent for synthesis, is the notion that consciousness is the advent and creator of unnatural atmospherics.[9] This phenomenon manifests strongly in horror fiction, Ligotti's natural home, and is especially clear in those stories that can generate an unsettling 'psychosphere.'[10] In horror fiction one

---

Peter Reed and David Rothenberg (Minneapolis: Minnesota University Press, 1993), 40-51.

[7] Alongside the aforementioned thinkers Zapffe and Metzinger, Ligotti draws on a number of major figures in the tradition of pessimism that the reader must mine from his notes since there is no bibliography provided in *Conspiracy*. However, the following sample constitutes a representative entry-point into the line of thinking he draws inspiration from: Arthur Schopenhauer, *Studies in Pessimism*, trans. T. Bailey Saunders (New York: Cosimo Classics, 2007), Emil Cioran, *The Trouble with Being Born*, trans. Richard Howard (New York: Seaver Books, 1976) or, more recently, David Benatar, *Better Never to Have Been: The Harm of Coming Into Existence* (Oxford: Oxford University Press, 2006).

[8] TD, 1:3. Ligotti, *Conspiracy*, 50.

[9] Ligotti, *Conspiracy*, 183.

[10] An innovative term deployed by Pizzolatto denoting, one must infer, the psychological atmosphere of a locale. Rust mentions it first in TD, 1:1. For an introduction to the genre of horror fiction see Terry Heller, *An Aesthetics of the Tale of Terror* (Illinois: University of Illinois Press,

often begins with a character who happens to be in tune with the more sinister strands operative in a specific locale.[11] On the way from Erath, scene of Dora Lange's murder, Rust informs us, 'I get a bad taste in my mouth out here. Aluminum, ash...'[12] These specific words feel strange given the context, but the message is clear: there is something off about this place. In the final episode the taste returns on the ride to Carcosa.[13] The atmospheric concentration of aluminum and ash is strong enough to let Rust sense that they have found their man.[14] Crucially, then, it is the atmosphere (psychosphere) that affirms the detection. It is for this reason that I wish to stress the significance of Ligotti's vicarious influence on *True Detective* since his pessimism has as its premise the introduction of atmospherics by consciousness.[15] It is precisely this addition that justifies Ligotti's belief that consciousness is an error.[16] The problem of consciousness is the cluster around which the show's most forceful truths combine and to this end let us examine Ligotti's specific arguments.

In strictly philosophical terms human consciousness is considered by Ligotti to be structurally paradoxical in as much as the will-to-know allows one to see the nature of existence a little

1987). A special mention, given his influence upon the genre and Ligotti in particular, must go to Edgar Allan Poe, the original master of the horror tale. See Edward H. Davidson, *Poe: A Critical Study* (Cambridge: Harvard University Press, 1966) for a classic study of Poe's immense and long-standing influence on the genre.

[11] There are numerous references made to Rust's hyper-sensitivity throughout the series (visions, neural damage and so on), but it is emphasised strongest in TD, 1:2.

[12] TD, 1:1.

[13] TD, 1:8. The vocabulary of the cult, to be discussed in more detail later, borrows heavily from Robert W. Chambers, *The King in Yellow* (Hertfordshire: Wordsworth Editions, 2010).

[14] Namely, Errol Childress. Errol is a member of a complicated and powerful family network that are suspected to have been engaged in ritual murders for numerous generations. Ultimately, however, Errol turns out to be the embodiment of the Yellow King the detectives are hunting. Appearing briefly in previous episodes, his status as main adversary is confirmed in TD, 1:8. Errol is the illegitimate child of Sam Tuttle (in turn the father of the powerful Reverend Billy Lee Tuttle and Governor Eddie Tuttle). Adding to their grip is Sheriff Ted Childress.

[15] Ligotti, *Conspiracy*, 183.

[16] See Ligotti, *Conspiracy*, 16.

too clearly, thus undermining the will-to-live.[17] Thinking, the 'core' of consciousness, operates in an unnatural manner in as much as only thinking entities can rationalise that the continuation of the species is an absurd or even unethical enterprise. We are, then, aberrations from nature, for whom the meaninglessness of life beyond brute reproduction can become apparent. Which might not be an issue if life was not filled with so much suffering. That all this suffering occurs just to create beings who, in their turn, will also suffer is the ground upon which pessimism is built. Consciousness also exhibits the peculiar characteristic of adding unrealities into reality. This is a facet of existing that is surplus to requirements for all other natural entities. Humans are strange entities once one grants that many of our fears are self-created. These non-existent fear-fictions pale in comparison to the meta-fictions we design to cover over the pointlessness of existence as such.[18] Such a strategic response, designed to repress the pessimistic train of thought, simply spells out the sheer oddness of the brain: it lets you see the emptiness at the heart of life, knows that this knowledge is problematic if you want to stay alive, and thus helpfully encourages you to delude yourself in one way or another. Anyone breaking the code of silence placed on how it goes with existence is reminded that, as Marty tells us, 'People round here don't think that way.'[19]

In many ways, Pizzolatto follows the simple formula of horror-fiction, but blends it with the *noir* detective genre. In the former genre one traditionally foreshadows something ominous and intangible, escalates its presence in the narrative, and then

[17] This strain of thinking is rigorously argued for in Ray Brassier, *Nihil Unbound: Enlightenment and Extinction* (London: Palgrave Macmillan, 2007). Brassier provides a brief 'Foreword' to Ligotti's text and is known for his own uncompromising views, which are more nihilistic than pessimistic, but operate with the same critical eye for undermining optimistic banalities. For Brassier, philosophy 'should be more than a sop to the pathetic twinge of human self-esteem' (xi).

[18] On the four methods, taken from Zapffe, of coping with the overabundance of consciousness, see Ligotti, *Conspiracy*, 31. In this instance, we can safely consider meta-fictions as a form of 'Anchoring.'

[19] TD, 1:1.

confirms that there is something off-kilter about this world.[20] That there is a war going on behind things, as Reverend Tuttle warns us.[21] For Ligotti some masters of this method are M.R. James, Arthur Machen, Edgar Allan Poe, H.P. Lovecraft and, significantly, Robert W. Chambers, of *The King in Yellow* fame.[22] The achievement of *True Detective* is to have blurred, as these writers do, the line between natural and supernatural explanation. That's why it is important that there are scenes in *True Detective* where you can't quite tell if the Tuttle/Childress clan are simply human-all-too-human figures of evil or if they are actually attuned to something forgotten, old and not quite rationally explicable. For instance, consider the reaction of Miss Delores when she sees the devil nets in Rust's notebook and is reminded of Carcosa.[23] Her rant, with mentions of 'him who eats time,' and even the visceral nature of her response, seem to speak to something otherworldly.[24] But then, moments later, her daughter seems fairly relaxed and neither detective seems overly perturbed by what has just happened.[25] Or consider the earlier encounter at Reggie Ledoux's compound where his exchange with Rust includes the warning that 'I know what happens next. I saw you in my dreams. You're in Carcosa now with me.'[26] When you watch this scene again and again it's hard to shake off the

---

[20] Ligotti expresses the core motif, the first, as follows: 'Something terrible in its being comes forward and makes its claim as a shareholder in our reality, or what we think is our reality and ours alone,' Ligotti, *Conspiracy*, 57.
[21] TD, 1:2.
[22] See Ligotti, *Conspiracy*, 57.
[23] TD, 1.7. Miss Delores is the former domestic servant of Sam Tuttle (the family patriarch as far as we can discern from the show).
[24] TD, 1:5. Her phrase here also echoes Rust's claim in the same episode that 'death created time to grow the things that it would kill.'
[25] TD, 1:5. Except maybe Rust who hopes she is wrong that death is not the end. Although by this point we are also witnessing a slight transition in his character; a certain tint of humour has crept into his pessimism absent from his previous musings.
[26] TD, 1:5. Reggie Ledoux is a co-conspirator with Errol and by extension likely the Tuttle network as well. However, his precise position or status is not made entirely clear. Given his brief dialogue it is implied that he has bought into the cult of the Yellow King heavily.

manner in which this line is delivered as if Errol is speaking through Reggie.[27]

Ultimately all this boils down to well-executed storytelling. Pizzolatto eases into his tale shades of psychological, cosmic and existential horror giving the entire show its distinctive atmosphere. This is true even if the bulk of the show focuses on fairly normal concerns and relationships. The atmospheric props are deployed selectively, hint by hint, but they are all operating with the promise of a final descent into primitiveness. In the manner of Conrad's *Heart of Darkness*, another text discussed by Ligotti, we are sailing toward a remote outpost where, it seems, anything goes and of which many rumours abound.[28] When we first catch sight of Reggie's compound it is presented as a jungle-scape replete with machete-wielding monster.[29] In this case, however, nobody has gone native per se, but rather we are working our way back in time from the (supposedly) civilised present. In the case of Dora Lange this means dredging up old, obscure things which, though not always forgotten, are somewhat repressed. The crimes of the Tuttle/Childress clan are both known and unknown, bordering on folklore, and thus they form a psychospheric traumatic memory for the region, but specifically for those on the fringes. These constitute, after all, the pool from which their victims are drawn on the basis of their powerlessness within the wider society.

There are many instances of this folkloric psychosphere remaining at the edge of memory for this fringe populace. The devil nets are our first clear example. Early on a pastor tells us his Aunt used to occupy children by making them create 'bird traps' or 'devils nets' which he attributes to her having a strain of Santeria to her beliefs.[30] Mary Fontenot's Aunt believes the devil net found out in her shed was possibly something she made in school.[31] We even see Dora Lange as a child in a picture, at what

---

[27] TD, 1:3. Note that Reggie is introduced in a brief shot in the previous episode as if he were the Yellow King.

[28] Ligotti, *Conspiracy*, 207. See Joseph Conrad, *Heart of Darkness and Other Stories* (London: Wordsworth Editions, 1998).

[29] TD, 1:5.

[30] TD, 1:1.

[31] TD, 1:1.

looks to be a *Courir de Mardi Gras* festival.[32] These were characterised, as Rust notes later, by Winterfests featuring antlers, masks, and blindfolds.[33] All this is sufficient such that meddling in occult-practises is enough to satisfy the local population when it comes to explaining Errol's actions. His gang is explained away handily as a paedophile ring with Voodoo elements.[34] The motif of the Yellow King could be read, then, as Pizzolatto's take on Lovecraftian time. We have, first, an atmospherics of the deep landscape, spreading back before the pipelines, before the Depression, before the plantations, originating perhaps in the pirate hideout days.[35] In this first sense, the Yellow King is the sprawl; its tentacles reaching far back, all around us, before we were born, after we die.[36]

It is the second Lovecraftian sense, when the narrative touches on the cosmic repetitiousness of horrors, where the show gains its depth. This is evoked most explicitly with Rust's final vision and articulated throughout with spiral imagery and discussion of eternal recurrence.[37] Spiral imagery permeates the show, whether at the original crime scene or Reggie Ledoux's distinctive tattoo, but the final cosmological vision is perhaps most significant since it occurs just prior to the confrontation with Errol.[38] This is the point where local horror (Carcosa) and cosmological horror (Rust's vision) finally synchronise atmospherically in the show. It is here where the locus of truth in *True Detective* is rendered explicit. To be conscious is to be

---

32 TD, 1:2.
33 TD, 1:7.
34 TD, 1:8.
35 To riff on Rust's wonderful historical track-back when discussing the roots of the sprawl in TD, 1:7.
36 TD, 1:8. This is how Betty, Errol's incestuous lover, describes Errol to Marty in another instance of blurring the lines between the natural and supernatural. In my own reading I take this to imply the Yellow King, qua sprawl, has existed and will continue to exist after Marty (and Rust) die. That is, she is not, though this is admittedly a more direct reading, referring to Errol specifically. However, if we consider that the sprawl does survive Errol's death then the Yellow King does, indeed, live on.
37 See Friedrich Nietzsche, *The Will to Power*, trans. Walter Kaufmann and R.J. Hollingdale (New York: Vintage Books, 1967) on the notion of eternal recurrence of the same.
38 TD, 1:8.

complicit in the sprawl of atmospherics. All bind themselves to a crime they cannot hope to solve through their continuance. Or their non-continuance. This is the circle proper. If we were to walk hand in hand into extinction it all still happened. Nothing can ever erase this and the evidence will rest in eternal stasis. Trapped in complete silence it will repeat without end.

Nothing Grows in the Right Direction: Scaling the Life of the Negative

Ben Woodard

In all its known permutations, the negative (whether coded as pessimistic, nihilistic, anti-natalist, etc.) is predominantly seen as the outgrowth of a twisted psyche, an error that should end in suicide before it leaks out of the head, before spraying indiscriminately outward like a ballerina holding an open jar of acid while doing a pirouette. Put otherwise, the inklings that life is not great, or that meaning is fragile, or maybe the continuation of the human species might not be the best idea, are generally taken to be thoughts which one should keep to themselves.

Yet a scalar and directional conflict exists which the affirmationist or optimist overlooks. That is, the negative is presumed to be inherently inward-turned even when it manifests itself externally despite the fact that the nihilist super-villain is far rarer than the affirmationist one. Evil deeds are generally more about selection bias of the overly-narrow affirmation, of the protection of some to the death of the others. Thus the preemptive cut-off of the negative position found in the statement 'why don't you just kill yourself?' is the first line of defense. Once the negative escapes the gravity of the easily dismissed would-be self-destructive ego the optimist or affirmationist stumbles to defend their territory.

Rust Cohle's answer to 'why do you get up in the morning' bears some ambivalence: either due to biological programming or to bear witness.[1] The former suggests the naturalist propulsion of species being, the animal response in the wake of cultural disgust, whereas the latter plays into the long-view, that the cultural capacity to witness, to export intelligence in the recording of data, holds some meager value while subsequently

[1] TD, 1:1.

bracketing human extinction whether prior to or following the death of the sun.[2]

Thus the second breach is passed – the conflation of the negative with the apathetic is surpassed in that the negative does not preclude labor, the avoidance of suicide (or death more generally) is not cowardice nor selfishness but as Cioran put it 'always too late.'[3] And, the eventual extinction of the human does not interrupt the production of information, the bearing witness, but only the form we view as most impressive. Having arrived at this point the question becomes: does the negative, as it is portrayed in *True Detective*, differ in kind from the affirmationist or positive gesture as an engine for disciplined thought taking reason as the choosing of a direction on ever-wider scales?

1. Biological Negativity or 'The Secret Fate of All Life'

Life goes wrong most of the time, or perhaps it goes where it wants to go, fueled by death drives and desire.[4] Or, when life goes right, in a biological sense, what goes right? If life is successful in its reproduction what is selected for reproduction is only the functional capacities of the organism, those capacities collectivized under the name intelligence which effectively predict the future via appropriate responses to stimuli thereby keeping the organism alive.

Either way life is a high-risk gamble against entropy where, as far as we know, the house always wins.

An affirmationist or pessimistic orientation then would be one bound to particular forms of temporality – of what to do with finite lifetimes, or what orientation does one take to a life-

---

[2] TD, 1:1.

[3] E.M. Cioran, *The Trouble with Being Born*, trans. Robert Howard (New York: Seaver Books, 1976), 169.

[4] I am borrowing this phrase from Giuseppe Longo. See G. Longo, M. Montévil and S. Kauffman, 'No Entailing Laws, but Enablement in the Evolution of the Biosphere,' in *Proceedings of the 14th Annual Conference Companion on Genetic and Evolutionary Computation (GECCO '12)* (New York: ACM, 2012), 1379-1392.

world? Or as Seneca puts it: 'Nothing is ours but time'[5] and yet time is a loan we cannot repay.

To qualitatively imbue life with some sanctity or evanescence pushes the human towards the path of vitalism[6] yet one that in order to talk about Life one must forget life – since to acknowledge the forces which make possible and animate the latter is to admit those that unfailingly destroy it and even any kind of ground it could possibly stand on. Thus the vitalist track ends in a place that itself denies the place it stands on while it triumphantly espouses that 'it's the journey, not the destination.' Or, it is the meaning without the matter. Or, as Henri Bergson puts it in *Creative Evolution*: 'For a conscious being, to exist is to change, to change is to mature, to mature is to go on creating oneself endlessly.'[7]

Such a qualitative seal of the topic of life brings about a combat between the pessimist and the optimist beyond quantitative measure. As David Benatar puts it in *Better Never to Have Been*, optimists and pessimists differ on two levels – on the factual and the evaluative senses (or quantitative and qualitative).[8] If whether or not there is more suffering than pleasure in the world cannot be appropriately measured (though Benatar argues there's demonstrably more suffering) then the disagreement becomes the future oriented sense of evaluative judgments. The evidence we have is that life will end, that we 'are all already dead,'[9] so that life, which is subject to the context of non-life conditions which tend toward entropy, is qualitatively

---

5 Lucius Annaeus Seneca, *Moral Epistles*, trans. Richard M. Gummere, 3 vols., Loeb Classical Library (Cambridge, MA: Harvard University Press, 1917-25), I.3.

6 By vitalism I am referring to the philosophical tradition which generally asserts that life is fundamentally non-mechanical and qualitatively separate from inorganic matter because of a life force or elan vital. Vitalism can be traced from ancient Greek thought through theories of spontaneous generation, to various versions of privileging the organic in German and French thought (Blumenbach for the former and Bergson for the latter).

7 Henri Bergson, *Creative Evolution* (New York: Dover, 1998), 7.

8 David Benatar, *Better to Never Have Been: The Harm of Coming into Existence* (Oxford: Oxford University Press, 2006).

9 See Ray Brassier, *Nihil Unbound: Enlightenment and Extinction* (London: Palgrave Macmillan, 2007).

'good,' attempts to retroactively inject the capacity for experience into a biological condition. The pessimistic view attempts to scale the various long-views before returning with a judgment – life is less than great because of oncoming disasters. Or, put in another sense, in the affirmationist view the future is a thing to be avoided in the activity of the present while the pessimistic view absorbs current knowledge about the future and lives for it (at least to minimize suffering along the way even if it increases suffering in the meantime).

Pessimism in this sense attempts to highlight the limit conditions of being 'sentient-meat' in Cohle's words.[10] The shaky ladder of evolutionary leaps does not bode well for our prospects in the short to medium run while physical and ecological models paint a dim portrait of the longer views. Yet because of, and despite of this, we are capable of engaging in a feast of ratiocination, exercises in puzzle-solving, of directing our survivalist hardware and software to far-afield problems. In this sense the aforementioned vitalist 'journey of meaning' pales in comparison to the errancy of reason without end. Thus the question never posited to Rust, as to know why he solves crimes as a pessimist, is answered not only in being good at it, but in the sterility of reason it allows suggesting a kind of Stoicism.[11] Quoting Seneca: 'Along the whole path of life Reason must be our guide, all our acts, from the smallest to the greatest, must follow her counsel; as she prompts, so also must we give.'[12]

That which seems to be an exception (or at least impressive output) of the mishmash of evolution is what allows us to stratify and date the epochs in which biological life is placed – perforating it with errors before stamping it with an expiration date. Thus, while the vitalist gesture purportedly rooted in the moment, in the present attempts to affirm life as such, it does so only through a denial of future orientation beyond that of the individual person (which, similar to the pessimistic view, must

---

[10] TD, 1:8.

[11] Broadly construed Stoicism is a philosophy (beginning in Greece in the 3rd century BC) that argues for a unified account of thought and nature through a reduction of ones one susceptibility to emotional swaying i.e. to bring one's will in accord with nature.

[12] Seneca the Elder, *Moral Essays*, trans. John W. Basore, 3 vols., Loeb Classical Library (London: W. Heinemann,1928-1935), III:85.

be selective within that life or appeal to the factual quantitative measuring of pleasure versus pain). While skeptical of the very capacity of measuring pleasure versus pain, the future orientation of pessimism allows a better sense of this even to be attempted. That is, if the now is the measure of life then the capacity to measure pain against pleasure can only be attempted through a desubjectification of the experiencing agent through time i.e. degrees of suffering are the likely condition of a human being born here and in a particular place.

Benatar argues that the pessimists can win the combat even with an appeal to the past. Namely, that there exists, he argues, an asymmetry between the statement 'the absence of pain is good' whereas 'the absence of pleasure is not bad.'[13] Thus the 'why don't you just kill yourself line' takes on another valence – it assumes that there is no more or less neutral state, that the pessimist must always be pessimistic anyway as the optimist must always be optimistic, once again admitting the temporal deadness of the logic behind the critique.[14]

Admitting the temporal deadness of the logic behind the critique simply reaffirms what we already know about the 'secret goal of all life': to spread its potentiality to exist in other forms (progeny) or to act as if there is no long view but only within the constraints of biological time. As Rust puts it: 'death invited time to grow the things it would kill.'[15]

So many of the projects designed to deny this level of negativity, by those 'so certain they were more than a biological puppet,'[16] brings us to the collective or social level of the pessimist.

---

[13] See Benatar, *Better to Never Have Been*, 40-41.

[14] In his *Conspiracy Against the Human Race*, Thomas Ligotti ties this position to the emergence of consciousness. Namely, Ligotti argues that the unknowing which comes with consciousness occurring in nature sets us apart from nature in such a way that installs fear which leads to madness, indifference, or willful ignorance. See Thomas Ligotti, *The Conspiracy against the Human Race* (New York: Hippocampus Press, 2011).

[15] TD, 1:5.

[16] TD, 1:3.

2. Existential Negativity or 'I lack the Constitution for Suicide'

If suicide is always-already too late if, as Cioran puts it (or as Rust puts it 'damage is done, you've grown up, it's already too late'),[17] if only optimists commit suicide, can we annex the outward turned psychological core of affirmation i.e. what becomes of pessimism if its external as use approaches that of optimism? Can it be said to the affirmationist, 'Why don't you just live yourself or affirm yourself?' The clunkiness of the phrase again points to the erasure of scale in the affirmationist gesture – what is good for the self is good for all – the ego expands ever outward the positive spark for all construction. Yet the rampancy of the ego requires its isolation while postulating artificial limits and cooperations down the line.

True Detective demonstrates that once our detectives are deep into the hunt the pessimistic speeches turn more to civilization, to religion, and in general to culture as ramifications of our biological frailties.[18] Biological programming gets recuperated and socially redistributed visions, faiths, and acerbic personalities take the reins of uncertain ends creating a world where 'people go away,'[19] Marty is quick to isolate the crime as the result of a twisted mind, as 'one instance' yet Rust is convinced its nature is too complex, it is 'iconic, planned, impersonal.'[20]

The potential egresses of the ego quickly come into focus on the show – 'there's a certain victory in knowing what you are'[21] where even the agency of God becomes a kind of existential threat: 'He knows you more than you know yourself" screams the preacher – this is the theological nightmare which becomes the

[17] TD, 1:2.

[18] This is particularly evident in the detective's encounter with the tent preacher in TD, 1:3 but continues as more is discovered about the ministry schools in the closing episodes of the series.

[19] TD, 1:2.

[20] TD, 1:1.

[21] TD, 1:3. Cf. Robert Chambers, *The King in Yellow* (Hertfordshire: Wordsworth Editions, 2010), Act 1, Scene 2.

social nightmare – your face is not your own, so take off your mask![22]

The principle thread of the *King in Yellow*,[23] that our faces are masks, that our outward-presentations are alien to our character, is a familiar trope to the crime drama or the thriller – the killer who hides in plain sight. Our detectives visiting the tent churches, question the stabilizing effect of collectivity – Marty: 'some folks enjoy community,' whereas for Cole serious questions are raised by those who 'gotta get together and tell themselves stories' – it's simply a cover for manipulation – one monkey tells the other monkey that the sun said 'for you to give me your . . . share.'[24] Community is simultaneously collectivization of labor and dwelling while also an added strata for manipulation. It is arguably the scaling of the social form which has allowed for particular forms of crime to evolve more ornately – anonymity resulting from sheer human numbers being one of the more well-cited factors.[25]

Cohle's approach to the camouflaging form of the social institution runs against the affirmationist approach by which collections overwhelmingly function to magnify the already existent positivity of the group's members which banks on iconography while indexing the oldness of basic beliefs without shearing their superstitious baggage. Such baggage affirms sociality for its own sake rather than a leftover from long-obsolete defensive or hunting groupings prior to settling for agricultural oppurtunism. Affirmation is construed as a seamless transition between the individual and social expression – the role and location of criticality disappears.

Pessimism is aligned against all of the social instead of its particularly damning or troublesome expressions or popular myths. Carcosa, the Yellow King, the devil traps, are composed of the same logic downsized and hidden away, complicit in a far more direct notion of sacrifice had they the time to fester. It would seem stability bred with desire, where the former restrains

---

22 TD, 1:3.

23 As suggested, Robert Chambers's *The King in Yellow* is one of the central references in *True Detective*.

24 TD, 1:3.

25 This is suggested throughout the series but is made especially evident regarding the 'sprawl' of anonymity in TD, 1:7.

the latter as it grows, determines the tension of affirmation and negation and that the corrupt forms of faith or ideology cannot be wed to either overwhelmingly.

A structural lesson exists in the difference between the assumption of the affirmationist or optimist view being automatically turned outward whereas the pessimistic is seen as self-pitying, myopic, or apathetic. Again this orientation misaligns the temporal-spatial fields or direction of pessimism. Following Benatar, the long-view or future-oriented nature of pessimism does not cry over spilled milk (which it would be if the negativity was only locally activated and locally focused) but illuminates future ends, things which have not yet, but will most likely, be spilled.

The legitimate or central question becomes how the hyper locality of suffering can be collectivized and not turned back in on itself in such a way that necessitates an enchantment of 'life,' at least in the human sense. Cohle's criticizing of the human who thinks 'this is all for me'[26] comes full circle in his own confession of wanting that little bit of 'deeper darkness' that looked like love in the half-open eyes of death.[27] In *On the Heights of Despair*, Cioran writes: 'There is no valid justification for suffering. Suffering has no hierarchy of values. The most interesting aspect of suffering is the sufferer's belief in its absoluteness. He believes he has a monopoly on suffering.'[28]

3. Justice without Meaning or 'This Giant Gutter in Outer Space'

The end of *True Detective* can be read as the collapse of the proper scaling of the negative – of love reasserting itself as the connective cosmic tissue against which all assailants find themselves ineffective. The last line, 'the stars are winning'[29] – that the emergence of stars in the sky speaks to the potential of creation against negation or even void is metaphor

[26] TD, 1:3.
[27] TD, 1:8.
[28] E. M. Cioran, *On the Heights of Despair* (Chicago: University of Chicago Press, 1992), 54.
[29] TD, 1:8.

masquerading as physics. It assumes that any creation in the human field of vision is creation regardless of the depths of space and time. It is weakness masquerading as optimism, masquerading as mystery.[30]

The demand or even the request for a satisfactory ending is written off as naïve wanting, as assuming that all is knowable when in fact it is little more than a desire for some coherence, some temporary ground to the line of inquiry, not as an end of all ends. The journey as *mysterium* undoes the possibility of its path other than being driven by solipsism or dreamy shares of inquiry. The negative is not apathetic but has reasons that affirmation knows not of because it admits itself to the possibility of unfreedom, the unfreedom of time, or nature, or matter, that does not bathe finitude in a fine light but engenders it, moves the story along for a while before crushing it. That is just how things go.

Because of scalar uncertainty of the application of the negative, notions such as justice, as wanting to solve the crime, are not themselves negated but are viewed as distributive modes. As Schelling put it, the law of the world (the *Weltgesetz*) is that 'all possibilities occur in equal measure' and none are suppressed.'[31] That is, justice is the distribution of creation according to our access, to ideation. Schelling's notion of justice is simply to spread out creation and minimize destruction – it is not attached to a human morality but to natural tendencies viewed anciently and broadly.

What is meaning, in terms of things being meaningful (not what is the meaning of a word for instance) other than to skew the scalability of reason into the shapes of unreason (or, what is arguably worse, to demolish the difference between reason and bad reason, between reason and reason badly used either in the

---

[30] While there is some guesswork involved in whether the stars we see in the sky are more dead or more alive, the crux of the matter is that the status of the stars must take into account their long-life span, the time it takes for their light to reach the earth in relation to our relatively short-life span. This is to say nothing of the low amount of baryonic matter vis-à-vis the amount of dark matter making up the cosmos as we understand it.

[31] F. W. J. von Schelling, *Darstellung Lecture 21*, trans. Iain Hamilton Grant (Unpublished, 2013), 2.

name of enlightenment or in the name of madness). As various thinkers adherent to a new form of rationalism have argued, one must take care to separate the disastrous history of modernity attributed to reason broadly construed and the necessity of reason to create a future oriented project as such.[32]

The bias against pessimism, beyond assuming it leads to apathetic inaction, assumes that humans cannot reduce or even redirect their pathological desires into meaningless procedures or procedures without self-directed importance. Does collectivity presuppose positivity and if so on what grounds? Malignant tumor cells get along just fine without it. Again, as mentioned above, this assumption dissolves once the scalar asymmetry between pessimism and optimism's exporting has been rendered inert.

There is an assumption that a degree of self-attention can lead to a collective attention – to some program of 'we're all in this together.' The uncertain temporal and spatial bounds of this togetherness, of an abstract care, does not adequately invoke a sense of direction (the sewing together of time and space scaled properly); it becomes the collective management and canceling out of an assumed selfishness or at least its thinning out to appear civil.

So what, what to do with this 'giant gutter in outer space?'[33] If this comment is not simply Travis Bickle on a planetary scale, the hope for a great rain to wash it all away, then what is the only collective organization to end it all – to walk 'hand in hand into extinction'[34] – to become fully anti-natalist, to join The Voluntary Human Extinction Movement?[35] Maybe? The lingering conflict between scaling the negative and the positive is that of a future of stability versus a future of less-stable construction where affirmation becomes more or less effective forms of management, whereas pessimism becomes work in the shorter term because of the acknowledgement of the knowledge of ends hunting the present. Every labor has its exhaustion, and

---

[32] See, for instance, the work of Reza Negarestani and Peter Wolfendale.

[33] TD, 1:8.

[34] TD, 1:1.

[35] The Voluntary Human Extinction Movement is a group that formed in 1991 that calls for the cessation of human reproduction for the sake of the Earth's environmental stability.

is nested in a geology of traumas,[36] and where the weight of time and the strain of space is mediated by the degradation of memory and the splitting apart of the body – there is only this body, this shadow, this darkness. There is a labor to darkness. As Boehme put it: 'It is not to be thought that the life of darkness is sunk in misery and lost as if in sorrowing. There is no sorrowing. For sorrow is a thing that is swallowed up in death, and death and dying are the very life of the darkness.'[37] That is, while darkness is self-closing – it is still an activity, a direction – its long temporality being 'tied off'[38] or flattened does not undo its passage, nor does it necessitate we must lighten or enchant this passage.

Quoting Thomas Ligotti: 'There was nothing recognizable in that sky – certainly no familiar visage spread out across the night and implanted in it. There was only this blackness above and this blackness below. There was only this consuming, proliferating blackness whose only true and final success was in merely perpetuating itself as successfully as it could in a world where nothing exists that could ever hope to be anything else except what it needs to thrive upon.'[39]

So setting aside Cohle's cosmological appeal to the gassy emergence of the stars, the love as deeper darkness cannot be a place to return to, there is no cosmological laying down of one's burdens nor is there a piling of wreckage, the Benjaminian lawn ornament,[40] to our 'not being able to go on.' Our backs are not

---

[36] The concept of trauma as an ostensibly spatial arrangement comes from the work of Reza Negarestani. See especially his *Cyclonopedia: Complicity with Anonymous Materials* (Re.Press, 2008), as well as 'Undercover Softness: An Introduction to the Architecture and Politics of Decay,' *Collapse* 6 (2010), 379–430.

[37] Jacob Boehme, quoted in Cormac McCarthy, *Blood Meridian: Or the Evening Redness in the West* (New York: Vintage Books, 1992), 2.

[38] TD, 1:7.

[39] Thomas Ligotti, 'This Shadow, This Darkness,' in *Teatro Grotesco* (New York: Virgin Books, 2008), 280.

[40] I am here referring to Walter Benjamin's reading of Paul Klee's painting *Angelus Novus* in one of his theses on the philosophy of history. In a well-known passage Benjamin claims the angel of history sees the rubble of the past pile up before it while it moves toward the future to which its back is turned. See Walter Benjamin, 'Theses on the

turned away from the past, the past rests on our backs, there is no finitude to love, only the long dead things we think we might find again. The cutting loose of location or individuation from ground.

'Nothing grows in the right direction'[41] because growth makes space for death in greater swathes with the entropic percolation of space-time. Growth, as the negentropic high-risk gamble against physics, the wrestling outwards of space-and time as matter, is a post-postponement of disintegration concomitant with its invention – while no-thing grows in the right direction, nothingness grows right in every direction, as directionality – the detective needs no meaning, no love, no heart to chase it. Only a body and a shadow flat against a darkness. Or to modify a phrase from Seneca:

'Reason, too, advises us to die, if we may, according to our taste; if this cannot be, she advises us to die according to our ability, and to seize upon whatever means shall offer itself for doing violence to ourselves. It is criminal to "live by [detection]"; but, on the other hand, it is most noble to "die by [detection]."'[42]

Philosophy of History [IX],' in *Illuminations*, ed. Hannah Arendt (London: Pimlico, 1999), 249.

[41] TD, 1:7.

[42] Seneca the Elder, *Epistles*, II:71. Here I am replacing 'robbery' with 'detection.'

True Detective, Jean-Luc Godard, and Our Image Culture: 'This May Well be Heaven, this Hell Smells the Same'

Niall McCann

> It is when history is denied that it is most unmistakably at work.
>
> – Roland Barthes, *Writing Degree Zero*

> History decomposes into images, not into narratives.
>
> – Walter Benjamin, *The Arcades Project*

Set in the present day but reflecting on the past – Louisiana in the nineteen-nineties – *True Detective* tells the story of two homicide detectives, Marty Hart and Rust Cohle, who, despite their initial dislike for one other, become a successful team as they attempt to solve a series of occult-related murders. As a filmmaker, the first thing that attracted me to *True Detective* was its aesthetic; the closest to European and Asian Cinema of any television series I have come across. From the six-minute tracking shot in Episode 4 (with its use of magic realism, and its wide panoramic framing of the landscape) to the use of two Hollywood stars, it could be argued that not only does *True Detective* owe more to cinema than to television in terms of its aesthetic but, also, as I will go on to detail, that it assumes a filmic critique of the visual culture that surrounds us, and the grand narratives this culture represents.[1]

Right from the very start, it would seem, the creators of *True Detective* chose to use a carefully exacted aesthetic, whereby the central protagonists – played by Matthew

---

[1] TD, 1:2.

McConaughey and Woody Harrelson – are presented against the bleak industrial landscape of Louisiana.[2] This juxtaposition (which ultimately marries the plot to the landscape) is a recurring motif throughout the series, and manifests most frequently in scenes depicting the detectives traversing the state in their car.[3] As noted by Marco Bohr in his piece 'Exploring the Visual Style of *True Detective*,' 'this strong emphasis on Louisiana's industrial landscape . . . evokes a comparison to Richard Misrach's series of photographs entitled "Cancer Alley.'[4] In this work, photographed in Louisiana in 1998, Misrach documented communities living in abject poverty closely located

Richard Misrach, from the series 'Cancer Alley,' in *Petrochemical America* (Aperture 2012).

to high-pollution petrochemical industries. Bohr notes of how 'Misrach's photographs clearly allude to the notion that a toxic industry has sucked all life out of nearby communities already

[2] Strongly evident in TD, 1:1.
[3] See for example TD, 1:1, TD, 1:5 and TD, 1:8.
[4] Marco Bohr, 'Exploring the Visual Style of True Detective,' *Visual Culture*, http://visualcultureblog.com/2014/03/exploring-the-visual-style-of-true-detective/.

struggling from extreme levels of poverty.'[5] In *True Detective*, the cinematography suggests a similar critique, as the cooling towers and chimneys of Louisiana's industrial belt loom large over social deprivation and crime, visually connecting and linking the two.

I would argue that this filmic critique is employed by the show's creators to point to a deeper motive or causation for crime, namely, the poverty inflicted on vast swathes of the population due to the dominant economic system of capitalism. Wherever we follow Hart and Cohle we are led further and further into extreme destitution. Nevertheless, the obscenity of crimes like murder, rape, sexual violence, kidnapping and child abuse are consistently contrasted against scenes of real beauty. A good example of this is when we arrive at the 'Bunny Farm' in Episode 2. The scene is shot through the detectives' car window as it approaches an illegal brothel hidden in amongst trees. The framing of the scene through the window of the car creates a mise-en-scène that, according to Bohr, 'uncannily references Botticelli's "Primavera,"' an apt moniker for a world which contains such beauty and wonder, but in which the majority of people live below the poverty line.[6]

Many of the tropes in *True Detective* recall the work of Jean-Luc Godard. Since the beginning of his career in cinema, and along with his peers in the French New Wave, Godard was obsessed with the genre of detection. Indeed, one could argue that all of Godard's films are about detection, namely, a process which privileges questions over answers. Recalling his 1985 film *Détective*,[7] Godard, 'in order to finance *Je vous salue, Marie*,' as Colin MacCabe recounts, 'had to make the star vehicle Détective with Johnny Hallyday and Natalie Baye.'[8] Just as a television show such as *True Detective* being produced without star names attached seems highly unlikely, one could argue here that these 'stars' stand in for capitalism, which is reified in our image industry. In Godard's *Détective*, as Anna Dzenis, notes: 'the

[5] Bohr, 'Exploring the Visual Style.'
[6] Bohr, 'Exploring.'
[7] *Détective*, directed by Jean-Luc Godard (1985; Paris: StudioCanal, 2005), DVD.
[8] Colin MacCabe, *Godard: A Portrait of the Artist at Seventy* (London: Faber & Faber, 2005), 286.

pleasure of this layered, mutating image, just like the pleasure of the "detective" story, is to be found in its investigations rather than in its solutions, in its questions rather than its answers.'[9]

In viewing *True Detective*, and recognizing its roots in the hard-boiled genre of Dashiell Hammett and Raymond Chandler's Marlowe, rather than that of Edgar Allan Poe and Agatha Christie's Poirot, it would seem clear that it is the mystery rather than the 'solving' of it which draws in the series' audience. It could be argued that the series' creators had no more interest in the actual mystery of the story than that of a framing device to hang other more critical ideas on. It is not where you are going but how you get there that counts. As we learn at the end of *True Detective*, and perhaps every detective story, mysteries often remain just that, never to be solved.

Godard's continuing interest in the cross-section between cinema and capitalism and the effect cinema has on audiences to shape their view of the world is mirrored in the structure of *True Detective*. *True Detective* is a show about storytelling first and foremost.[10] The first season of *True Detective* ends like it began, with someone telling a story: in Episode 1, driving along with his new partner, Rust describes himself as a pessimist.[11] And yet, in the very last episode, Episode 8, Rust states: 'Y'know, I think the light might be winning.'[12] As Daniel Colucciello Barber argues in this volume, what this scene reveals is nothing more than some weird primordial need for humans to tell each other stories. This need to tell ourselves stories is a theme which is returned to throughout the first season of *True Detective*. All the characters in the series lie to themselves in order to live, be it Hart about his family and his marriage, Cohle about his never-ending quest to solve the case, or the indistinct congregation of people at some errant church listening to a preacher.[13] All are in need of a narrative.

If we were to take Jean-Francois Lyotard's idea that grand narratives have failed us, and apply it directly to *True Detective*,

---

[9] Anna Dzenis, 'Détective,' http://sensesofcinema.com/2002/cteq/detective/.

[10] Cf. Daniel Colucciello Barber, 'Affect Has No Story,' in this volume.

[11] TD, 1:2.

[12] TD, 1:8.

[13] The latter occurs in TD, 1:3.

we would immediately see that this is what the mise-en-scène represents.[14] Lyotard proposes an extreme simplification of the postmodern as an 'incredulity

Richard Misrach, *Untitled (New Orleans and the Gulf Coast)*, 2005.

towards meta-narratives.'[15] This could almost be a tag line for *True Detective*. Here, all the people we encounter through our protagonists are lost: economically, socially, politically, romantically, religiously; regressing into barbaric acts and violent gestures against a world that has abandoned them. No longer do their stories explain the world, they have been exposed as mere fairy-tales. One is reminded of the B.S. Johnson line – another writer who had no time for narrative – in his second novel *Alberto Angelo*: telling stories is telling lies.'[16] Stories, rather than pointing towards some kind of truth, obfuscate and hide the real from us; offering nothing more than an easily

---

[14] Jean-François Lyotard, *The Postmodern Condition: A Report on Knowledge*, trans. Geoff Bennington and Brian Massumi (Minneapolis: University of Minnesota Press, 1984).

[15] Lyotard, *The Postmodern Condition*, xxiv.

[16] Quoted in the preliminary front matter of Jonathan Coe, *Like a Fiery Elephant: The Story of B.S. Johnson* (London: Picador, 2004).

digestible version of our world, one that is comforting and easily consumable, and one that shields us from the horrors of existence.[17]

True Detective borrows from a wide-range of contemporary literature. Philosophically including, amongst others, Ray Brassier's *Nihil Unbound*, and Eugene Thacker's *In The Dust of This Planet.*[18] The show's creator and writer Nic Pizzolatto has himself spoken in-depth about these influences, and some of his other more obscure references, such as the series of short-stories entitled *The King in Yellow.*[19] I would suggest that through its clear and constant visual and textual referencing *True Detective* reminds us that we live our lives through stories, whatever that story may be. However, the question remains, what if these stories do not explain what we need them to? What if it is a nightmare instead of a dream?

Richard Misrach, *Swamp and Pipeline, Geismar, Louisiana*, from the series 'Cancer Alley,' neg. 1998, print 2012.

The title of *The King in Yellow* refers to a story within a story, a fictional play that forms the leitmotif in a series of short stories by Robert W. Chambers. Of the stories in question, the first four mention this play explicitly – a play which is said to induce despair or madness in those who read it. The stories describe 'Act i' of this play as quite ordinary, but upon reading 'Act ii' it is said

[17] Cf. Paul J. Ennis, 'The Atmospherics of Consciousness,' in this volume.
[18] Ray Brassier, *Nihil Unbound: Enlightenment and Extinction* (London: Palgrave MacMillan 2007) and Eugene Thacker, *In the Dust of Planet* (Winchester: Zero Books, 2011).
[19] Michael Calia, 'Writer Nic Pizzolatto on Thomas Ligotti and the Weird Secrets of "True Detective,"' *The Wall Street Journal* (February 2, 2014), http://blogs.wsj.com/speakeasy/2014/02/02/writer-nic-pizzolatto-on-thomas-ligotti-and-the-weird-secrets-of-true-detective/.

to drive a person mad with the revealed truths; it is here that we find the hell called 'Carcosa,' the lair where Pizzolatto's *True Detective* reaches its climax.[20]

One of the most overt references to Chambers' work in Pizzolatto's show is the idea of a document which is unwatchable due to the awful truths it will expose. In place of *The King in Yellow*, then, we have, in *True Detective*, a VHS tape featuring the death of one Marie Fontenot. We are never privy to what is on this tape. Much like the *The King in Yellow*, we only glimpse a brief moment at the beginning, but the impending horror is explicit. When we see Hart watch the tape, the camera cuts away and we hear his screams, and when our two protagonists show the tape to a former colleague, the camera cuts away again.

This idea of the unwatchable provides us with a link to what is perhaps the predominant concern of Jean-Luc Godard. For Godard it is this very notion that is the pervasive legacy of the Holocaust, namely, our inability as a visual culture to 'show' or 'watch' what happened. One of the crucial aspects of a cinematic approach to the Holocaust has been the presence or absence of footage of the camps themselves.[21] Godard has continually stated his belief that,

> . . . the camps were surely filmed in every which way by the Germans, so the archives must exist somewhere. They were filmed by Americans, by the French, but it wasn't shown because if it had been shown it would change something. And things must not change. People prefer to say never again.[22]

Godard's point here is made in reference to Claude Lanzmann's *Shoah* (1985), a film which features no archival footage at all.[23] Lanzmann's film is made up entirely of images filmed in the nineteen-seventies and nineteen-eighties featuring people the

---

[20] Robert W. Chambers, *The Yellow Sign and Other Stories* (Oakland: Chaosium, 2004). Cf. TD, 1:8.

[21] See MacCabe, *Godard.*

[22] Richard Brophy, *Everything Is Cinema: The Working Life of Jean-Luc Godard* (New York: Metropolitan Books, 2008), 510-511.

[23] *Shoah*, directed by Claude Lanzmann (1985; London: Eureka Entertainment, 2007), DVD.

director interviewed. That is to say, Jews who had survived the camps, Germans who had participated in their running, and Poles who had lived in their vicinity. This awful, almost unparalleled event in our history is here recalled through its enduring presence; as Richard Brophy describes Lanzmann's work, 'this is a film about History which takes place entirely in the present.'[24] Nevertheless, it is in its very inability to *show* the horrors that took place that mires this work for Godard, and highlights one of the central issues at the heart of our image industry; namely, the manner in which we use images not to show, but to conceal, not to understand, but to obfuscate.

The Holocaust actually represents a break in the history of cinema, a break caused by the fact that 'nobody filmed the concentration camps, no one wanted to show them or see them.'[25] Godard's thesis reflects his belief in the power of cinema, and his assumption that the overwhelming popularity of cinema would have compelled a worldwide outcry against the Holocaust, had it been documented, or recreated on screen. This failure, for Godard, signified 'the abandonment of cinema's documentary essence in favor of its spectacular side.'[26] The resultant postwar success of typically American cinema meant that the intrinsically historiographic aspect of the film was lost because in his view, 'the very essence of America is its lack of history.'[27] One could argue that it is this very break in the history of our image industry which heralds the dawn of not just American cinema but of capitalism, with which it is forever entwined. This is a system which utilizes the media, movies, news reports and television programs to disable the critical faculties of the public.[28] In order that we too, like Rust, can say, 'yes, the light is winning,' rather than look, think, or question the unpalatable horrors of our existence.[29]

---

[24] Brophy, *Everything Is Cinema*, 510.
[25] Ibid., 513.
[26] Ibid., 512.
[27] MacCabe, *Godard,* 293.
[28] See Noam Chomsky and Edward S. Herman, *Manufacturing Consent* (New York: Pantheon Books, 1988).
[29] TD, 1:8.

One attempt made by Hollywood to show the unshowable was Steven Spielberg's *Schindler's List*.[30] This film was released in December 1993 and entered the public arena in the guise of a

Richard Misrach, from the series 'Cancer Alley,' in *Petrochemical America* (Aperture 2012).

fictional successor to Lanzmann's *Shoah*, and was made, quite obviously, by a Jewish man. The narrative which Spielberg imposed on the camps to explain them, however, is necessarily misleading, and actually prevents any form of understanding; though it should be stated, and it is important to register, Spielberg's film did raise awareness of the Holocaust for a new generation; as MacCabe recalls, 'I was astonished when I took my daughter to see Schindler's List, and she informed me that she simply did not know anything about this history.'[31] The shoe-horning of the Holocaust into a story of personal success, imposing a narrative in order to 'explain' it, when this moment more closely represents the greatest failure of explanation in

[30] *Schindler's List*, directed by Steven Spielberg (1993; California: Universal Studios, 2004), DVD.
[31] MacCabe, *Godard*, 327.

human history is, as MacCabe states, at best problematic and at worst shows a 'contemptible view of history [itself].'[32] History, it would seem, is now a product to be marketed and sold.

As Frederic Jameson claims, under the contemporary climate of capitalism a 'relentless process of commodification [has] occur[ed], not merely across space but across time as well.'[33] One of the hallmarks of late capitalism is the plunder of the very often grave substance of the real lives of the past in order to cater for the idle amusement of the often surreal lives of the present. As with *Schindler's List*, historical figures, events and styles are extracted from their original context to reappear in the guise of pastiche.[34] According to Jameson this harnessing of the past principally 'as a resource for the production of the commodity serves to erode the crucial sense of historical time.'[35] The inevitable outcome is that of a widespread historical amnesia, indeed, a strategic amnesia one might add, that is central to and symptomatic of the depthlessness of our society.[36]

Richard Misrach, from the series 'Cancer Alley,' in *Petrochemical America* (Aperture 2012).

[32] MacCabe, *Godard*, 327-328

[33] Jameson, *Postmodernism, Or, The Cultural Logic of Late Capitalism* (London: Verso, 1991), 16.

[34] Ibid., 16-25.

[35] Ibid., 16.

[36] Ibid., 6.

In returning to Godard's concern with the camps, to that which is unwatchable or unshowable, to that from which we avert our gaze, it could be said that this is not simply a failure of cinema, but is an integral aspect of capitalist society. As Slavoj Žižek notes:

> Think about the strangeness of today's situation. Thirty, forty years ago, we were still debating what the future will be: communist, fascist, capitalist, whatever. Today nobody even debates these issues. We all silently accept global capitalism is here to stay. On the other hand, we are obsessed with cosmic catastrophes: the whole life on Earth disintegrating, because of some virus, because of an asteroid hitting the Earth, and so on. So the paradox is, that it's much easier to imagine the end of all life on Earth than a much more modest radical change in capitalism.[37]

This kind of system, of which the image industry is a constant invigilator (against critical thinking), not only hides from our view the horrors of the past and the continuing horrors of the present, but in fact perpetuates their occurrence. If we cannot understand the past then we are constantly doomed to repeat it. Within this context one can understand exactly why Adorno once said that it is impossible to write poetry after Auschwitz.[38] Since the Holocaust, our cinema and visual culture has become a funereal art form, one which mourns its own passing. A monster, slowly eating and regurgitating itself, mourning the meaning that has been lost in a sea of intertextuality.

---

[37] *Žižek!*, directed by Astra Taylor (2005; New York: Zeitgeist Films, 2006), DVD.
[38] Theodor W. Adorno, *Prisms* (Cambridge, MA: MIT Press, 1982).

Richard Misrach, *Community Remains, Former Morrisonville Settlement, Dow Chemical Corporation, Plaquemine, Louisiana*, from the series 'Cancer Alley,' neg. 1998, print 2012.

As *True Detective* unwound it became clear that the cardinal concern of the series was never in actually 'solving' the murder mystery *à la* Poe but rather in the idea that there is a need in our society for a convincing and satisfactory narrative.[39] For a 'conclusion' to it all. One in which everything is made clear, explained and expunged. This is played out in the very last episode, before which we glimpse the same empty images that heralded the show's beginning, only this time they are seeped in darkness. It is here that we are reminded that 'time is a flat circle.'[40] This sentence, quite literally betrayed by the fact that our protagonists think they have caught their killer, in the end merely serves to show that we are destined to begin again, until we can, as a society, create narratives which look at the world afresh. Until then we too are destined to repeat the horrors of our past.

---

[39] TD, 1:7-8.
[40] TD, 1:5.

Ultimately, through this thoughtful mise-en-scène, and what is for the most part an intelligent script, *True Detective* forces us to face up to our own need for a 'nice ending.' That this 'nice ending' leaves more questions than answers, should simply serve to remind us that we too as a world need to ask more.

‘True Dick’ – Using Misdirection and Self-Seriousness to Update the ‘Buddy Cop’ Trope for the Tumblr Generation: The Accelerated Acceptance and Premature Canonisation of *True Detective*

Daniel Fitzpatrick

We should probably begin with that title. The symposium for which this paper was prepared was announced six episodes into *True Detective’s* eight episode run. By that stage the spectacle of hyperbole surrounding the show had become as fascinating as the show itself. If anything, the show had already lost some of its lustre by this point, dropping one of its central conceits in anticipation of a finale that would delight some but disappoint just as many. The juggernaut of endlessly expanding column inches devoted to seemingly every aspect of the show continued to grow and grow regardless. HBO had certainly captured something, riding the tide of a perfectly timed ‘McConaissance’ (the popular term for Matthew McConaughey’s sudden decision to take himself seriously as an actor). Previous to this shift, McConaughey was known mostly as an ‘actor-in-search-of-a-shirt,’ appearing in sleepy roles in formulaic romantic comedies. Then a series of more spirited performances (*Killer Joe* [2011], *Mud* [2012]) began to raise his status to that of ‘serious actor.’ *True Detective* would cement this shift. The show’s marketing had focused primarily on the movie-star bona fides of McConaughey and co-star Woody Harrelson,[1] and the marketing

[1] Interestingly both actors got their starts in television, Matthew Mc Conaughey as a soon-to-be-murdered gardener, mowing lawns in an episode of the forgotten NBC show *Unsolved Mysteries*. It is worth noting here that even at this early stage of his career McConaughey was already rebelling against the repressive influence of shirts (fighting the

of the show, as well as its critical reception, seemed from the outset to speak of a condescension to the medium, implying that a TV series like *True Detective* could only ever be taken seriously if it transcended the limits of its medium and became something else entirely.

True Detective's reception is embedded within a contemporary critical and social-media environment , a so-called 'recap culture,' which necessitates instant, fully formed reactions as websites battle it out for attention. There is little room here for reflection; immediacy is key, and so it remained to be seen to what degree an academic seminar, a seminar announced before the show had completed its short run, would either extend or problematise these tendencies. In my experience, this could go either way, and my concerns in this regard resulted in a title that, upon first glance, may have suggested that I was trolling the entire enterprise. This is only partly true.

True Detective is exciting, entertaining, and at times inspired, with two exceptional performances at its centre and a few more scattered around the periphery. This was always good and sometimes great television. It was also often inconsistent in its thought processes—a tendency which grew more pronounced as it approached its conclusion. It was as close to an 'auteur' project as television was likely to get, envisioned in its entirety by its writer Nic Pizzolatto who worked with a single director (Cary Fukunaga) for the show's run. In spite of this, the final work felt like the product of contradictory personalities working at cross purposes. It is a show that would seem to be about philosophy, or at least demonstrably able to engage with complex philosophical ideas, but it is also weighed down with contradiction and struggles to articulate a clear philosophy of its own. It is also

---

good fight). Also worth noting here are some nice intertextual references, as while McConaughey's character name in the show is credited as Larry Dickens after he is introduced, we get testimony from the character's mother, credited onscreen as Dorothy Lang, which is easily abbreviated to Dora Lang, the murder victim in McConaughey's return to the televisual sphere. This begins to explain why detective Cohle gets so involved in the case, Dora Lange being his mother in a previous extratextual incarnation. Time truly is a flat circle. His co-star Harrelson also got his start in television as the lovable but dim barman Woody in the long-running sitcom *Cheers*.

often highly familiar, excessively reliant upon well-worn tropes. At the show's best, these tropes are employed knowingly and playfully, playing out a metacommentary on familiar narrative devices. At other times, however, the show seemed oblivious to the hoariness of these devices, treating them with a more po-faced earnestness. In spite of aspirations to the contrary, the show remains deeply embedded within its medium. However, the discourse of condescension that surrounded it suggested that any product of television would only ever be taken seriously if it transcended its medium, a discourse written directly into HBO's marketing strategy: 'It's not TV, it's HBO.'

More serious considerations of the products and histories of television eventually led to the emergence of Television Studies as a distinct discipline of study. It remained to be seen to what degree a symposium on *True Detective* would address the tendencies of this wider discipline. As with Film Studies before it, Television Studies has always been a hybrid discipline, borrowing extensively from other more established disciplines, particularly during its initial phases. Early interest in the medium was rooted primarily in a social studies framework,[2] and these tendencies aligned Television Studies in its formative period with the emergence of a cultural studies paradigm. In terms of more popular discourse, the subtext of many early considerations seemed to be either 'is television bad for you?' or 'how bad for you is television?' Little attention was given to a closer analysis of the actual products of television, nor was there a suggestion that this attention would be either justified or useful. However, as the products and histories of the medium began to be treated as adequate and valid objects of study, these tendencies would be reversed in favour of a more exclusively hermeneutic approach.

In a contemporary context, television, as an object of study, is far more likely to be considered via a literary-studies approach in which TV shows are 'read' and treated as self-contained 'texts.' Interpretation is key and generally little consideration is given to the wider contexts in which these texts are embedded. This wider tendency is typified, for example, by Kim Acass and Janet Mc

[2] Raymond Williams's *Television: Technology and Cultural Form* (1974) would be a key text in this regard.

Cabe's 'Reading Contemporary Television' series.[3] It is a shift that remedies, while overcompensating for, an earlier tendency to treat television solely as medium. For these contemporary approaches the medium is often evaded, obscured, or otherwise treated as invisible. This shift has become typical of what is now referred to as a 'golden age' of television, an era in which television has attracted attention from a wide array of interests, beyond the confines of its own discipline. With *The Wire, Mad Men,* and so on, television is granted a cultural pedigree it previously lacked; television viewing is no longer something to be ashamed of. The 'Reading Contemporary Television' series tackled several texts of this era, from *Ugly Betty* to *Deadwood* and the priority here was immediacy: 'this series is distinct in that it sets out to immediately comment upon the TV zeitgeist.'[4] This tendency is extended through the contemporary click-bait 'recap culture' of television criticism.

A somewhat different tendency is at work in the 'popular philosophy' publishing niche of William Irwin's 'Philosophy and . . .' series. These books cover a wealth of diverse material (*Veronica Mars and Philosophy*, *30 Rock and Philosophy*), but here the texts are being considered by a discipline outside of Television Studies as an opportunity to reapply thinking in relation to a populist medium. As the titles demonstrate this is a philosophy-first approach and the starting point is rarely the objects of study themselves but rather the ways in which these texts can be used to elucidate existing aspects of philosophical thought. Each of these approaches offers invaluable insights into their texts but their contribution to wider considerations of the medium or to the field of Television Studies generally is harder to gauge.

Television's neighboring discipline of Film Studies has suffered from many of these same issues and is by no means absolved of them yet. It too initially borrowed heavily from a literary studies framework, prioritising the 'text' and interpretation above all else, and treating films as 'ontological

3 This series, published by Macmillan, now has upwards of twenty entries.

4 Quote taken from an online iteration of the book series' jacket blurb, Kim Acass and Janet McCabe, *Reading Contemporary Television*, http://us.macmillan.com/series/ReadingContemporaryTelevision.

self-contained entities.[5] This tendency would eventually prove too reductive with insufficient acknowledgement granted to what makes an experience of 'film' different to that of a literary text, alongside a concomitant attempt to reduce film to literary principles. Here film becomes a 'language' like any other, a language which can be read in terms roughly similar to those established in literary forms; a 'shot' is the equivalent of a 'phrase', a 'scene' a 'sentence' and so on. These approaches resurface in relation to television in a climate in which the highest praise a television show can receive is for it to be compared to the 'Great Novel.'[6] *The Wire* as a contemporary equivalent to Dickens is one of the most commonly cited of these clichés, an aspect the show even reflexively commented upon in its final season.[7] Within Film Studies these tendencies underwent a shift in the late eighties/early nineties when a group of influential writers and theorists, mostly concerned with early film, prioritised wider ontological perspectives and granted greater consideration to history and context in relation to their objects of study.[8] A comparable tendency has been slower to emerge in relation to Television Studies, particularly in terms of a more general discourse. If an object of study like *True Detective* is to be considered valid it must be considered the 'Greatest of All Time,' transcending, and reducing the visibility

5 Siegfried Schimidt, 'Literary Studies from Hermeneutics to Media Culture Studies,' *CLCWeb: Comparative Literature and Culture* 12 (2010): 2, http://docs.lib.purdue.edu/clcweb/vol12/iss1/1/.

6 Adam Kirsch and Mohsin Hamid, 'Are the New 'Golden Age' TV Shows the New Novels?,' *The New York Times*, February 25, 2014, http://www.nytimes.com/2014/03/02/books/review/are-the-new-golden-age-tv-shows-the-new-novels.html.

7 The show elaborates its portrait of Baltimore through a focus on its various institutions and Season five introduces a focus on its press. Within this context a press editor repeatedly refers to the 'Dickensian aspect' of a particular story, a story that had been at least partly fabricated, a way for the show's writers to playfully acknowledge, and mock, the discourses that had built themselves up around the show, even within its run.

8 This tendency eventually becomes absorbed under the heading 'new film history,' Thomas Elsaesser considers the impact of this shift in 'The New Film History as Media Archaeology,' *Cinémas: Revue D'études Cinématographiques* 14 (2004): 75.

of, its medium. If and when a text like *True Detective* is considered in relationship to any wider histories of the medium in which it is embedded, these histories will be highly localised.

Alan Sepinwall described the impact of *The Sopranos* as the 'big bang' of contemporary television,[9] a revolution in what we understand to be television's potential and a moment typically seen as marking the starting point of our current golden age. This is now where most histories begin, creating a 'year zero' and discarding as irrelevant anything that occurred before this date. This is of course at least the third of such 'golden ages' cited in relation to television. The first was in the 1950s, when television began its domination, reaching out to larger and larger audiences.[10] This was also an important era for live broadcasting and for earlier iterations of the kinds of 'anthology' shows to which *True Detective* owes a significant debt. The second golden age comes in the 1980s,[11] as more heavily serialised shows like *Hill Street Blues* and more formally inventive shows like *Moonlighting* highlight an expanding set of possibilities for the medium. Our current golden age then typically takes in usual suspects such as *The Wire*, *Deadwood*, and *Mad Men*, but is occasionally expanded to include more 'populist,' or at least less 'serious,' fare, shows like *Lost,* or *Arrested Development*. For Brett Martin, these shows became 'the signature American art form [and] equivalent of what the films of Scorsese, Altman, Coppola, and others had been to the 1970s or the novels of Updike, Roth, and Mailer had been to the 1960s.'[12] This is also been a golden age made up predominately of male show-runners

---

[9] Alan Sepinwall, *The Revolution Was Televised: The Cops, Crooks, Slingers, and Slayers Who Changed TV Drama Forever* (New York: Touchstone, 2013).

[10] Max Wilk, *The Golden Age of Television: Notes from the Survivors* (Mount Kisco, NY: Moyer Bell, 1989).

[11] Robert J. Thompson, *Television's Second Golden Age: From Hill Street Blues to ER* (Syracuse: Syracuse University Press, 1997).

[12] Martin is the author of *Difficult Men: Behind the Scenes of a Creative Revolution: From The Sopranos and The Wire to Mad Men and Breaking Bad* (2013) and is cited here in Hope Reese, 'Why Is the Golden Age of TV So Dark?,' *The Atlantic*, July 11, 2013, http://www.theatlantic.com/entertainment/archive/2013/07/why-is-the-golden-age-of-tv-so-dark/277696/.

with shows dominated by dysfunctional male anti-heroes, a tendency *True Detective* exhaustively reiterates.

Even before the show began broadcasting commentators had already started discussing this 'revolutionary' text and its 'novelistic' approach in inflated terms.[13] By the time of its fourth episode, with its attention-grabbing long-take, the show was already cited as 'the best TV series ever made.'[14] Before the show's premiere, director Cary Fukunaga described it as 'this thing I saw as being an eight-hour movie, rather than just an episodic television show'[15] and Matthew McConaughey took a similar position when he described his decision to commit to the project: 'it was a 450-page film, is what it was.'[16] Comparisons between television and cinema are highly symptomatic of this current golden age, with texts regularly being referred to as 'cinematic' in their scope and ambition, with television also regularly described as potentially displacing cinema in terms of importance and ambition.[17] These comparisons have a longer history, but they typify the contrary position contemporary televisual texts inhabit, where in spite of a growing recognition of the products of the medium, shows like *True Detective* have to

---

[13] Allen St. John, 'How HBO's 'True Detective' Will Change The Way You Watch Television,' *Forbes*, January 13, 2014, http://www.forbes.com/sites/allenstjohn/2014/01/13/how-hbos-true-detective-will-change-the-way-you-watch-television/.

[14] 'I want to be sincere and tell you that I think True Detective is the best TV series ever made, and that I've basically held that opinion since the third episode' Shane Ryan, 'True Detective Review: 'Form and Void,'' *Paste Magazine*, http://www.pastemagazine.com/articles/2014/03/true-detective-review-form-and-void.html.

[15] Neil Drumming, 'True Detective' Director Cary Fukunaga Explains the Show's Dark Humor,' http://www.salon.com/2014/01/09/true_detective_director_cary_fukunaga_explains_the_shows_dark_humor/.

[16] ''True Detective': What We Know About Season 2,' *Chicago Tribune*, March 10, 2014, http://articles.chicagotribune.com/2014-03-10/news/sns-rt-entertainment--20140220_1_nic-pizzolatto-rust-cohle-television-show.

[17] The New Yorker, 'The Big Story: Is Television the New Cinema?,' *The New Yorker Blogs*, January 12, 2012, http://www.newyorker.com/online/blogs/culture/2012/01/the-big-story-is-television-the-new-cinema.html.

transcend the unspoken but assumed problematics and limitations of the medium to be taken seriously. It is not sufficient for a show like *True Detective* to achieve greatness in relation to its medium, and other products of its medium, instead it must become something else entirely, most typically a novel or a film.

A rigid hermeneutical approach which reduces television to self-contained texts, along with a tendency to describe it almost exclusively in relation to products of other mediums, tends to obscure the histories and specificities of this medium. A show like *True Detective*, which employs an A-list cast, a single director through its run, and has an ambitious visual coda, is interesting also for the ways in which it speaks to and remains embedded within its context as a product of television. Rather than rely on this rhetoric of transcendence, *True Detective* can also usefully be considered alongside other currently airing shows like *Enlightened, Louie, Rectify, Hannibal, Broad City,* and *Top of the Lake*. Each of these texts in their own way offers viewing pleasures as innovative as anything *True Detective* has to offer, with each also simultaneously demonstrating an acute understanding of both the capacities and limitations of its medium and offering a means to manipulate and foster these aspects accordingly. Each is in turn as instructive as anything this current golden age has produced, while also offering a diversity of perspectives lacking in many of these texts to date.

Beyond the conventional hermeneutic, literary-studies approach, what other perspectives that can be brought to work in relation to a text like *True Detective*? Siegfried J. Schmidt, writing about literary studies but making an observation that is also applicable here, outlines a wider shift 'from Hermeneutics to Media Culture Studies.'[18] He begins with a classical hermeneutic position favoring 'exclusively text-immanent analysis' and excluding 'the contexts in which literary texts are produced, distributed, received, and post-processed,'[19] positions reiterated in relation to *True Detective*. We have the opportunity to consider also those aspects excluded by these perspectives and in

[18] Siegfried Schmidt, 'Literary Studies from Hermeneutics to Media Culture Studies,' *CLCWeb: Comparative Literature and Culture* 12 (2010): 2.
[19] Ibid.

relation to *True Detective* these aspects can be particularly instructive. It is the elaborate nature of the show's reception and 'cultures of response' however that are most likely to be lost to history.

Phillip Maciak raises some of these same issues in his review of two publications which tackle this current golden age: 'while *The Sopranos* and *Lost* and *The Wire* will likely remain in circulation for generations to come, the circumstances of their original serialisation will be lost, and with them the frenzied, often generative, cultures of response.'[20] Outside of the more familiar critical responses to *True Detective*, it is in these discourses that we find key correctives to the rhetoric of transcendence that otherwise surround the show.

'True Detective Conversations,' the first of several memes that sprang up in relation to the show, a tumblr site was one of the more insightful. Each entry contained three sequential 'screencaps' from the show, in which Cohle responds to a question put to him by Harrelson's Hart. A funny moment in and of itself here it is twinned here with various imagined pieces of dialogue, in which Hart tries to engage Cohle in topical small-talk:

> Hart: Weathers been pretty crazy lately don't you think?
> Cohle: I think the craziest thing about the weather is society's desire to make objective truths like 'it is cold outside' into lengthy conversations.
> Hart: perplexed

Or,

> Hart: Did you watch the Super Bowl?
> Cohle: I don't think there's anything 'super' about brain trauma.
> Hart: perplexed

[20] Phillip Maciak, 'Kill The Leading Man: Two Histories of 21st Century Television,' *Los Angeles Review of Books*, August 14, 2013, https://lareviewofbooks.org/review/kill-the-leading-man-two-histories-of-21st-century-television.

As with most memes, the more you read the funnier and more cutting the joke becomes so that even basic non-sequiturs function:

> Hart: What's your favourite Winter Olympics event?
> Cohle: Curling
> Hart: perplexed

The 'truedetectiveseason2' meme was slower to emerge. Begun as an actual online conversation about possible casting decisions for the show's second season, it quickly devolved into a means by which to re-embed *True Detective* within contexts it seemed eager to transcend. '#truedetectiveseason2' reminds us of the degree to which the show relied upon well-worn 'buddy-cop' tropes, tropes endlessly reiterated by both television and film. This meme ran for weeks on end with images of pre-teen nineties TV stars the Olsen Twins in detective overcoats or other unlikely detective pairings, such as Tom Hanks and his dog in *Turner & Hooch* or Sylvester Stallone and his mom in *Stop or My Mom Will Shoot*, all accompanied on twitter with the hashtag #truedetectiveseason2. Later entries would even lose their connection to the show entirely, becoming instead layered meta-responses to the meme itself.

In addition, there were also an abundance of video parodies and responses to the show, the sharpest of which was the 'yellow king theory' clip, a sharp deconstruction of the tone of typical responses to *True Detective*. In voiceover, a narrator's describes his personal 'theory' of *True Detective*, distinguishing himself from the average viewer through his more acute engagements with the text: 'I am someone who watches TV with a careful eye for detail.'[21] In the clip an actor dressed up as a 'yellow king' is dropped into key scenes from the show. These additions are deliberately unsubtle as he dances around and directly addresses the camera, but 'Kyle's' observations remain oblivious to their obviousness – 'blink and you'll miss him.' The creators of the clip are satirizing a discourse that prioritises interpretation above all and in which even the most mundane observations are reframed as profound and insightful revelation.

---

[21] 'True Detective: Yellow King Theory,' 2014, http://www.youtube.com/watch?v=X8zTSDFiI24.

A question raised by critical responses to *True Detective* is why this show has become such a magnet for theoretical interpretation, often at the expense of other equally innovative shows?[22] Some of the claims are made in relation to the show's innovative anthology structure, whereby each season is set to play out an entirely different narrative with a new set of characters and cast. This is a format that brings a text's generic aspects to the fore, aspects that will ultimately grant the show continuity. This model was not innovated by *True Detective*, but was first successfully reinvented by FX's *American Horror Story*.[23] Another perspective that might be usefully brought to work in this regard, then, is a 'genre studies' framework, for this is after all a show that seems to be playfully aware of its genre convictions.

In terms of its genre trappings, *True Detective* remains deeply embedded within the tropes of television, with McConaughey's detective just one in a long line of exceptionally gifted crime-solvers who don't like to play by the rules. The actor replaces here an endlessly repeatable variation of doctors who solve crimes, psychics who solve crimes, robots that solve crimes, dogs that solve crimes, females that solve crimes (imagine?), a man with a 'mind palace' that solves crimes, with a philosophical nihilist that solves crimes. The show also reiterates a familiar Holmes/Watson dynamic in its central pairing, a trope in which

---

[22] HBO's *Enlightened* for example draws from a small pool of directors but also feels like an auteur project for its writer Mike White, working in collaboration with a brave and committed performance by Laura Dern. Similarly, *Top of the Lake* feels very much a Jane Campion project, a mystery thriller in the *True Detective* mode with a shared tendency toward religious symbolism. Here the Jesus figure however is a young, sexually abused girl (she evens gets her own resurrection scene), her father a violent self-flagellating criminal, and the show's God-figure a long-haired, female, trash-talking leader of a women's refuge. Neither text, however, corresponds so clearly with the established codes of this 'golden age,' rejecting their focus on the male anti-hero. Compared to both these shows, *True Detective*'s representations seem conservative and familiar, the show ultimately far too enamored with its charismatic central pairing to interrogate their position with a more critical eye.

[23] It is a format that also has a longer history reaching back beyond this current reinvention, a particularly popular format in the 1950s with shows like *Twilight Zone* or *Thriller*.

one of the two is always assigned to be the more obviously gifted but both will ultimately be necessary to solve the mystery. *True Detective* is a detective story that refuses to play fair or apply consistency with the rules of detective stories. It lazily constructs a conclusion to its central mystery that would be acceptable in an action thriller but is grossly insufficient to the detective or mystery narrative the show initially announced itself as. The 'green paint' revelation that unlocks the case, while it does allow Hart to fulfill his necessary role as the 'Watson' of the partnership, would likely have resulted in Pizzolatto being forcefully ejected from 'The Detection Club' for example.[24] Ultimately, *True Detective* replaces its initial concerns with the tropes of a *Silence of the Lambs* style thriller in a manner that doesn't function as an instance of creative genre-bending but rather as sloppy and inconsistent storytelling.

The tendency for television shows working within a modern social-media environment to overload their texts with intertextual reference, references that can then be picked up on, explored and endlessly picked apart by an on-line fan base with Wikipedia at the ready, is well established. *Lost* had earlier reaped the benefits of this approach, a show in which a single throwaway reference to Flann O'Brien's *The Third Policeman* led to an unprecedented spike in online sales of the novel.[25] *True Detective* also comes laden with intertextual reference, from

---

[24] The 'Detection Club,' a group of well-known detective writers who met regularly, established in the 1930s a code of ethics used to establish a fair relationship between the reader and the central mystery. An oath taken at these meetings included affirmations like the following: 'Do you promise to observe a seemly moderation in the use of Gangs, Conspiracies, Death-Rays, Ghosts, Hypnotism, Trap-Doors, Chinamen, Super-Criminals and Lunatics; and utterly and forever to forswear Mysterious Poisons unknown to Science?' See http://elegsabiff.com/2013/04/20/a-z-challenge-rules-of-the-detection-club-circa-1929.

[25] In this instance a writer on the show hinted that the book was chosen 'very specifically for a reason,' but ultimately the showrunners would admit they had never read the book although they had heard it was 'very interesting' ('Lostpedia - The Third Policeman,' *Lostpedia*, http://lostpedia.wikia.com/wiki/The_Third_Policeman.

Thomas Ligotti to Robert Chambers to Alan Moore.[26] These references have also led, for example, to an equally unprecedented spike of interest in the Chambers text from which the show's concepts of 'Carcosa' and the 'Yellow King' are borrowed. Through these references, engaged viewers are offered a means to unlock the show's secrets, granting a more active involvement, and while these references are often essential and enrich our experience of the show, in its weaker moments they can make it seem like a grab-bag of half thought-through allusions.

The logical extension of this tapestry approach, as well as the reworking of existing tropes, may eventually be the kind of 'big-data' programming that has already been trialed with Netflix's *House of Cards*. Netflix was in the online streaming business for some time before they started to invest in original programming and as a result they had a lot of accumulated data, drawn from over thirty million subscribers, information that would directly inform the particulars of their move into original programming. This data demonstrated that a high proportion of Netflix viewers liked movies with Kevin Spacey, that a high proportion of these also liked political dramas, and that a high proportion of these also liked movies directed by David Fincher. This information directly informed their decision then to invest a $100 million for two seasons of *House of Cards*,[27] a show which combines each of these aspects. If Netflix is to be believed,

---

[26] I would add here one overlooked intertext in relation to *True Detective* which may be of import: the comic book *Fatale*. The two texts are either eerily or suspiciously similar depending on where you sit, I would lean toward the latter. The main difference being that *Fatale* follows through on the allusions *True Detective* merely flirts with. Both have well organised cults that transcend the limits of time and space, both contains references to a text that will drive its readers insane, both have 'spaghetti monsters' but in *Fatale* they are true Lovecraftian tentacle creatures living among us.

[27] Mark Sweney, 'Netflix Gathers Detailed Viewer Data to Guide Its Search for the Next Hit,' *The Guardian*, February 23, 2014, http://www.theguardian.com/media/2014/feb/23/netflix-viewer-data-house-of-cards, and David Carr, 'For "House of Cards," Using Big Data to Guarantee Its Popularity,' *The New York Times*, http://www.nytimes.com/2013/02/25/business/media/for-house-of-cards-using-big-data-to-guarantee-its-popularity.html.

television's next golden age and the future of intertextual programming may well be automated.

THE NONSENSE OF DETECTION: TRUTH BETWEEN SCIENCE AND THE REAL

Scott Wilson

> I always speak the truth. Not the whole truth, because there's no way, to say it all. Saying it all is materially impossible: words fail. Yet it's through this very impossibility that the truth holds on to the real.
>
> – Jacques Lacan[1]

1: THE TRUTH OF NONSENSE

Nic Pizzolatto's *True Detective* aligns, it is suggested, 'criminal detection and nihilistic terror' thereby saving, impossibly we might add, 'the significance of detection from forensic positivism.'[2] But surely it is the relentless realism of scientific positivism, dedicated to the 'uncovering and exposure' of matter that unfolds the most forbidding landscape, where significance vanishes over a horizon of extinction such that there is nothing to be known because the creatures that might know something are already dead.[3] The heroically implacable pursuit of the scientific logic of reality's disenchantment and dissolution promises to

---

[1] Jacques Lacan, *Television: A Challenge to the Psychoanalytic Establishment*, ed. and trans. Jacques-Alain Miller (New York: Norton & Norton, 1990), 3, translation modified.

[2] Nicola Masciandaro, 'True Detection,' http://thewhim.blogspot.com/2014/03/true-detection-in-works.html.

[3] Cf. 'Against the anglo-historicist forensic norm of truth as something still there to be known, the crime show refreshingly advances the essential negativity of knowing, namely, the fact that truth is not an object of knowledge, but a swampy, lived matter of uncovering and exposure which perforce must stay open to its own most pessimal possibilities' (Masciandaro, 'True Detection').

unravel all forms of human consolation more effectively than pessimistically peering into a *mise-en-abyme* of apophatic negativity. And yet, the paradoxical figure of the criminal detective appropriately called 'Rust,' clutching his big notebook of clues even as he scorns the error of consciousness, gazes intently at the nonsensical yet ominous signs that shimmer above the disintegrating skyline of an unbinding cosmos, as if they contained 'the secret truth of the universe.'[4]

Rust Cohle's contention that consciousness is an error, which implies that there must be some truth somewhere against which this error might be judged, takes a moral as much as a pragmatic dimension.[5] The 'tragic misstep in evolution' implies both that consciousness is an evolutionary error producing self-consciously anxious beings who hesitate to act with the amoral efficiency of other predatory animals, and that consciousness is also a *moral* error in the sense that self-awareness enhances and exacerbates physical pain and suffering.[6] Schopenhauer's famous comment from *The World as Will and Idea* that every time a man swats a fly he implicitly 'acknowledges that the fly suffers less from being killed than he suffers from being annoyed by it,' anticipates this idea concerning the higher capacity for suffering in complex beings relative to apparently simpler life forms.[7] Indeed it is possible to contend that there is no 'physical' pain as such, that is not a product of consciousness. That pain is a faculty of the brain and consciousness is evident in phenomena such as the phantom limb and general anaesthetics. Indeed for contemporary science the reality or existence of consciousness and pain – the firing of neuronal C-fibers – outside of human brains and brains like them is highly questionable.[8]

---

[4] TD, 1:2.

[5] TD, 1:1.

[6] TD, 1:1.

[7] See Scott Wilson 'Musca Amusica,' in *Melancology: Black Metal Theory and Ecology*, ed. Scott Wilson (Winchester: Zero Books, 2014), 215. Arthur Schopenhauer, *The World as Will and Representation Volume I*, trans. E.F.J Payne (New York: Dover, 1966), 310.

[8] See V.S. Ramachandran and Sandra Blakeslee, *Phantoms in the Brain* (London: Harper Perennial, 1998). See also Georges Rey, 'A Reason for Doubting the Existence of Consciousness,' in *Consciousness and Self-Regulation, Vol 3*, eds. R. Davidson, G. Schwartz and D. Shapiro

Ever since the post-linguistic turn of the nineteen-eighties and the rapid development of cognitive neuroscience, scientists have become increasingly sceptical about the utility and even reality of 'top-down concepts such as thinking, consciousness, motivation, emotion, and similar terms,' doubting that they 'can be mapped onto corresponding brain mechanisms with similar boundaries as in our language.'[9] The eliminative materialism of Paul and Patricia Churchland famously denounced and rejected the 'folk psychological' mysticism of conventional concepts 'such as belief, desire, pain, pleasure, love, hate, joy, fear, suspicion, memory, recognition, anger, sympathy, intention and so forth.'[10] For the Churchlands folk psychology is simply bad theory that results in the frequent examples of bad human behaviour that we see all around us (e.g. the violent and passionate results of beliefs, desire, pain, pleasure, love, hate etc.) and should be replaced by a theory based in the grey matter of the brain, an eliminative materialist 'successor theory.'[11] For Thomas Metzinger, a philosopher following in the wake of cognitive neuroscience, the 'self' that is notionally regarded as the centre and owner of these traits and emotions, is likewise regarded as an illusion; Metzinger's *Being No One* (2003) and *The Ego Tunnel* (2009) contend that 'there is no such thing as a self.'[12]

This contention renders the profession of criminal detection absurd. Since there is no question of a self, no 'who' to question about the question of being or not being, the search for 'whodunit' is utterly redundant. This is why there can be no pure science of detection or criminology. The biological puppet made of 'sentient meat,' to use the words of Cohle, that is the object of science, cannot be held responsible for its actions.[13] Criminal

(New York, Plenum, 1983), 1-39 and Paul Churchland and Patricia Churchland, *On the Contrary: Critical Essays 1987-1997* (Cambridge, Massachusetts: The MIT Press, 1998).

[9] György Buzáki *Rhythms of the Brain* (Oxford: Oxford University Press, 2006), 10.

[10] Churchland and Churchland, *On the Contrary*, 3.

[11] Churchland and Churchland, *On the Contrary*, 3.

[12] Thomas Metzinger, *The Ego Tunnel: The Science of the Mind and the Myth of the Self* (New York: Basic Books, 2009), 1. See also Thomas Metzinger, *Being No One: The Self-Model Theory of Subjectivity* (Cambridge, Massachusetts: The MIT Press, 2003).

[13] TD, 1:8.

investigations logically concern a subject of crime, that is to say a legal subject supposed to be responsible for his or her actions that is of no concern to a radical neuroscientist, for whom there can be no crime. Not even the interesting legal distinction between criminality and insanity can be a concern since there is no such thing as madness any more than there is sanity, simply processes that operate, or do not. It is true that few neuroscientists are willing to pursue the social or legal implications of their theories, partly because, as Metzinger suggests, 'they often underestimate the radical nature of their positions.'[14] This seems to be the case with the Churchlands themselves and their promise of a 'superior social practice' that will come with the displacement of Folk Psychology by a theory based in a properly scientific account of 'human cognition and mental activity' which falls back on a kind of liberal pragmatism that expresses the pious hope that 'a deeper understanding of the springs of human behaviour may permit a deeper level of cognitive interaction, moral insight, and mutual care,' without explaining why the former should imply the latter.[15] As Freud might have noted, one could just as well recoil in horror at the thought of untapping the deep wellspring of human behaviour.

The notion of crime is dependent upon law – religious and political laws, not natural laws – and this law absolutely requires that there be some locus of truth, authority and justice guaranteed by God or something thing like it (a master or master signifier) somewhere on the horizon to arrest the infinite regress of rationalizations. Certainly God disappeared a long time ago, but that does not mean he hasn't left a world of sin behind him.
Is the true detective, then, the forensic one who is utterly confined by error: the error of consciousness that is disclosed by the truth immanent to scientific method as an infinite locus of endless confutations? Or at least according to Karl Popper's Humean critique of inductive reasoning that holds that no amount of empirical confirmations of a particular natural law or process can demonstrate its operative necessity; as Jacques-

[14] Metzinger, *The Ego Tunnel*, 130.

[15] Churchland and Churchland, *On the Contrary*, 35. See also Scott Wilson, 'Science and Truth,' last modified May, 2011, http://www.thelondongraduateschool.co.uk/thoughtpiece/science-and-truth-on-an-unconscious-that-isn't-one-but-something-of-the-one-2/.

Alain Miller re-iterates in an essay on science and psychoanalysis: 'the history of science is a continuum of conjectures and refutations.'[16] There are other theories of science, of course, but for the most part science is regarded as a locus of trial-and-error in which non-error concerns the production of a number of (mathematical) correspondences that appear to cohere with certain regularities or iterations found in nature so that they can be said to constitute laws, such as the law of evolution. Faith in these laws and the scientific method that discovers or produces them is essential and to this extent the faith in science is analogous to religious faith. It is unthinkable that laws might change arbitrarily or for no reason – or indeed for laws to become nonsensically paradoxical. For example, while science conceives of the world as having evolved, this conception is dependent on the consistency of this law and the necessity that laws themselves do not evolve.

It was the nineteenth-century philosopher of science and religion Émile Boutroux who in *The Contingency of the Laws of Nature* (1874) first posed the question of whether or not it was thinkable that laws themselves evolve and change.[17] This is a point made by Jacques Lacan when he asserts that 'it is not at all clear to me why the real would not allow for a law that changes,'[18] something re-iterated more recently by Quentin Meillassoux in his own musings on the contingency of natural laws and 'hyper-chaos.'[19] The laws sought by science are those that by definition must be consistent, but such consistency is ultimately a matter of faith and therefore quasi-religious. The trace of God operates in the method wherein science seeks Him (or the Devil) in the details.

---

[16] See Karl Popper, *The Logic of Scientific Discovery* (London: Routledge, 1959), cited in Jacques-Alain Miller, 'Psychoanalysis and its place among the sciences,' *Psychoanalytical Notebooks* 27 (2013), 10.
[17] See Émile Boutroux, *The Contingency Of The Laws Of The Nature*, trans. Fred Rothwell (Chicago and London: The Open Court Publishing Company), 1920.
[18] Jacques Lacan, *The Triumph of Religion* (London: Polity Press, 2013), 81.
[19] Quentin Meillassoux, *After Finitude: An Essay on the Necessity of Contingency*, trans. Ray Brassier (London: Continuum, 2009).

However, Cohle's method of detection is not that of a forensic scientist picking through the maggoty debris and DNA. Rather, he appeals to a different, more psychological tradition of detection that has historically drawn on psychoanalysis, another method of detection (of the workings of the unconscious).[20] Certainly, Cohle's specialism, his mode of interrogation, seems to owe much to certain founding assumptions about truth in psychoanalysis. In his essay on psychoanalysis's place among the sciences, Jacques-Alain Miller recalls Popper's critique of inductive reasoning because it is the complement of his devastating disqualification of any place that psychoanalysis might have therein.[21] Psychoanalysis has no place among the sciences precisely because in its concern with error, with parapraxes and slips of the tongue, it is never wrong; everything has significance for psychoanalysis and nothing happens by accident.

The serious problem with psychoanalysis is that it is always true. When in the absence of any suggestion, to cite the well-known example, an analysand blurts 'the dream is not about my mother!' we know for sure that he is telling us precisely the opposite. Psychoanalysis is always true, then, because it appeals to a 'truth' that is not the opposite of falsehood; it appeals to a truth which stands over or 'grounds' both the true and the false – or the error and the slip – which is related to the very fact of formulating any kind of utterance or action: 'for I can say nothing without positing it as true. Even when I say 'I am lying' I am saying nothing but "it is true that I am lying,"' for example.[22]

This is another dimension of the truth of detection that is well embodied by Cohle. Rust's speciality is getting people to tell the truth, or rather to acknowledge the truth that they speak, not least because he knows they are speaking the truth all the time.

---

[20] Psychoanalysis is a theory of the unconscious founded by Sigmund Freud (1856-1939). See Sigmund Freud, *The Standard Edition of the Complete Psychological Works of Sigmund Freud*, translated from the German under the general editorship of James Strachey, in collaboration with Anna Freud, assisted by Alix Strachey, Alan Tyson, and Angela Richards, 24 vols (London: Hogarth Press and the Institute of Psycho-Analysis, 1953-1974).
[21] Miller, 'Psychoanalysis.'
[22] Freud, *Complete Psychological Works*.

The truth is pouring out of them, you just have to be able to hear or see it. 'You just look them in the eyes,' says Rust, 'the whole story is right there. Everybody wears their hunger and their haunt, you know.'[23] We learn about Cohle's talent for analysis during episode three while he is himself being interrogated. His little boasts about his prowess in this regard are all part of the game of rivalry and show and tell that he is playing with the detectives and with the viewer.[24] Disconcertingly, as he talks about his special facility for seeing the hunger in the eyes and hearts of suspects, he pulls out a pocket-knife and starts making little model men out of his empty beer cans.[25] In effect what he is doing is demonstrating, through the production of these symbolic objects, how the subject (that is also the subject of crime) is produced. As Cohle never ceases to claim throughout the series, this subject is a fiction whose identity is both illusory and crafted. 'As sentient meat,' Rust says, 'however illusory our identities are, we craft those identities.'[26]

We know the subject is not the same as the 'biological puppet' made of sentient meat.[27] Rust's rather brilliant model of the subject is the aforementioned empty beer can.[28] To produce this subject we must first, as he demonstrates, empty the can of its beer, that is to say its substance (the substance that one enjoys), must be evacuated in order to reveal a central emptiness. Around this void the beer can's representational regime circulates: the battery of signifiers that bear the name and label of the brand. In Cohle's case this is the *Lone Star* beer label that designates his identification with Texas. The subject of the signifier and identity, the little fictional man (or woman) who acts in the world, is then crafted out of this basic structure: the hole that supports the symbols.[29] Cohle's laconic subject of

[23] TD, 1:3.
[24] TD, 1:3.
[25] TD, 1:3.
[26] TD, 1:8.
[27] TD, 1:3.
[28] TD, 1:3.
[29] Crime we could say is generally motivated by the fact that confronted with your empty can of beer, you suspect that someone else has drunk it, or spilled it, or that it tasted of piss, or indeed was empty to begin with. This is 'beer logic' that is not unrelated to the 'kettle logic' described by Freud. See Freud, *Complete Psychological Works*, IV: 119-20

enunciation is this empty *Lone Star* beer can, a little point of light: a pin-prick or hole in the black firmament of the universe that further supports the notion of the universe as a whole that nevertheless remains incomplete precisely because of the existence of this *Lone Star* that is the individual subject. It is for this reason that the wish to have never been born or the desire to follow Emil Cioran's instruction to rid oneself 'of the traces of this scandal [of birth]' is to repair or fill in the hole so that the universe might become whole again.[30] It is the *Lone Star* fantasy, as Nicola Masciandaro writes, of being 'surrounded by a voidal cosmos whose blackness is at once lamenting your birth and sucking you into the unending paradise of never having been.'[31] And that is why one cannot speak the whole truth; because it is precisely speech that punctures the hole in the universe.

2: MACHO NONSENSE

Since it is not possible to speak the whole truth, truth requires a metaphor and part of the disappointment of *True Detective* it seems is that it fails to deliver this metaphor just as it fails to give up on the little pin pricks of subjective light. In spite of its heroic promise, the series continually deviates from the aligned paths of 'criminal detection and nihilistic terror' and fails to disclose either a master criminal or Lovecraftian monster.[32] It even loses interest in the possibilities of conspiracy and political corruption. Worse, in the poetic finale Cohle affirms the victory that is implied by the very existence of starlight: 'once there was only dark...the light's winning.'[33] This apparently sentimental deviation from both the usual path of hard-boiled realist crime fiction and the Southern Gothic horror to which it seemed intriguingly conjoined no doubt accounts for much of the generic disappointment with which television critics greeted the end of the series. Two examples are characteristic. Describing the series

[30] Emil M. Cioran, *The Trouble with Being Born*, trans. Richard Howard (New York: Seaver Books, 1976), 19.

[31] Nicola Masciandaro, 'I Am Not Supposed to Be Here: Birth and Mystical Detection,' *Black Sun Lit*, http://blacksunlit.com/2014/05/.

[32] Masciandaro, 'True Detection.'

[33] TD, 1:8.

that promised so much as ultimately 'second rate,' *The Times* TV critic Hugo Rifkind dismissed the finale as:

> Poor. For weeks now, we've heard about a spaghetti-faced monster with green ears. What with all the spooky twisted twigs, politicians and witchcraft, this sounded like Ancient Rome. But no. It turns out he'd just been painting a house. Are we happy, really, that something painted on so vast and creepy canvas – with corrupt senators and ancient mysteries – ends up with a slapdash decorator?[34]

Following hard upon this disappointed reaction, criticism turned back on the series and it began to be denounced for its apparent misogyny. A subsequent piece in the *Sunday Times* entitled 'Women-Haters, Us?,'[35] concurred with Emily Nussbaum's contention in *The New Yorker* that it was all a load of 'macho nonsense,'[36] suggesting that for the *Sunday Times* at least part of the problem was the perceived failure of 'machismo' to deliver a satisfying climax.[37] Nussbaum's judgment was posted before the last episode – she had already got bored with it – and does not concern the denouement so much as the 'shallow' profundities of Rust Cohle. Nussbaum prefers Marty, a much more interestingly 'flawed and real' character for her than Cohle – 'a macho fantasy straight out of Carlos Castaneda' – whose 'dorm-room deep talk' fails to compensate for the paper-thin stereotypes of women on show – they're either dead bodies or eye candy, resentful wives or 'crazy pussies.'[38]

---

34 Hugo Rifkind, 'Hugo Rifkind on TV,' *The Times* (April 19, 2014), accessed May 31, 2014, http://www.thetimes.co.uk/tto/arts/tv-radio/article4066438.ece.

35 Pizzolatto quoted in Jonathan Dean, 'Women-haters, us?' *The Sunday Times* (April 20, 2014), accessed May 31, 2014, http://www.thesundaytimes.co.uk/sto/culture/film_and_tv/article140 0195.ece.

36 Emily Nussbaum, 'Cool Story, Bro: The Shallow Talk of *True Detective*,' *The New Yorker* (March 3, 2014), accessed May 31, 2014, http://www.newyorker.com/arts/critics/television/2014/03/03/14030. 3crte_television_nussbaum

37 Dean, 'Women-haters, us?'

38 Nussbaum, 'Cool Story, Bro.'

In his own defence, Nic Pizzolatto told the *Sunday Times* that 'the thing that's absolutely essential is that it is a closed-point-of-view story, and everything you see is from the point of view of the two detectives.'[39] This authorial suggestion at least alerts viewers to the idea that the world of *True Detective* is a highly subjective, 'unreliable' one, as they say in literary studies. Viewers are thus invited to disregard in any easy sense that this is an objective world guaranteed by God or science. Rather, viewers must consider the nonsense that plagues the partial perspective of the subject. As Nussbaum attests, these variations in perspective are caused by the 'irritating' nonsense that is based on sexual difference.[40]

One of the proverbs on a banner behind Reverend Theriot's make-shift pulpit stretched across the inside of his marquee bears the legend: 'Lean not on your own understanding.'[41] The preaching of God's own nonsense is always worth heeding, at least for pedagogical purposes. After all one is never going to learn anything new if one already understands and therefore knows and anticipates it. Paradoxically, but logically nevertheless, it makes good sense to pay attention to nonsense, that is to say that which one does not understand. The 'macho nonsense' to which Emily Nussbaum is alert points in the first instance to sexual difference, the 'serious muddle' that poses an intractable barrier between men and women which for psychoanalysis is fundamental.[42] 'We will never get to the bottom of the relationship between speaking beings that we sexuate as male and the speaking beings that we sexuate as woman,' writes Lacan.[43]

In her short *The New Yorker* review Nussbaum offers a perfect illustration of this impasse herself. On the one hand, she is at a loss to account for the appeal of a ridiculous fantasy figure like Rust Cohle, and yet in her own preference makes what most men would regard as the inexplicable choice of Marty.[44] The

---

[39] Dean, 'Women-haters, us?'

[40] Nussbaum, 'Cool Story, Bro.'

[41] TD, 1:3.

[42] Nussbaum, 'Cool Story, Bro.'

[43] Jacques Lacan, *The Triumph of Religion* (London: Polity Press, 2013), 78.

[44] Nussbaum, 'Cool Story, Bro.'

preference is gratuitously offered, and seemingly perversely raises the question of how any woman could choose the adulterous, chauvinistic, self-centred Marty over the ethical and super-cool Rust? One of the main functions of Marty seems precisely to be a dumb foil to Cohle's brilliance and illustrate his point about 'sentient meat' dedicated to pursuing its moronic satisfactions.[45] And yet, Nussbaum follows in this preference a certain tendency evident in *True Detective*. Throughout the series women are throwing themselves at Marty. Even his wife keeps coming back. He's a huge success with women, yet all this seems to do is make him more miserable.

Nussbaum prefers Marty because, she says, he's both 'flawed and real' relative to the fantasy-phallic figure of Rust – phallic not simply because he's clearly 'ripped,' but because he stands out as the series' signifier of desire and being.[46] Indeed, there's something of the Woman [who doesn't exist] about him.[47] Men both desire and want to be him. Certainly Marty desires him and this desire is also perhaps part of the 'problem' with the series in so far as it both stimulates yet frustrates desire in a very classically 'feminine' way. Every time the series adopts the generic form of a no-nonsense piece of detective fiction progressing through the slow accumulation of evidence towards a revelatory climax, the narrative becomes deflected by the 'bromance' of Rust and Marty's on-off relationship. Indeed, the detective fiction increasingly becomes the backdrop and condition of the inter-subjective relationship between the two protagonists. In this the series takes on a much more traditionally 'female' structure.

In Lacanian terms, it could be said that far from being 'macho,' then, *True Detective* is dominated by a 'feminine' position of being, that of the structure of the *pas-tout*, the 'not all' or 'not whole.'[48] When Emily Nussbaum says she prefers Marty because he's both 'flawed and real' she is indicating that her desire is not directed to the 'phallus' (the signifier of wholeness), but towards the signifier that is lacking in the Other,

---

[45] TD, 1:8.

[46] Nussbaum, 'Cool Story, Bro.'

[47] See Jacques Lacan, *Encore: Seminar XX* (New York: Norton & Norton, 1998).

[48] See Lacan, *Seminar XX*.

that in psychoanalysis is written S (Ø).[49] It is also why Marty, the father-failure, is the figure who is much more attuned with the senseless universe than Rust who, in his attempt at aligning 'criminal detection with nihilistic terror,' is still trying to make sense of it.[50] Marty knows that this is a stupid idea and is evidence of Rust's 'panic.'[51] Marty's position (and perhaps also that of Emily Nussbaum) is that of the fetishistic cynic who knows perfectly well that the universe is senseless but carries on anyway, seeking little bits of *jouissance* and therefore meaning here and there in the guise of a 'crazy pussy.'[52]

3: THE NONSENSE OF THE REAL

Critics giving bad reviews to pieces of work generally operate according to an economy whereby the profit (in self-aggrandizement) of their judgment cannot be fully enjoyed unless it has previously invested credit in the work under consideration. Thus before the damning verdict on *True Detective* was delivered concerning its sexual politics and ultimately disappointing ending, the series was highly commended for its look or style; especially the way the desolation of Louisiana is conveyed. For example, before dismissing the series' 'misogynist 1970s attitudes,' Jonathan Dean of the *Sunday Times* concedes that 'everyone thinks it looks great, as oil tankers glide across backgrounds, bringing space to the small screen.'[53] Even Nussbaum appreciates its 'piquant scenes of rural degradation.'[54] Of course part of the function of Cohle's profundities is to draw our attention to this aspect of things: 'this place is like somebody's memory of a town, and the memory is fading. It's like there was never anything here but jungle.'[55] But not only does Cohle draw our attention to the degradation of the place and its desolation, he connects this with

[49] Lacan, *Seminar XX*, 78.
[50] Masciandaro, 'True Detection.'
[51] TD, 1:3.
[52] TD, 1:4.
[53] Dean, 'Women-haters, us?'
[54] Nussbaum, 'Cool Story, Bro.'
[55] TD, 1:1.

the general emptiness and meaninglessness of the universe, this senseless desert in which 'consciousness was a tragic misstep': 'It's all one ghetto, man. A giant gutter in outer space.'[56] It is curious that it is this aspect of the series that unites TV critics, fans and aficionados (not to mention the contributors to this volume of essays) in mutual approval. Far from 'nihilistic terror,' the contemplation of Louisiana's swampy yet derelict terrain of depravity and depression seems to offer some kind of comfort and satisfaction.[57]

It is a commonplace to suggest that it is because of the absence of some kind of unifying ideal, guarantee or grounding principle (like God or matter, say) that the universe appears to be without meaning or purpose. For psychoanalysis, it is not so much that the absence or displacement of such a 'paternal' or 'master' signifier results in the disappearance of the semblance of meaning, but rather its deregulation and dispersal in fragments of *jouissance.* Ironically, designating the universe as uniformly 'senseless' promises to reorganize it into a unified field and thus give it a consistency that is perhaps reassuring. In the series Louisiana is both the figure for the desertified universe and yet at the same time pulsates with swampy perversion, promising monsters and conspiracy that fail to fully inflate into life. The landscape is relentlessly horizontal, but tangled, rhizomatic and labyrinthine, filled with erring nonfungible signifiers comprising the nonsense of detection: 'I don't like this place,' states Cohle, 'nothing grows in the right direction.'[58]

The failure of the paternal metaphor or name-of-the-father is a very familiar premise for crime fiction these days that produces a number of compensating versions of villainous psychopathology that the flawed yet heroic detective defeats, usually through violently blowing him away in a manner that renders him virtually indistinguishable from his enemy, thus obscuring the hole in the law with a bigger more bloody cinematic one.[59] *True Detective* both acknowledges and

---

[56] TD, 1:1.

[57] Masciandaro, 'True Detection.'

[58] TD, 1:7.

[59] On the 'name-of-the-father' see Jacques Lacan, *The Psychoses: The Seminar of Jacques Lacan, Book III*, trans. Russell Grigg (London: Routledge, 1993).

thematises this problem in different ways. With Rust this acknowledgement is also a warning, as he says to a prostitute: 'of course I'm dangerous, I'm police. I can do terrible things to people with impunity.'[60] For Marty, the identity of law and its subversion offers the promise of more entangled and conflicted enjoyment as he has himself tied up with his own handcuffs.[61] This gesture from episode two underscores what by now viewers have already recognized, that the response to the failure of paternal law is not here the familiar one of psychosis but rather perversion.

In *True Detective* we do not see the construction of a delusional metaphor in the form of a super-villain that holds together some kind of global conspiracy (in spite of numerous suggestions that this is where the series is going). Rather, the arcane signs of Carcosa are disclosed to refer to nothing but themselves, just child-like scribbling, the nonsensical writing of a signifier 'outside the Other' that promises to restore *jouissance* to the desertified universe. Eric Laurent in his essay 'Feminine Positions of Being' could almost be describing the milieu of *True Detective* when he writes:

> The mission of the pervert is that he has to do with a desolate world . . . his mission is to make everyone enjoy and to enjoy more. To enjoy more does not mean more pleasure; one very quickly leaves the terrain of pleasure to enter into more horrible spaces, but which are part of the relentlessness of his mission...and it is what makes Lacan call him a soldier working for an obscure god to whom he sacrifices all his interests in order to return to the world the surplus *jouissance* it lacks.[62]

The pervert is the 'soldier' toiling in the field of maternal demand, that is to say (mummy's) little soldier who has to regenerate the land that has been rendered a 'dead desert'

---

[60] TD, 1:2.

[61] TD, 1:2.

[62] Eric Laurent, 'Feminine Positions of Being,' in *The Later Lacan*, eds. Bogdan Wolf and Véronique Voruz (New York: SUNY Press, 2007), 230.

because of 'the king's sin.'[63] In *True Detective* this regeneration is effected through the arcane writing into existence of the obscure God, the Yellow King in the labyrinth of Carcosa that is supposed to expiate the sins of the father. Lacan writes of perversion in the form of a pun, as the *père version* that is a veering by way of the father in the default of the paternal metaphor's failure to substitute for maternal demand. For Lacan, perversion is 'the sole guarantee of this function of father, which is the function of the symptom, as I have written it.'[64]

In the absence of any paternal figures who aren't sunk, like the Tuttles, in sin and debauchery, women are split in the series into three phantasmatic types: the superegoic, the obscene and the sacred that correspond, it could be suggested, to the imaginary, real and symbolic registers. The main maternal figure is Marty's wife Maggie, an exemplary instance of the griping superegoic wife and mother who features recurrently in recent American detective movies and TV series, the wife who constantly makes demands on her guilty husband or partner tying him or her down and deflecting him or her from his symbolic role as police.[65] The superegoic wife of maternal demand is supported by the 'crazy pussies' who in *True Detective* summon the horror of incestuous *jouissance*: Marty's wayward daughter whose burgeoning sexuality causes her father so much anxiety and Errol Childress's sister-mother-lover.[66] Capping off this paring are all the dead or 'sacred' women, the girls who are sacrificed or killed. Supremely, the senseless death of Cohle's own daughter is symbolic precisely to the degree that it impeaches the symbolic order in its totality by operating as the signifier of the lack in the Other.[67]

---

[63] Eric Laurent, 'Feminine Positions,' 230.

[64] Jacques Lacan, 'Seminar of 21 January 1975,' in *Feminine Sexuality*, eds. Juliet Mitchell and Jacqueline Rose (Basingstoke and London: Macmillan, 1982), 167.

[65] In *The Wire*, for example, it is not just McNulty's and Daniels's wife who perform this function. Even the lesbian cop Griggs has to endure the cliché of a wife moaning about her long working hours and drinking with the boys. See *The Wire: The Complete Series*, created by David Simon (2002-2008; Burbank CA: Warner Home Video, 2008), DVD.

[66] The latter appears in TD, 1:8.

[67] TD, 1:2.

The standard Freudian text on perversion is 'A Child is Being Beaten,' in which what we would now call child abuse becomes the phantasmatic framework for perverse *jouissance*.[68] Perversion provides the backdrop and setting for *True Detective* where everything grows the wrong way; it sets the horizon of (self-) disgust and *jouissance* in relation to which everyone gets off one way or another. It is not just that the prime abuser, Errol Childress, is himself an abused child sunk in an incestuous relation with his sister-mother in a perpetual childhood, picking up victims from various schoolyards. It can be seen even with the two detectives themselves, betrayed in the *jouissance* of their reaction to the snuff video.[69]

Central to the series and the psychic state of its main character, the death of Cohle's daughter is 'senseless' except in so far as it 'spared [him] the sin of being a father.'[70] In one sense, no doubt, the whole series could be said to be simply the guilt-ridden fantasy of Cohle, whose Ligottiesque profundities and Nietzschean ruminations are nothing but an alibi, drawing attention both away and towards his inability to free himself from melancholy and mourning: his failure as a father to protect his daughter becomes universalized to the degree that the entirety of the symbolic order is indicted.[71] Nevertheless, his daughter's death, even as it confirms the senseless cruelty of life saves him from sinking into the cynical and perverse milieu of the Louisianan swamp. At the same time, at the heart of the Texan *Lone Star* tin-man is a father-less hole of despair, emptying beer can after beer can as if this might one day drain the last dregs of his depression.

The landscape of *True Detective* is both real and phantasmatic in so far as it provides the objective correlative of

---

68 Freud, *Complete Psychological Works*, XVII.

69 TD, 1:7.

70 TD, 1:2.

71 Friedrich Nietzsche (1844-1900) is the nineteenth-century German philosopher who in various texts proclaimed the death of God and the relativism of all values. See, for example, Friedrich Nietzsche, 'Thus Spake Zarathustra,' trans. Walter Kaufmann, in *The Portable Nietzsche* (New York: Viking Press, 1968) and Friedrich Nietzsche, 'The Genealogy of Morals,' trans. Walter Kaufmann and R.J. Hollingdale, in *On the Genealogy of Morals and Ecce Homo* (New York: Random House, 1967).

the psychic terrain of someone who is evidently clinically depressed, but whose depression is an entirely reasonable response to a predicament that is both personal and cosmic. If psychoanalysis has one thing to teach us, it is not that conclusions can be too simple (Freud refused to apologize for the monotony of his conclusions); it is on the contrary that such simplicity is neither held in common nor easily understood. 'If you say "I am depressed,"' writes Jacques-Alain Miller, 'there is no way the meaning you give to depression is the same as your neighbour's.'[72] Any meaning, if there is one, is entirely particular to the person concerned whose truth can only emerge in the gaps and failures of those words that are used to render oneself understandable. That is why 'an analyst is someone who professionally will not understand you' precisely in order to encourage the truth to emerge from the misunderstandings that disrupt the fantasy of self-knowledge.[73]

If we translate this to art and its critical reception, we could suggest that in so far as *True Detective* aligns psychic and aesthetic fictions, it similarly illustrates through the nonsense of detection this 'strange and different theory of truth and the real,' that is to say, a real 'which is not exactly external reality,' but nor in its intimacy is it foreign to it either.[74] In his final moments (from which he recovers) Rust says 'yes' to the darkness, an affirmation that is supported by an affect that that he attributes to the love of his daughter.[75] No doubt it is a delusion that Cohle, in earlier episodes of the series, would have scorned. But perhaps it is also a tacit acknowledgement that it is not the question of delusion that is important. It makes no more sense to posit the cosmos as an object of pessimism any more than as the object of an optimism that the former requires in order to offer itself as an alternative. This is something that is suggested in the way that the disappointment of Cohle's apparent revelation of an afterlife is nursed for some of his fans by the hope that his delusion is the banishing summons of an optimism that awaits the inevitable return of an even more crushing pessimism. Optimistic or pessimistic, delusion is inevitable, just as faith is integral to the

[72] Miller, 'Psychoanalysis,' 18.
[73] Miller, 'Psychoanalysis,' 18.
[74] Miller, 'Psychoanalysis,' 18.
[75] TD, 1:8.

belief in any law or prospect whatsoever, be it religious, scientific, natural or psychoanalytic. What differentiates the 'true detection' of *True Detective*, we might propose, does not ultimately concern any law. Rather, it concerns the fictional divination of, and fidelity to, the real of science that is betrayed in the secret truth of its impossibility and nonsense.

THE CORPSE IS THE TERRITORY: THE BODY OF DORA KELLY LANGE IN *TRUE DETECTIVE*

Erin K. Stapleton

Fig. 1 Dora Lange as she is found (demonstrating the 'theatrical capacity' of criminality).

The body of Dora Kelly Lange, the first victim found by Rust Cohle and Marty Hart in Season 1 of *True Detective*, gives the series an initial orientation for the narrative of investigation.[1] Dora's body, as displayed by her killer (or killers) is studied by the investigative partnership of Cohle and Hart and provides a surface, or territory of symbolic eruptions for the detectives to pursue. Of far more interest in death than she could have been in life, Dora provides a locus of necrophilic intensity for the partners, as their lives become consumed by the details of hers. The relationship between Hart and Cohle—along with other relationships in their lives—is arranged around the intimate knowledge of Lange's corpse (as well as that of other bodies that appear during the course of their investigation). The corpses of

[1] TD, 1:1.

crime (as well as other physical evidence) overwhelm the narrative of the series, which is uniquely characterised by the tracing of decay over time. Through the use of recorded interviews and the dramatisation of recollections, the series traverses the temporality of the story through the territories of the character's bodies, as they recount, in the present, details of their past experiences. The show orients the audience in time (1995, 2002, 2012) by carefully exacting a particularly unkind ageing process (to a greater or lesser degree) unevenly on each of the living characters' bodies, which serves to demonstrate the physical effects of living imperfect lives in the shadow of crime, and the corpses it creates. The disparity between the spoken recollections (in at least some aspects of the events) and the past scenes themselves draws attention to the unreliability of witness, imagination as much as memory, in contrast to the seemingly material inertia of the corpses that punctuate and structure the story.

FROM SACRIFICE TO CRIMINALITY (PRODUCING THE CORPSE AS SACRED OBJECT)

Fig. 2 Rust pulls the knife from his stomach.

'Rules describe the shape of things.'[2]

---

[2] TD, 1:3.

The specificity of the dead (human) body is essential to the transgression that appears both in the ritual that creates it, and in the investigation following the discovery of the corpse. The dead body, as Patricia MacCormack has argued, is the body at its most dynamic, 'in death, the body can be actually, physically reorganised' in a way that is impossible while maintaining living function.[3] The crimes inferred in *True Detective* bear a resemblance to the story of the serial killer Gilles de Rais (ca. 1404-1440), whose crimes and trial would later be presented in an account alongside an analysis by Georges Bataille. In this analysis, Bataille writes that Christianity has created the need for extravagant violence by requiring confession and forgiveness, 'Christianity is even fundamentally the pressing demand for crime, the demand for the horror that in a sense it needs in order to forgive.'[4] This, he argues, is exemplified by Gilles de Rais, who was associated with Joan d'Arc's campaign, and subsequently inhabited a series of castles where he raped and murdered children. In *True Detective*, the actual crimes committed remain somewhat vague, however, the narrative (and particularly the videotape Cohle steals from the home of Billy Lee Tuttle) implies that they include the ritualised rape and murder of children procured for this purpose by a church-based organisation that provides schooling in low socioeconomic areas.[5] Just as Gilles de Rais appears, for Bataille, as a response to Christianity, in *True Detective* the practice of Christianity facilitates these crimes.

The performance of criminal transgression and the artifacts it produces, which appear in the tableaus of corpses in *True Detective*, betray what Bataille refers to as the 'theatrical capacity' of criminality.[6] Bataille writes that the criminal practice of Gilles de Rais was framed by an evolving ritual that seemed more concerned with the witness of death (the sacrifice), 'to see

---

[3] Patricia MacCormack, 'Necrosexuality,' in *Rhizomes: Cultural Studies in Emerging Knowledge* 11/12 (2006), http://www.rhizomes.net/issue11/maccormack/.

[4] Georges Bataille, *The Trial of Gilles de Rais*, trans. Richard Robertson (Los Angeles: Amok Books, 2004), 16. Cf. Daniel Colucciello Barber, 'Affect Has No Story,' in this volume.

[5] TD, 1:7.

[6] Bataille, *Trial of Gilles de Rais*, 15.

death at work,' than the pursuit of sexual or erotic pleasure.[7] The sacred expenditure (the waste) inherent in killing a child, in Bataille's analysis, constitutes an absolute site of criminality to which all crime (as it transgresses articulated social boundaries) would appear to aspire. It is, as Bataille has often written, the task of literature to imagine the possibilities of these transgressions, and to mythologise them, while exploiting this 'theatrical capacity' of crime itself. In *Erotism*, Bataille even identifies within the literary genre of the detective novel an opportunity to witness violent expenditure without the risk of the criminal act itself.[8]

The practice of sacrifice, as a communicative tool, is tangibly embedded in the establishment of communities. Sacrifice produces knowledge and communal relationships where the destruction of the use-value of a sacred object occurs. For Bataille, sacrifice as a tool of social formation begins with practices of animism, and the killing of specific animals as simulacral representations of mystical deities.[9] The development of static communities (the architecture of settlement) coincided with the 'domestication of animals' in the Neolithic period, which (at least in Western European cultures) robbed them of their sacred function.[10] The bodies of animals became utilities of production, the mundanity of which undermined the system by which they could be made sacred objects. Bataille's work on Gilles de Rais further indicates that monotheism, and in particular, Christianity, produces both the need for and solution to the appearance of evil.[11] By removing sacrifice as a fundamental operation of religion (where the sacrifice of Christ cannot be exceeded) the need for expenditure remains unresolved in the community. Humanity has produced civilisation, as Bataille writes (after Freud) by developing a structure of taboos that must (to a greater or lesser extent) produce fear, and only be transgressed under certain

[7] Ibid., 14.

[8] Georges Bataille, *Erotism: Death and Sensuality*, trans. Mary Dalwood (San Francisco: City Lights Books, 1957/1962/1986), 86-87.

[9] Bataille, *Erotism*, 81.

[10] Ibid.

[11] Bataille, *Trial of Gilles de Rais*, 16.

circumstances.[12] As a result of this structure, physical impulses and desires (such as the desire for sexual acts, the desire to kill and so on) are framed as a set of prohibitions. Transgressing these prohibitions becomes the locus for expenditure and, by extension, for the designation of criminality.[13] Communities delineate opportunities for controlled transgression (which Bataille discusses in terms of the 'festival') in order to limit the opportunity for transgression in a manner that reinforces the structure of social order against an uninhibited return to animality.[14] Whereas in pre-Christian society, one of these opportunities is constituted by sacrifice (particularly of animals, as totems or simulacra of particular deities), with the crucifixion of Christ, the organisation of Christianity severs the sacred potency of animals from humanity, framed by the exclamation 'Felix Culpa!' or 'Oh happy fault,' which removes the possibility of expenditure from animals by producing (through destruction) the sacred body of Christ.[15]

Christianity's contribution to criminality, as it severs the possibility of animal sacrifice as expenditure, is also a contribution to what Bataille designates 'literature,' where the representation of horror provides a substitute or consumable simulacrum of expenditure.[16] Echoing this, Pierre Klossowski positions the artist as a simulacral criminal, as the representation of a criminal act and the act itself, which simultaneously arise from an indistinguishable impulse, where, if one can depict a 'monstrous act,' one also has the capacity or 'the strength to bring it about.'[17]

---

[12] Bataille, *Erotism*, 37.

[13] A position further affirmed by David B. Allison in 'Transgression and the Community of the Sacred,' in *The Obsessions of Georges Bataille: Community and Communication*, ed. Andrew J Mitchell and Jason Kemp Winfree (Albany: State University of New York Press, 2009), 84.

[14] Georges Bataille, *The Accursed Share*, Volume II, trans. Robert Hurley (Brooklyn: Zone Books, 1976/1993/2007), 89.

[15] Bataille, *Trial of Gilles de Rais*, 16.

[16] For a more detailed explanation of how this simulacrum functions, see Erin K. Stapleton, 'BAD COPIES: the Experience of Simulacra in Interactive Art,' *Rhizomes* 26 (2014), http://www.rhizomes.net/issue26/stapleton.html.

[17] Pierre Klossowski, *Nietzsche and the Vicious Circle*, trans. Daniel W. Smith (London: Continuum, 2005), 156.

The quasi-mystical explanations for crimes committed in *True Detective* both contextualise and obscure the rituals practiced to perform them as well as the corpses they produce.[18] In this context 'the corpse is territorialised by forensic medicine and religious ideology,' where the intimate knowledge of the corpse is exchanged between investigation and ritual—that is to say, the maintenance of capitalist economies (continued productivity) and the expenditure concomitant with a pursuit of the sacred.[19] The narrative explores and further complicates the relationship between the outwardly fundamentalist Christian context in which the crimes are committed, and the ostensibly pagan rites performed on the bodies of the victims. The rituals practiced and alluded to are neither pre-Christian nor Christian but in using human victims (and the implication of sexual violence in addition to sacrifice) the crimes respond to the conservative Christianity from which they originate, and seek to exploit the opportunities for the pleasure of transgression such a structure offers. When Lange's body is discovered, Cohle refers to it as a 'paraphilic love map'—an object of multiple fetishes and transgressions—a plethora of semiotic abjection is performed on her flesh.[20] The process of sacrifice has severed the utility of her body (its usefulness as the arrangement of a living being) allowing the territory of Lange's corpse to become reorganised through and as the topography of the investigation-as-narrative.

[18] TD, 1:1. As the investigation into Dora Lange's killer (or killers) begins in the initial episode, the first of numerous iterations of the Christian phobia of 'Satanism' (met by Cohle's rolling eyes) is introduced by Reverend Tuttle, who, as indicated above, is later found to have kept footage of his participation in these very same 'Satanic' crimes in his house.

[19] MacCormack, 'Necrosexuality,' 7.

[20] TD, 1:1.

THE BODY AND THE CORPSE

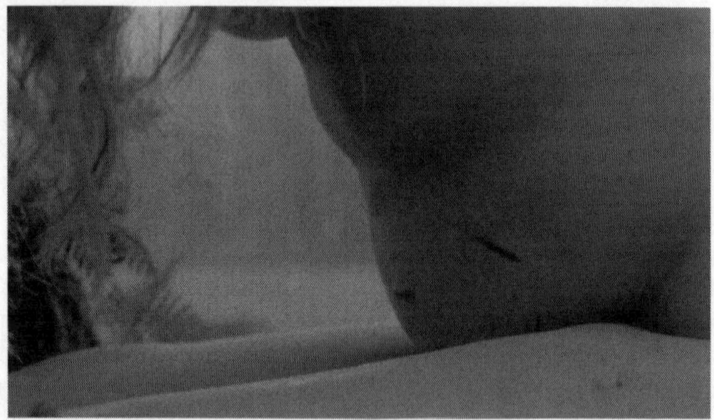

Fig. 3 Dora Lange's body is found posed, with 'shallow contusions' to her abdomen.

> For as the body is one, and hath many members, and all the members of that one body, being many, are one body: so also is Christ. (1 Corinthians, 12:12)[21]

In *True Detective*, the territory of detection is constructed materially. The investigative process (and the narrative result of that process) is located solely in the physical appearance of the evidence (the corpses, scars, locations and images). Dora Lange's corpse provides the initial territory or orientation through which the communities of *True Detective* are formed. When her body is discovered, the community of Rust and Marty, as partners in detection begins to be articulated.[22] The relationship produced between the two is a homosocial bond, that is to say, it approaches and implies a homosexual intimacy which precludes their ability to sustain relationships with partners who reflect their apparently traditional sexual interests, and this binds them to one another throughout the almost twenty year period over which the case spans.[23] The corpse itself is found beneath a

[21] As partially quoted by Rust Cohle in TD, 1:2.

[22] TD, 1:1.

[23] Homosexual, in that they share a sexual partner in Marty's (ex)wife, Rust also exercises moral judgement over Marty's sexual activity, and

singular, twisted tree in an overgrown field. A symbol, on the upper back, recalls a Minoan 'running spiral,' and the corpse is crowned by a contemporary revision of Minoan 'horns of consecration.'[24] In the detectives' investigation of the ritual practices of the murder, along with the possibility of other similar events, the details of those practises remain spectral to the narrative but appear to contain Tree Cult[25] and Animist elements.[26] This combination of pre-Christian tradition, around which the sacrificial community is arranged, situates the performance of theses murderous events outside of the Christian social order in which they are found. However, these are rituals performed with the knowledge (and erotic power) ascribed to the transgressions they represent, and are therefore not a practice of a return to animality, but an expression of violent expenditure.[27]

they repeatedly share the physical, confined intimacy of tight camera frames. In the final scenes of the show, their bodies are in excessive contact: Marty attempts to stop the bleeding from Rust's stab wound, Marty presents Rust with a box containing cigarettes, tied with a ribbon (and they joke about marriage) and Marty hugs Rust, and then assists him to walk away from the hospital.

[24] Donald Preziosi and Louise A. Hitchcock, *Aegean Art and Architecture* (Oxford: Oxford University Press, 1999), 144, 150.

[25] Caroline Tully, 'The Sacred Life of Trees: What Trees Say about People in the Pre-Historic Aegean and Near East,' *Australasian Society for Classical Studies: Selected Proceedings* 33 (2012): 7, http://www.ascs.org.au/news/ascs33/.

[26] The practice of Animism—the designation of animals as being sacred or of having a mystical purpose, particularly in prehistoric religions—was discussed by Victorian-era anthropologists and in particular by E.B. Tylor in *Primitive Culture* (1871) and Edward Clodd in *Animism: the Seed of Religion* (1905). For a more contemporary discussion of these practices, through an analysis of Tylor, see also the essay by Martin D. Stringer, 'Rethinking Animism: Thoughts from the Infancy of Our Discipline,' in *Journal of the Royal Anthropological Institute* (1999).

[27] Stuart Kendall, 'Introduction,' in George Bataille, *The Cradle of Humanity: Prehistoric Art and Culture* (New York: Zone Books, 2009), 20.

Fig. 4. Close-up detail of the spiral painted on Dora's back.

The configuration of community positioned in opposition to the alienation of the individual human body is central to the narrative of *True Detective*. The series sets up a relational dialectic between the family man, Marty Hart, and his partner, the extinction-nihilist, Rust Cohle. Cohle, having been recently transferred to the detective unit in Louisiana, is not well-liked by his colleagues. He is set apart by his refusal to assimilate—a gesture inspired in part by his intellectual capacity and in part by his insistence on espousing the futility of the continued existence of humanity.[28] As the intimate community between Cohle and Hart is formed around the corpse of Lange, and is reintensified by the discoveries of further murder victims, this pattern continues in relation to the disappearance of all the other relationships in their lives.

True Detective is far from unique in the televisual medium in using the image of a (murdered) female corpse as a vehicle through which to compose a relationship between men investigating the crime of her demise.[29] One approach that the

[28] TD, 1:1. Rust's inability to get along with his colleagues is initially demonstrated in the first episode of the series, where his refusal to be cordial causes a physical incident with another detective at the CID (Detective Geraci). In addition to his speech to Marty in the car, in which Rust argues in favor of the extinction of humanity, and his propensity to say 'odd shit,' as observed by Marty, Rust also insists upon illuminating the ludicrous nature of religion for the by then long-suffering Marty when they visit a tent revivalist congregation in TD, 1:3.

[29] Other examples include: *Twin Peaks* (1990-1991), *The Killing* (2011-present), *Broen/Bron* (2011-present), *The Bridge* (2013), *The Tunnel* (2013).

series takes is at least in part inspired by *Twin Peaks*, such that the narrativisation of murder that provides a catalyst for the series is almost forgotten in the protagonists' unraveling lives. The story-telling of the corpse, that apparition of the discontinuity, or continuity of the exuberance of life, arranges the trajectories of the living protagonists as they negotiate their investigation, as Cohle says 'everybody is nobody'—every living body, that is.[30] The performance of assembling a personality is predicated on our experience of physicality as an interaction between the competing impulses that flood our bodies and the way in which other bodies interact with our own. In *Volatile Bodies*, Elizabeth Grosz writes (after Alfonso Lingis) that archaic societies deployed the physical surface of the body (the skin) as an inscriptive surface through which to communicate.[31] This is a way for a society to wear the agreement of commonality on its surface, conveying status and purpose through scarification, tattooing and other rituals of physical (painful) sacrifice.[32]

Fig. 5 Cohle's tattoo becomes more prominent in the unsanctioned raid on the lair of Reggie and Dewall Ledoux.

30 TD, 1:1.

31 Elizabeth Grosz, *Volatile Bodies: Toward a Corporeal Feminism*, (Bloomington: Indiana University Press, 1994), 138-139.

32 For discussion of sacrifice as the price of admission to a community, see also Moira Gatens, *Imaginary Bodies: Ethics, Power and Corporeality* (London and New York: Routledge, 1996) 21-28.

In *True Detective*, the bodily surfaces of the characters informs shifts in both their outward personalities, and what little of their thoughts they reveal. Marty, once bullish, self-righteous and controlling, has lost his grip on the women around him and the resolution that allows him to do his job. His physical transformation from fit, blonde, square-jawed police detective to bloated late-middle-aged man reflects this loss (the former giving the viewer a spectral glimpse into the character's past, the latter more closely reflecting his current appearance). A motif used to sustain the appearance of Rust in the 1995 period of the story, is his small, circular mirror, mounted above a light switch in his apartment.[33] This mirror, which causes Marty some consternation for its oddness, is used by Rust to gaze into each of his eyes at intensive moments.[34] The reduction of mirror usage to the reflection of a single eye (each eye in turn) is reminiscent of the Bataillean eye—the Judas-sphere of communicative engagement and source of both erotic and violent intensities.[35] This correlates to the appearance of Rust's body in the 2012 period of the story, which is dominated by a tattoo.[36] This tattoo, of a bird, that reaches from the bottom of Rust's bicep to the middle of his forearm, is a point of distinction, and a point of contact between the community of killers (who all have tattoos and scars) and the community of detectives (who do not).

Given the 'nobody' status of the experience of humanity, the 'somebody' of *True Detective* becomes, in the first instance, the corpse of Dora Lange. Her absence, and the reconstruction of the details of her life that it inspires, produces her identity. She can be someone in death, if not in life. The inability to be 'somebody'

---

[33] TD, 1:1. (The mirror is noticed by Marty when he visits Rust's apartment for the first time. As he looks around the room, in a manner befitting a conventional detective, he non-verbally, but pointedly registers the mirror, along with the prodigious collection of crime-related books as odd.)

[34] TD, 1:4. Rust gazes in the mirror at each of his eyes, in a way that conjures a dissociation between the appearance of the eye, and the arrangement of subjectivity of which it is a part.

[35] Georges Bataille, 'Eye,' in *Encyclopaedia Acephalica*, trans. Iain White (London: Atlas Press, 1995), 43. The eye is a recurrent theme in both Bataille's theoretical and literary works.

[36] Rust Cohle's tattoo appears when he rolls up his sleeves while being interviewed (TD, 1:1).

is facilitated by the necessity of communication. Removed from the exchange of communication, the discontinuity of Dora ceases, and therefore, the continuity of life in general is restored. She (as the appearance of an identity) now becomes apparently inert and finite while she is detected through the imagination of memory, in particular that of Cohle's.

EXTINCTION, EXISTENCE, AND CONTINUITY

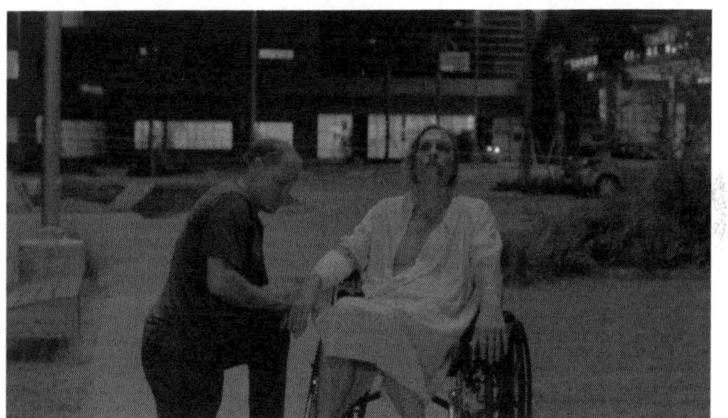

Fig. 6. Star-gazing at the end of the world.

> '[L]ife may be doomed, but the continuity of existence is not.'[37]

Human thought on extinction is characterised by the theorisation of an end to the discontinuity of the individuated experience of humanity, as Cohle says to Hart shortly after they first encounter Lange's corpse:

> We are things that labour under the illusion of having a self, this secretion of sensory experience and feeling, programmed with total assurance that we're each somebody. When in fact, everybody is nobody.[38]

---

[37] Bataille, *Erotism*, 23-24.
[38] TD, 1:1.

Theories of extinction are based on the premise of continuity, where the end of human life (the Anthropocene era) will signal the opportunity for the continuity of living as it exists in general, or, as is argued by Claire Colebrook, the discontinuity of life in general can be exceeded in turn by the continuity of images.[39] The paradox of the various iterations of extinction theory, and in particular those that welcome the demise of humanity, is that acts of linguistic expression, and particularly of writing, are quite simply, an expression of a desire for immortality.[40] Although the structure of language falls hopelessly short of expressing the discontinuous experience of our inner lives, the continued desire to attempt communication, and therefore to live beyond our discontinuity, is an expression of the conceit of this arrangement of individual being.

Death disrupts (destroys) the discontinuity of the experience of life, as it resides in the discrete experience of the individual body. For Bataille, the discontinuity of life is expressed by the individuated experience of identity, while continuity is expressed in the continuation of life in general, regardless of the death of discrete bodies.[41] The relationship between, and the development of the identities of Rust and Marty are affected by the territory of Dora Lange's corpse. Their lives map the territory of her body. When Bataille establishes links between eroticism, death and the impulse to reproduce by introducing the concept of 'discontinuous' and 'continuous' forms of life, he notes of how the existence of discontinuous organisms produces the very conditions through which these organisms experience themselves as unique and distinct from other bodies.[42] The sensation of discontinuity produces

---

[39] Claire Colebrook, *Death of the Posthuman: Essays on Extinction, Vol. 1* (Ann Arbor: Open Humanities Press with Michigan Publishing, 2014), 28.

[40] Georges Bataille, *The Accursed Share, Vol. 1*, trans. Robert Hurley (Brooklyn: Zone Books, 2007), 11. Bataille implies this when he writes that *The Accursed Share* project is something 'that the author would not have written if he had followed its lesson to the letter' (11).

[41] Bataille, *Erotism*, 15.

[42] In Bataille's *Erotism*, 'discontinuous' designates organisms that reproduce sexually, where two organisms contribute genetic material to the production of a unique organism, while 'continuous' designates organisms that reproduce asexually, single-celled organisms that

alienation from other beings because, as Bataille states, 'if you die, it is not my death,' as the distinct perspective that 'I' experience is separate from 'yours,' and can never be communicated, regardless of the linguistic or representational efforts we might make.[43] The discontinuity of individual being that appears in opposition to the continuity of life in general, explains, for Bataille, the human (and animal) desire for the production of community.[44] The discontinuity of our lives means that the experience of the orientation through which we view the world dies with us, but the simulacral gestures that are language (writing) and orders of visual representation (art) are the discontinuous being's feeble attempt at continuity; 'like someone's memory of a town, and the memory's fading.'[45] As Klossowski observes, by writing and speaking we form a gestural simulacrum of ourselves and our position, which, while not accurate, extends beyond ourselves and affects other discontinous beings (and in this misrecognition, we become immortal).[46]

The final scene of the last episode of *True Detective* is a coda of Rust's nihilism.[47] His near-death experience has apparently softened his horror for the uselessness of life, and the situation of impasse constituted by everybody existing as nobody in particular. He tells Marty that while he was comatose he could feel himself devolving into a formless materiality that included his dead loved ones who, it would seem, were waiting for him until the time came when they would all return to an indistinguishable darkness. While he expresses his disappointment in his coming to consciousness, Cohle also articulates a position that appears at odds with the aggressive pessimistic position he had assumed through the series. Marty

---

bifurcate the nucleus of the cell into two distinct nuclei, thereby making two copies, or clones, of themselves, for example (12).

[43] Bataille, *Erotism*, 12.

[44] Bataille, *Inner Experience*, trans. Leslie Anne Boldt (Albany: State University of New York Press, 1988), 83-85.

[45] TD, 1:1.

[46] Pierre Klossowski, "Of the Simulacrum in Georges Bataille's Communication" in *On Bataille: Critical Essays*, trans Leslie Ann Boldt-Irons (Albany: State University of New York Press, 1995), 147-148.

[47] TD, 1:8.

invites Rust to look up at the stars in the hope that it will appease his grief at the repeated experience of losing his father and daughter. When Rust looks up at the sky he says, 'it's all one story, the oldest, light versus dark,' to which Marty adds: 'it seems to me the dark has a lot more territory.'[48] In Cohle's response, 'Well, once there was only dark. If you ask me, the light's winning,' there appears to be a latent nostalgia for the monotheistic dialectic between 'good' and 'evil' reawakened here in the spirituality of a near-death experience. However, if the exchange of light and dark is taken as thermodynamic rather than moral, where intensities of energy exist in the material of the discontinuous body, the pinpoints of light in the encroaching darkness become a metaphor for the exchange between the continuity of active material existence, and the discontinuity of the intensive energy of individuated being.[49] This is a position further confirmed by the title of the final episode, 'Form and Void,' in its allusion to the modality of volatile energy implicated in an active materiality. Therefore, the superficial appearance of spirituality in the face of death can be equally understood as a musing on the relationality between the discontinuity of the experience of the individual organism, and the continuity of (active, material) existence in general.

The appearance of a corpse provides the intensive locus for communication, as well as the narrative topology of *True Detective*. The repetition of the sacrificial killings, the echo of the practice of which is first uncovered by the discovery of Dora Kelly Lange's corpse, gives the series a foundation for the relationship between the two detectives, as well as the rupture of alienation that gradually degrades their lives. Whether the narrative clumsily recuperates a form of spiritualism from the apparent nihilism underlying forensics, or simply reiterates the brevity and discontinuity of the experience of singular identity, the dynamic mirage of the corpse remains at its rotting heart.

---

[48] TD, 1:8.

[49] Gilles Deleuze, *Nietzsche and Philosophy*, trans. Hugh Tomlinson (London: Contiuum, 1962/1983/2005), 42-43. This point is inspired by Gilles Deleuze's description of thermodynamics in relation to Friedrich Nietzsche's understanding of the physical sciences of his era, and how that understanding informs the operation of the eternal return.

THE FLAT DEVIL NET: MAPPING QUANTUM NARRATIVES IN *TRUE DETECTIVE*

Caoimhe Doyle & Katherine Foyle

The format of *True Detective* presents two testimonies describing the same events, two overlapping but not identical stories, both presented as truths. Likewise, the following may be read either as a single narrative with two inconstant and inconsistent narrators or as two independent analyses seeking to detect some of the same truths. [CD&KF]

> There is a god in man,
> and in nature.
> He, who sits in the dark,
> is the bringer of light.
>
> This beauty,
> the sign of an open eye.
>
> Call him, to black flame
> Call him, bringer of light
> Call him, to black flame
> Call him, call him, call him . . .
>
> – Gogoroth, 'Sign of an Open Eye'[1]

> You know, I kind of look forward to the day that I die . . . if you think about it, time isn't linear. Every moment that has ever happened, or that will ever happen, is happening right now. We just chose to live in this moment to create some illusion of continuity. So really we have already died, and we've also not yet been born.
>
> – Jessa, *Girls*[2]

[1] Gorgoroth, *Ad Majorem Sathanas Gloriam* (Regain Records, 2006).

> Murder, is something that is intricately connected with society in a number of ways. And with [*True Detective*] what we wanted to do is not so much to create a 'whodunit' as to create something which asked 'what happened?' Where we could trace all of these complex threads from the heart of the murder and see what kind of areas they lead us in to. Areas of history, occultism, mythology, architecture, social considerations. All of these played a part in shaping the world that the crimes happened in, and it seemed to me to be important to investigate all of those possibilities to try and create a map of this event that included all of those strange foreign areas that aren't generally included when one considers a murder. I was not concerned with 'whodunit' I was concerned with 'what happened' I was concerned with the 'whydunit' aspect of the thing.
>
> – Alan Moore, *Mindscape of Alan Moore*[3]

'Little old Beetle goes round and round
always the same way you see,
until he ends up right up tight to the nail.
Poor old thing.'

– School Girl, *The Wicker Man*[4]

'Do you think I care what you wrote?
You don't control my fate,
otherwise I wouldn't be here
I'm not just some character in your book
and you . . . are not my God.'

– Dustfinger, *Inkheart*[5]

---

[2] *Girls,* 'Deep Inside,' season 3, episode 4, dir. Jessie Peretz, 2013, HBO.

[3] Alan Moore speaking about the creative process for the graphic novel *From Hell* in *Mindscape of Alan Moore,* directed by DeZ Vylenz (2005; London/Amsterdam: Shadowsnake Films, 2005), DVD.

[4] *The Wicker Man,* directed by Robin Hardy (1973; London: StudioCanal, 2002), DVD.

[5] *Inkheart,* directed by Iain Softly (2008; Los Angeles: New Line Cinema, 2009, DVD. Based on the book of the same name by Cornelia Funke.

In 1995 in the State of Louisiana, the body of Dora Lange was found raped and mutilated, thought to be the result of a ritualistic murder.[6] One year previously in Oslo, Norway, Varg Vikernes of the one-man Black Metal band Burzum was found guilty of the murder of Euronymous and the arson of three churches. Widespread media reports at the time attributed Vikernes's crimes to his membership of a non-existent 'Satanic Cult.'[7] During their investigations of the murder of Dora Lange, detectives Rust Cohle and Marty Hart discover a burned out church painted with mysterious symbols.[8] This seems to cement their view, and the view of most people who knew about the case at the time, that Dora Lange's murder was carried out by a similar Satanic Cult operating in Louisiana.

When Varg Vikernes speaks about Black Metal in his recent YouTube series 'World of Darkness,' he is speaking about it with the benefit of present day knowledge. In the first video of the series, 'The Temple of Elemental Evil,' Vikernes states that Burzum—and by extension (according to his reasoning) all Black Metal bands—took influence primarily from Role Playing Games or RPGs, false realities where players can take on quests in a fantasy land.[9] Vikernes, according to this video, seems to believe that these fantasy worlds are representative of what Europe was like 'in antiquity.' For Vikernes, RPGs were an attempt to 'make real the magic of our forebears' and so Burzum's music had the same aim: to 'make you emotionally awaken the ancient European mind set.' By this Vikernes does not just mean that the magic of these 'forebears' is made real inside the game, but

[6] TD, 1:1.

[7] See *Until the Light Takes Us*, directed by Audrey Ewell and Aaron Aites (2009; New York: Variance Films, 2009), DVD.

[8] TD, 1:2.

[9] Varg Vikernes, 'World of Darkness Part 1: The Temple of Elemental Evil,' http://www.youtube.com/watch?v=q_2l5nkhLjo.

rather it is made real through the game, and by extension through Black Metal music. [CD]

Fig. 1 *Top*: Cohle and Hart approach burned-out church in *True Detective*. *Bottom*: Cover of Burzum album, *Aske* [ashes]. Varg Vikernes himself is widely thought to have burned down this church, and taken this picture, but this has never been confirmed.

'Fans call what we see on the screen "canon," but we do not treat it as a sacred text: it does not have the canonical connotations of "literary canon" or "canon of Scripture." Screen canon is not "that which is good and true." . . . We used canon non-canonically, more in the way scientists would say "data."'"[10]

Let's explore the idea of fan fiction ('fanfic') as sacrilegious.[11] When quizzed about the literary validity of fan texts, many fan writers point to Dante's 'The Divine Comedy' as the originary fanfic.[12] Certainly it satisfies many of the criteria for fanfic: it subverts canon (in this case Biblical), the main character is a self-insert or 'Mary Sue'[13] on the part of the author–it's even a

---

[10] Mary Ellen, 'The Learning Curve: Hypertext, Fan Fiction, and the Calculus of Human Nature,' *Alternate Universes: Fanfiction Studies*, http://www.alternateuniverses.com/TLCpaper.html.

[11] 'Fanfiction' refers to any prose work based on existing texts (literary or otherwise). It is referred to by fandom participants as 'fanfic.' Fanfic can serve multiple purposes with regards to the 'canon' or 'source narrative' that informs it, including, but not limited to: continuing a completed text (as in a sequel); explaining gaps in narrative; augmenting or embellishing existing scenes or stories; developing and embellishing 'backstory' implied (by its mention or its absence) by the canon [meta]; hypothesising on romantic relationships alluded to (or absent from) canon [shipping]; hypothesising on sexual relationships featuring canon characters [previously referred to as 'lemon', term not in use at time of writing]; imagining an average, uneventful (although sometimes specific) occasion involving one or more canon character(s) [drabble]; placing characters from one narrative into another fictional universe or situation [Alternate Universe, AU], and so on. Generally speaking, fanfiction does not enjoy mainstream cultural status (unless it is disguised as 'profic, for example: the multiple recent reinterpretations of Sherlock Holmes stories; the MTV series *Teen Wolf*, based on the 1980s MTV movie of the same name; *Torchwood*; Dante's *Divine Comedy*; 'reboots' of science-fiction and comic book movies, gritty or otherwise; *Fifty Shades of Gray*).

[12] Molly McArdle, 'Where Do Books Go After They End?,' *The Toast*, February 10 2014, http://the-toast.net/2014/02/10/harry-potter-and-books-after-they-end/.

[13] The term 'Mary Sue' originated from *Star Trek* fanfic *A Trekkie's Tale* by Paula Smith, parodying a trend of female original characters in fanfic who acted as 'author avatars' who possess unnecessary skills and positive traits (regarded as wish-fulfilment) and who often had a romantic relationship with a canon lead. Over time the accepted definition has broadened to include male characters, a variation known as a 'Marty Stu', typified by different traits, usually those culturally associated with masculinity (since a Sue's defining characteristic is perfection). See 'Mary Sue,' *TVTropes*,

crossover, with Dante meeting not only Biblical but literary figures on his journey. But ultimately in this example, Dante is reverent of, as well as referent to, his source material. The same could not be said of, for example, Satanism. In one of his recent YouTube videos,[14] Varg Vikernes derided Satanism and questioned its anti-Christian-ness, pointing out that subversive rituals like Black Masses, by their very sacrilege, are derivative of Christian rites, since subversion as well as worship requires intimate engagement with source material. In this way, Satanic texts could be seen as fan works of Christian canon. To paraphrase Richard Berger, fanfic is the 'profound' text to canon's 'sacred' one.[15] Or as Reza Negarestani would have it: 'To do rigorous theology is to perforate the Divine's corpus with heresies.'[16]

In this framework, Nic Pizzolatto is a theologian rather than worshipper at the church of pessimism. And *True Detective* is fan fiction of pessimist texts (not only purely theoretical texts by any means, since the series was heavily influenced by the weird fiction of Thomas Ligotti, the work of H.P Lovecraft, and the graphic novels of Alan Moore, to name a few). Moreover, *True Detective* is sacrilegious crossover fanfic starring a pair of Mary Sues. [KF]

Vikernes does not admit this, but his current accounts of Black Metal culture in the early 90's may be influenced by present day 'Metallectual' movements, specifically Black Metal Theory. Emerging in late in 2008 in connection with Nicola Masciandaro's paper 'What is This that Stands before Me? Metal as Deixis,' presented at *Heavy Fundametalisms: Music, Metal and Politics*, in Salzburg, Sweden,[17] Black Metal Theory is a

---

http://tvtropes.org/pmwiki/pmwiki.php/Main/MarySue

[14] Varg Vikernes, 'World of Darkness, Part II: Satan Incarnate!,' http://www.youtube.com/watch?v=YO3zLAS4FC8.

[15] Richard Berger, 'Screwing Aliens and Screwing with Aliens: Torchwood Slashes the Doctor,' in *Illuminating Torchwood*, ed. Andrew Ireland (Jefferson, NC: McFarland & Company, Inc., 2010), 72.

[16] Reza Negarestani, *Cyclonopedia: Complicity with Anonymous Materials* (Melbourne: re.press, 2008), 62.

[17] Nicola Masciandaro, 'What is This that Stands before Me? Metal as Deixis,' in *Reflections in the Metal Void*, ed. Niall W. R. Scott (Oxford: Interdiciplinary Press, 2012), 3-17.

phenomenological approach to Black Metal music, and put simply, is a thinking with–rather than on–Black Metal.[18] What Vikernes is doing in his video is essentially theorizing his own actions over twenty years previously, and so Black Metal Theory may be 'retroactively' influencing Black Metal. It is not difficult to make comparisons here between Vikernes and the protagonists of *True Detective*, unreliable narrators who have twisted the story to suit their current needs.

In *True Detective*, Cohle speaks in detail about 'M-brane theory.'[19] He states: 'In this universe, we process time linearly. Forward. But outside of our space time, from what would be a 4th dimensional perspective, time wouldn't exist. And from that vantage, could we attain it, what we'd see is our space time would look flattened, like a single sculpture of matter in a super position, in every place it ever occupied. Our sentience just cycling through our lives like carts on a track. See, everything outside our dimension that's eternity . . . eternity looking down on us. Now to us, it's a sphere. But to them, it's a circle.'[20] At first viewing, this theory seems complicated, but Cohle's version is simple enough: time is a continuous loop in which we are all trapped, cycling through the same lives over and over, unable to escape. If we track the progression of Cohle's thought as the episodes unfold, it becomes evident that the first time he hears

---

[18] The blog which bore witness to Black Metal Theory's emergence defines it as follows: 'Not black metal. Not theory. Not not black metal. Not not theory. Black metal theory. Theoretical blackening of metal. Metallic blackening of theory. Mutual blackening. Nigredo in the intoxological crucible of symposia' (*Black Metal Theory*, http://blackmetaltheory.blogspot.ie).

[19] More commonly known as M-Theory. 'M-Theory is the best candidate yet for the Theory of Everything. It also provides new insights into the search for the Multiverse, in more ways than one. The most obvious relates to the image of our entire Universe as a flat sheet of two-dimensional paper lying on a table, with an extra dimension at right angles to the surface of the paper, extending upwards in the third dimension. There is no reason why there couldn't be another sheet of paper on top of the first one, and another, and another—or a multitude of three-dimensional universes separated from one another in the eleventh dimension' (John Gribbin, *In Search of the Multiverse* [New York: Penguin Books, 2010], 153).

[20] TD, 1:5.

time described as a flat circle is from Reggie Ledoux, in 1995.[21] Due to the narrative bias of the show, we as viewers are conditioned to see this concept as Cohle's theory. In reality it is an important aspect of the show's mysterious cult. This becomes evident in the final episode when Errol proclaims: 'I have very important work to do—my ascension removes me from the disk and the loop, I am near final stage.'[22] Evidently the murders in *True Detective* can be seen as Errol's attempt to save himself from this flat circle of infinite repetition. In fact, Pizzolatto confirms this (insofar as the author can confirm anything about a narrative) when he says '[Errol] believes the murders, ritually enacted over a period of time, upon his death, permit him an ascension that removes him from the Karmic wheel of rebirth.'[23]

In 'The Expert's Guide to HBO's *True Detective* and Weird Comic Book Fiction,' Stewart and Stewart detail the personal philosophy of prolific comic writer Alan Moore. According to their view, it amounts to a belief that mythic structures stand outside space and time, or rather that if enough people believe in a story, or maybe even if enough people hear it, it becomes true. For Moore, Jack the Ripper is a modern day myth, which is why, in the graphic novel *From Hell*, in the quest for immortality that most serial killers seem to be embarking on in modern fictions, Jack the Ripper 'actually succeeds. He literally ascends [in the novel] to a weird vantage point from which he can see across time.'[24] In a way this is the same point made by Vikernes: 'if enough people give spiritual energy to dreams they will gain a life of their own.'[25] In reality though, what does it mean to be

---

[21] Ibid.

[22] TD, 1:8.

[23] Jeff Jenson, 'True Detective post-mortem: Creator Nic Pizzolatto on happy endings, season 2, and the future of Cohle and Hart,' *Entertainment Weekly*, http://popwatch.ew.com/2014/03/10/true-detective-post-mortem-creator-nic-pizzoletto-on-happy-endings- season-2-and-the-future-of-cohle-and-hart/.

[24] Adam Stewart and Mark Stewart, 'The Expert's Guide to HBO's True Detective and Weird Comic Book Fiction,' *Comics Alliance*, http://comicsalliance.com/true-detective-comic-books-weird-fiction-secrets-influences-alan-moore-grant-morrison-invisibles-hbo/.

[25] Vikernes, 'World of Darkness Part 1: The Temple of Elemental."

immortal? Only that you live on in stories, and Western culture's favourite stories are stories about murder.[26] [CD]

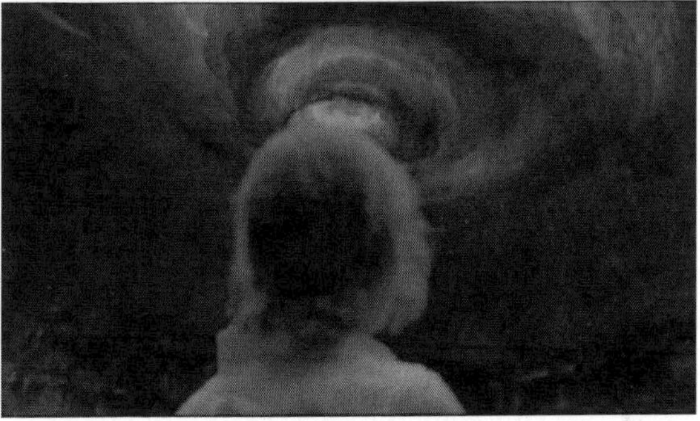

Fig. 2 *Top*: Birds whirl around as they leave the hut of 'the nameless saint' in *Byzantium* (Neil Jordan, 2013). This sight greets those who enter the hut to become vampires—i.e.

[26] This is made evident by the popularity of such TV shows as *C.S.I.*, *Criminal Minds*, *Breaking Bad* and of course *True Detective*. The murder mystery format has been a staple of TV and theatre for decades and the detective novel remains one of the most popular genres since the publication of the first Sherlock Holmes novel in the late 1800's. Moreover, any mass murder or murder of particularly shocking brutality is often described in gruesome and meticulous detail in the media (especially the tabloid presses). In fact it is theorized that many mass shootings, especially in the USA, take place in part precisely because the murderer knows he (I say he because it is almost always men) will be written and talked about, that his name will live on after his death (which is usually by his own hand, shortly after the shooting takes place).

immortal—before they are attacked by a malevolent version of themselves. *Bottom*: Cohle's hallucination of an astronomical event in the centre of the labyrinth, just before his violent showdown with Errol Childress.

In *Cybertext: Perspectives on Ergodic Literature*, Espen J. Aarseth defines ergodic literature as that in which 'nontrivial effort is required to allow the reader to traverse the text.'[27] Following this, he reclassifies all textual media requiring ergodic reading—hypertexts, role playing games, choose-your-own adventure books and so on—under the broad category of the cybertext, a classification based not on the level of interference of an individual reader, but on the structure of the text itself. Reading a cybertext is an exercise in inaccessibility, defined by the paths a reader does not choose and hence loses access to.[28] To illustrate the risks of this game-like narrative structure, Aarseth uses the motif of the labyrinth. Aarseth's labyrinth comes in two shapes, taken from Penelope Reed Doob's *The Idea of the Labyrinth* (1992): unicursal/the spiral, a single path with no choices required to reach the end; and multicursal/the maze where choices at critical points determine where the journey ends up and whether it succeeds. Aarseth dismisses out of hand a third possible labyrinth shape: the net, described by Umberto Eco in *Semiotics and Philosophy of Language* (1984) as one in which 'every point can be connected with every other point,' since it lacks the 'fundamental inaccessibility' of the spiral and the maze.[29]

Could a linear text like a novel or a single-arc, self-contained television series be a cybertext? Certainly not according to Aarseth's understanding; the structure wouldn't allow it. But what if the structure of such texts could be changed? What if a maze could become a net? Reza Negarestani has put forth the idea of Hidden Writing,[30] in which the reader of a linear text

[27] Espen J. Aarseth, *Cybertext: Perspectives on Ergodic Literature* (Baltimore: The John Hopkins University Press, 1997), 6.
[28] 'The concept of the cybertext focuses on the mechanical organization of the text, by positing the intricacies of the medium as an integral part of the literary exchange' (Ibid., 1).
[29] Ibid., 6.
[30] 'One of the initial symptoms of inauthenticity that Hidden Writing produces is positive disintegration, or more accurately, collectivization

becomes an archaeologist, using plot holes as sites to begin a process of exhumation.[31] As he puts it, 'reading through the plot holes of a story is possible only by devising a line capable of twisting in and out of them,'[32] even if such a line requires the original or main plot to be reconfigured. Hidden Writing, and indeed fanfic, could easily be grasped as ergodic readings of linear texts. The twists and turns of the main plot are red herrings to the ergodic reader or fan writer, who sees a plot hole as the site of an alternate narrative intersecting with the main one, or as Negarestani puts it, 'the entrance to the warren compound of the necropolis or the real underground network.'[33]

Despite his intentions, Pizzolatto seems to have created a holey text rather than a holy one. Consider viewing the plot of *True Detective* from an extra-dimensional perspective, just as in Cohle's vision of the universe as a flat circle. If we include the underground network of all the routes not taken—where every turning point is linked to every other, the main plot trapped inside it unrecognisable and inextricable—it would be a mess of intersecting lines: a flat devil net.[34] In fact the image of the devil net is flattened twice in *True Detective*. First by being drawn in Rust's ledger, and secondly when he shines a beam of light on a devil net, creating a flat shadow. Cohle literally illuminates the devil net, revealing Hidden Writing through its flattening. [KF]

---

of one author (voice) or an authorial elite, and its transformation to an untraceable shady collective of writers, a crowd' (*Cyclonopedia*, 62) Negarestani describes Hidden Writing as 'utilizing every plot hole, all problematics, every suspicious obscurity or repulsive wrongness as a new plot with a tentacled and autonomous mobility' (61). In the case of the novel (or indeed, although not explicitly stated in *Cyclonopedia*, the filmic text), the structure of the whole is perforated by plot holes. A plot hole, in this instance, is not simply a mistake but 'conveys the activities of a subsurface life' (61). In Hidden Writing, 'the central or main plot is reinvented solely in order that it may stealthily host, transport and nurture other plots' (61).

[31] *Cyclonopedia*, 64.

[32] Ibid., 60.

[33] Ibid., 64.

[34] Devil nets are a symbol used many times in *True Detective*, found at multiple crime scenes. Taken from real folk traditions, a devil net is a structure made of twigs tied together, meant to ward off evil.

Fig. 3 *Top*: Cohle shines a flashlight on a devil net. *Bottom*: 'Flattened' drawings of devil nets in Cohle's ledger.

'The body is not one member but many . . . now are they many but of one body.'[35] This is the answer given by Cohle when asked why he chose to become a homicide detective after his release from psychiatric care. Alan Moore believes this statement to be true in a very literal sense, he believes 'every human soul is in fact one human soul—it is the soul of the universe itself.'[36] According to Mircea Eliade, the cosmos, or the universe,

35 Corinthians 12:14, as cited in TD, 1:2.
36 *Mindscape of Alan Moore.*

symbolically takes the shape of a tree.[37] *True Detective* seems to revel in its obscure references, and an out-of-print Grant Morrison comic book of short stories from the late 90's is probably as obscure as it gets.[38] According to Stewart and Stewart, Morrison puts forward the idea that 'Lovecraft's Great Ones were in fact the human race seen from "above" – a billion eyed and tentacled super intelligence.'[39] Stewart and Stewart here use Eliade's symbology, giving the example of an upside down family tree as a visual link, a mass of intersecting branches all forming one being of thought stretching back into the past and out into the future. Or as Reza Negarestani might describe it: 'branches stretching out, numerous protuberances going astray . . . Viewed from afar, they look unbroken; up close, they are a mélange of sutures and amputated limbs'.[40] Importantly, this extra-dimensional perspective on the human race can only be obtained by someone who is, as Cohle puts it, 'outside . . . time,'[41] and this idea certainly gives weight to the various online readings of *True Detective* that make the point that there is no 'monster at the end' of the story except mankind.[42]

When reciting the quote from Corinthians above, Cohle traces out an odd pattern in the air with his hand. It seems to begin as a cross but quickly becomes less structured, crossing over itself numerous times, resulting in a vaguely triangular shape. The image left behind is reminiscent a devil net.[43] The

---

37 'One thing seems clear beyond doubt: that the cosmos is a living organism . . . the mystery of the inexhaustible appearance of life is bound up with the rhythmical renewal of the cosmos. This is why the cosmos was imagined in the form of a gigantic tree; the mode of being of the cosmos, and first of all its capacity for endless regeneration, are symbolically expressed by the life of the tree' (Mircea Eliade, *The Sacred and the Profane: The Nature of Religion* [New York: Harcourt, 1959], 148).

38 Grant Morrison, *Lovely Biscuits* (Oneiros Books, 1998).

39 Stewart and Stewart, 'The Expert's Guide."

40 Reza Negarestani, email correspondence, 11 March 2010.

41 TD, 1:5.

42 TD, 1:3.

43 Another obscure reference which Pizzolatto directly cites as an influence (specifically for the devil net) is *Sticks* by Karl Edward Wagner (short story first published in *Whispers*, March 1974). In *Sticks*, the protagonist is lead by a trail of stick sculptures to an abandoned house

devil net, of course, is yet another instance of intersecting and overlapping branches. Earlier in the same episode we are shown a panning shot of one of the devil nets from above.[44] Bearing in mind Morrison's being of thought, this 'single sculpture'[45] can become a flattened map of conscious thought, a trail that could be followed in any direction, from past to future, or non-linearly from any one strand (of thought) to another. [CD]

The unfinished hypertext *Star Trek* fanfic *The Learning Curve* (TLC) takes the movie *Star Trek V: The Final Frontier* as its labyrinth access site, or more accurately as one path through a labyrinth of possible paths. TLC makes the branched nature of narratives evident by placing a torch in the hand of the reader and inviting them to make the character's choices. Hyperlink colour indicates whether each choice is obviously weighted or unweighted, but even seemingly insignificant choices have consequences further along the narrative path. This cybertext format, rather than any specific quote or occurrence, conveys the essence of TLC: 'that life-altering choices are as apparently simple and uninformative as left versus right, that you cannot tell from the triviality of the choice how grave the consequences might be.'[46]

No matter how grim or unsatisfying the conclusions may be, only readers—from their position outside the narrative—have the power to choose a path through it, not characters. In the final showdown in the old stones,[47] Cohle is led down the 'right' path by a voice—ostensibly Childess's, truly the writer's—passing many openings without taking them. Every path Cohle's torchlight beam sweeps over is one that fans may excavate:

---

where he is attacked by an undead creature. Years later these sculptures become important symbols for a mysterious cult.

[44] TD, 1:2.

[45] TD, 1:5.

[46] Mary Ellen, 'The Learning Curve.'

[47] The 'old stones' is a phrase used by several characters in *True Detective* to refer to the Fort Macomb Ruins, site of the ultimate fight between Cohle and Childress. For example, Dora Lange's husband Charlie says, 'He said that there's this place down south where all these rich men go to, uh, devil worship . . . He said there's all these, like, old stones out in the woods, people go to, like, worship. He said there's just so much good killin' down there' (TD, 1:4).

choosing one path implies that many go unchosen. This is the glorious nature of fan fiction. The fan ergodically reads texts meant to be read in a linear way; from screen canon as a flat circle pierced by plot holes a fan can reveal a tangle of narratives that could connect them. Contemplating only the onscreen narrative of *True Detective* is to walk only one path in the labyrinth, to see only one twig in the devil net.[48] [KF]

Fig. 4 *Top*: Boys dance around the maypole in Robin Hardy's 1973 film *The Wicker Man*. *Bottom*: Cohle examines a devil net in *True Detective*.

[48] Or, to experience only one state in a superposition of states. Hugh Everett, famed for his work in developing a theory of the Multiverse, wrote: 'From the viewpoint of the theory, all elements of a superposition (all 'branches') are actual, none are any more real than the rest. It is unnecessary to suppose that all but one are somehow destroyed' (cited in John Gribbin, *In Search of the Multiverse* [New York: Penguin, 2010], 28).

According to John D. Barrow, one theory on the formation of the vacuum is as follows: '[Cosmic strings] will start by threading the Universe with a great network of lines of vacuum energy, like a web of cosmic spaghetti. As the expansion of the Universe proceeds, the network behaves in a complicated fashion. Whenever intersections of string occur, the string re-organises itself by exchanging partners.'[49] If the same string intersects with itself, what occurs is a loop, which will eventually expend all of its energy and vibrate from existence.

The flat devil net should be seen, then, as a symbol for the necessity of fanalysis (fan analysis). Mobilized by the ease of access to almost all information online, the flat devil net is an endless web of ideas and thought fuelled by the obsessive mentality which shows like *True Detective* spawn. A mass of roots with no known depth, or a sprawling expanse of branches with no known height.[50] Like the flat circle, the flat devil net has no beginning or end, but unlike the circle it has many intersections. If a television show is a flat circle, and it is, then it will eventually, like quantum loops, vibrate itself out of existence, or at least out of relevance. It is only though constant interaction, analysis, pestering,[51] and penetration, by fans, viewers, theorists et al. that a show maintains itself. The same can be said of any theory or mode of thought (in so far as any theory only interacting with itself will soon become irrelevant). In the spirit of Black Metal Theory's openness,[52] what we propose here is not just an opening of fiction to theory, which really is already the

---

[49] John D. Barrow, *The Book of Nothing* (London: Cape, 2000), 282.

[50] Cohle mentions the sprawl on a few occasions throughout the series, which serves as a metaphor for the vast reach of the cult and the crimes committed by them.

[51] Michael O'Rourke, 'The Mutual Pestering of Black Metal and Theory,' paper presented at *P.E.S.T. [Philial Epidemic Strategy Tryst]*, Eden Pub, Dublin, 10 November 2011.

[52] 'Black metal theory expresses a need to reopen music to the philosophy of music and philosophy to the music of philosophy, in a black way. If philosophy is thought, practicing the love of wisdom (philo-sophia), black metal theory is thought practicing the love of black metal' (Dominik Irtenkauf, 'Interview with Nicola Masciandaro,' http://thewhim.blogspot.ie/2011/02/interview-on-bmt.html. 'Not not black metal, not not theory, yes, yes black metal, yes, yes theory' (Michael O'Rourke, 'Mutual Pestering').

case, but an opening of theory to, or by, fiction. To allow TV characters the same relevance and reverence as philosophers and to not just speak about narratives philosophically, but to speak about philosophy narratively. The flat devil net is an image for the future of theory, and equally a theory for the future of image. [CD&KF]

> In the woods there grew a tree,
> and a fine fine tree was he.
> And on that tree there was a limb,
> and on that limb there was a branch,
> and on that branch there was a nest,
> and in that nest there was an egg,
> and in that egg there was a bird,
> and from that bird a feather came,
> and of that feather was a bed.
>
> And on that bed there was a girl,
> and on that girl there was a man,
> and from that man there was a seed,
> and from that seed there was a boy,
> and from that boy there was a man,
> and from that man there was a grave,
> and from that grave there grew a tree.[53]

[53] *The Wicker Man.*

Affect Has No Story

Daniel Colucciello Barber

> Men and women of the jury . . . You have said that you could try this case on the basis of evidence. What i am saying now is not evidence.
>
> – Assata Shakur[1]

The Negation of Story

We can begin with the scene of the crime. Not with one particular crime scene, this one or that one, but with the notion as such. The notion of the scene of the crime, or at least the phrase indicating this notion, is commonly used and just as commonly unthought. What is a crime scene? And how do we decide what belongs to it and what does not? In a sense, the scene of the crime is quite empirical, even positivistic. It is where the crime took place. But the taking place of a crime, the scene of its taking place, is something that is always being tracked and narrated. The detective story emerges from a scene where the crime took place, but the act of detecting why and how the crime took place, or what the nature of the crime is, is something that always leads beyond any strictly empirical crime scene. In *True Detective*, for instance, the detection of the crime and its scene leads us to other crimes with other scenes, it sprawls and swamps into various backwater sites, into files and the flooding of files, into every nook of the bayou, and into the homes of both the detected and the detectors.

Our traveling from place to place, the tracking and expression of the scene of the crime, takes place through story. In

---

[1] Assata Shakur, *Assata: An Autobiography* (Chicago: Lawrence Hill Books, 2001), 170. The 'i' is not capitalized in the original. Original text is italicized.

other words, the justification for going from the scene of the crime to other sites is the act of detecting the crime, and the link between the crime scene and these other sites is provided by narrative, or story. The term 'scene' connotes a specified place that is articulated within a larger frame of reference. Think, for instance, of a scene in a play or a film: it indicates something that is distinctively decisive, but that gains its distinctively decisive force from its embedding within a larger story. Accordingly, we can think of the crime scene as a concentration of something larger, or we can think of it as being expanded into a larger story. In either case, the scene of the crime is inseparable from the story of the crime; to have a crime scene is to have a crime story.

In *True Detective*, the story of the crime functions in various registers: the intentions ascribed to various characters, the conflicts between these characters' differing stories, and the totality of the show. We might also mention the various stories constructed by viewers. The point, however, is not to compare stories or to focus on their various registers, but to observe that story is being constituted, that story proliferates and reproduces, in various or multiplicitous ways, and that in doing so story ensures its survival. There is story, and there will be story. And it may be the case that we are supposed to believe that there has always been story. Here, we might recall Rust Cohle's remark, in the last episode of Season 1, while looking up at the sky: 'It's just one story, the oldest ... light versus dark.'[2] But the question I want to raise is whether there is, in reality, a story: Does story exist?

To ask this question is to turn attention away from the opposition that the show sets up between pessimism and optimism. Cohle, in the show's conclusion, seems to shift from one side to the other – siding with the light against the darkness, he seems to abandon his pessimism. This can be taken as a withdrawal from negativity. Yet to take it as such would be mistaken, for it would be to conflate pessimism's *division from* optimism with the enactment of negativity. Such a conflation must be refused – for pessimism, no matter how radically it is articulated, remains bound to optimism, or to the narration of itself through its divisive relation with optimism. Pessimism is articulated through the division from optimism, or as the story of

[2] TD, 1:8.

this division, yet negativity – as I will articulate it – refuses story's division or division's story. While pessimism can *appear* through story's division – the division, for instance, between darkness and light – negativity names a negation of story, or of story's divisive capacitation of appearance.

My interest, then, is to divert attention from Cohle's apparent turn from pessmism to optimism (as well as from his appearance, prior to this turn, as a narrator of pessimism). Instead of focusing on darkness and light in terms of pessimism and optimism, I want to analyze darkness and light according to negativity. Pessimism and optimism set up a division that can be continually undone and re-set; pessimism and optimism can shift back and forth as the story of darkness and light. In other words, pessimism and optimism dialectically constitute each other by dividing from one another, and in doing they belong to the constitution of story. Negativity, on the other hand, names the negation of story and division as such.

The Story of the Crime and the Story of Christ

We can begin understanding what it means to negate story by understanding the nature of story as it is mediated by *True Detective* – and to do this we must understand Christianity. The first reason for such a claim is that Christian themes are quite present within the show, such that talking about the show involves talking about Christianity. Here we might recall the various appearances of Christian practice, but we should especially recall Cohle's Christological figuration. The suffering detective is clearly depicted as Christ in the last episode,[3] but this outcome was already suggested in the first episode, when he tells his partner, Marty Hart, that he has a cross in his apartment for the purpose of meditating on Christ's experience of and preparation for suffering (in the Garden of Gethsemane).[4] The story of Cohle, from the first to the last, is framed by the story of Christ, by the story of the one who is said to be the first and the last, the one who teaches how to suffer meaningfully for justice.

---

[3] TD, 1:8.
[4] TD, 1:1.

There is, however, a second reason for claiming that understanding the nature of story, as mediated by *True Detective*, entails understanding Christianity. This reason has to do not with the appearance of Christian themes within *True Detective*, but rather with the way in which *True Detective*, as a story of division, can be connected to the story of Christ (and of Christianity in general), which is also a story of division.

While the story of Christ is often told as a story of salvation, it should be noted that to tell a story of salvation is also to tell a story of division. This is because the work of salvation requires the prior work of division; salvation depends on the capacity to be saved or damned. The division between these two contingent outcomes, these two possible directions, provides the background for the story of salvation envisioned in Christ and historically enacted by Christianity. Cohle is not far from this logic when he claims: 'Vision is meaning. Meaning is historical.'[5] For Christianity, meaning is found as the history – or, in terms of the detective, the timeline – of escaping damnation by finding salvation, or of failing to find salvation and ending up damned. And this macrological story of light's struggle to overcome darkness – 'The light shines in the darkness, and the darkness did not overcome it' – correlates with the micrological story of the self: I can take the side of light or dark; I can achieve my existence, I can become something, through the contingent taking of one side and not the other; I know I am this because I am not that.[6] In this sense, division and contingency constitute each other, and together they constitute a narrative of achievement.

The story of the crime is not simply analogous to the story of Christ, for the Christ story is already a crime story. We can understand the crucifixion as a crime scene that has become world-historical. Someone – that is, Christ – has been killed, and wrongfully so. There is a crime. The killing of Christ is a crime committed by humanity – in its entirety – against God.[7]

---

[5] TD, 1:2.

[6] John 1:5.

[7] I am here describing the structure of standard Christian theology in terms of the positions it establishes. While some might read these positions in terms of providence, or in terms of philosophical vectors (Hegelian, Nietzschean, or otherwise) surrounding the death of God –

Importantly, however, Christ is both divine and human. Thus Christ is both the God against whom the crime is committed, the victim, and the representative of the human criminals. He is the criminal, but also the victim – and because he is the victim, the one who makes the scene of the crime as a story of sacrifice, he opens the contingent possibility of salvific achievement for criminals. The story of Christ makes all humans into criminals who can be saved.[8] Yet for a human to be saved, to make the shift from contingently criminal to contingently saved, it is necessary for that human to rightly understand and confess this story.

INDISCERNIBILITY AND SPRAWL

There is salvation precisely because there is a story of a crime. When one is saved, one is saved from being killed by the criminal and/or from being damned as a criminal.[9] Salvation needs criminals, and the work of salvation, the work of moving from a criminal position to a saved position, needs a story. This story, which is experienced individually as confession,[10] is probably the

---

for an intriguing instance of such a reading, see Hans-Robert Jauss and Sharon Larisch, 'Job's Questions and Their Distant Reply: Goethe, Nietzsche, Heidegger,' *Comparative Literature* 34.3 (Summer 1982), 193-207 – I am interested in the positions as such, and specifically as they establish and are established by a crime story.

[8] This is true at the level of the structure of Christian theology. To be a human, according to Christian theology, is to be an individual that is both guilty of killing God and capable of being forgiven insofar as one confesses such guilt. This structure is exemplified at the very scene of Christ's crucifixion, where the criminal crucified alongside Christ is, upon confession, granted forgiveness (and entry to paradise) by Christ. See Luke 23:32-43. For a fuller discussion of this logic, see Gil Anidjar, 'Survival,' *Political Concepts: A Critical Lexicon* 2 (Winter 2012): no pagination, http://www.politicalconcepts.org/survival-gil-anidjar/.

[9] Criminality, of course, involves more than just murder. For the purposes of this essay, however, I am interested in criminality as murder. This is because both the crime against Christ and the crime(s) investigated in *True Detective* revolve around murder.

[10] Confession, in the ordinary or common sense of the contemporary, connotes an admission of fault or guilt. My interest in this term stems from the way in which it emerges in Cohle's skillful practice of procuring such admissions of guilt from individuals suspected of criminality, and

basic example of what Cohle criticizes when he says, 'Everybody wants confession, everybody wants some cathartic narrative.'[11] Yet Cohle, despite the critical position he takes, is a virtuoso producer of these stories; he is renowned for getting confessions from those positioned as criminals. As one individual, while being interrogated by Cohle, puts it: 'Please just tell me what to say. I want to confess.'[12]

Cohle's oscillation between critic and producer of confessional narratives is not surprising insofar as we observe the role of Christianity. For Christianity, justice is not about refusing criminality, it is about confessing criminality. It is about a certain style of criminality, about knowing how to tell the story of criminality in a salvific manner.[13] Accordingly, Christianity requires being contingently positioned as both criminal and victim, both damned and saved. It is this divisive yet inseparable positionality that provides the engine for the story; it is this same divisive yet inseparable positionality that makes the story's opposition of characters become indiscernible.

In *True Detective*, we see this becoming-indiscernible again and again. Cohle, when he produces confessions, cannot be fully distinguished from the evangelist (Joel Theriot).[14] And if Hart constantly does violence in the name of victims, especially women, so does Cohle, even if he is more subtle: his detective work is unthinkable apart from the story of his dead daughter, Sophia.[15] The division between Hart and Cohle, upon which the

---

the way in which the practice of confession is central – and etymologically linked – to Christian identity (where being Christian entails admitting one's guilt against and to God).

[11] TD, 1:5.

[12] TD, 1:3.

[13] As Talal Asad has remarked, 'a "bad conscience" is no bar to further immoral action, it merely gives such action a distinctive style.' See Talal Asad, 'Responses,' in *Powers of the Secular Modern*, eds. David Scott and Charles Hirschkind (Palo Alto, California: Stanford University Press, 2006), 230.

[14] TD, 1:3.

[15] Sophia died (at the age of two) as a result of being hit by a car while she was riding her tricycle. Cohle discusses this event, as well as the significant impact it had on his life, during an interview scene in TD, 1:2.

show frequently relies, does not ultimately stand up.[16] Furthermore, we might recall that when Reggie Ledoux – the murderer to whom the detection initially leads – dies as a criminal on his knees, he is in the same position as the woman who was his own victim, the woman at the original scene of the crime, the woman bound by rope in order to be bound to the meaning of a sacrificial death.[17] Nor should we forget another instance in which Cohle and Hart are both divided and bound together through a woman: they have a notable moment of tension over who gets to mow the lawn for Hart's wife.[18] Even as they are opposed to one another, they both remain men who want to mow the lawn; and even as these lawnmowing detectives are opposed to the criminals, the show's ultimate criminal, Errol Childress, first appeared as one who mows lawns.[19]

What I am pointing to is not a conspiracy – where indiscernibility produces the potential guilt of all. I am pointing instead to a 'sprawl' of connections.[20] Conspiracy needs a sprawl, but it cannot stay in sprawl; conspiracy needs to sprawl beyond divisions, beyond the empirical delimitation of a crime scene, but it also needs to make a story out of this sprawl; conspiracy tells us that the crime leads everywhere, especially to places where

---

[16] To set up a division between two central characters in order to then, by way of story development, undo this division is typical of the buddy-cop genre. In this sense, the setting up and undoing of the division between Hart and Cohle can be read in terms of genre. Yet I am interested in how this setting up and undoing of division may be read as belonging to a dialectical negativity (such as that named by Hegel) and thus as fundamentally distinct from the sort of negativity that refuses even the initial setting up of division.

[17] Ledoux's death occurs in TD, 1:5; the original scene of the crime occurs in TD, 1:1.

[18] TD, 1:3.

[19] Both the argument over who gets to mow the lawn for Hart's wife and the initial appearance of Childress occur in TD, 1:3. At this point, however, Childress is not imagined by Cohle and Hart to be a suspect. Yet Childress eventually becomes – in the final episode TD, 1:8 – the murderer to whom the detection of the crime leads. It is for this reason that I describe him as the show's ultimate criminal.

[20] Cohle, when explaining the complexity and scope of the network of criminality surrounding the murders he is detecting, remarks, 'Now, I don't know the sprawl of this thing, all right? The people I'm after, they're all fucking over,' in TD, 1:7.

you do not expect it, but in doing so it is still committed to the story of a crime. In other words, conspiracy is still committed to the existence of a crime and of criminals, which is to say that it is still committed to a story of salvation. So, when faced with the demise of salvific hope, when faced with the reality that there is nothing, no-body, to be saved, it makes sense to still seek to tell the story of a crime. The crime is already cathartic, even if incompletely so – for if there is a crime, then there are criminals, and the detection of criminals has meaning. Even if the criminals are never ultimately detected, or especially if they are still out there (as the not-yet-detected), the existence of criminals gives us something to work at, and to be saved from.

The sprawl of connections engulfs our ability to divide and identify positions, just as the floods keep engulfing the files.[21] However, the story of the crime does not stop producing positions, for it proclaims – in the face of this sprawling deactivation of division – that there is something to do, a meaning to be detected, a division to be made. When Hart says that Cohle 'sound[s] panicked,' he is right – but the panic is not about the evangelist's story being true, it is rather about the sprawl's refusal of any story at all, including a story that would explain the evangelist's error.[22] Cohle's panic, in other words, is about the 'pan-,' the all,[23] of the sprawl, which is all over and all too much for a story. Affection of the all-sprawl dissolves and drowns every story. Affect has no story, and so the story can be imagined only as a detection-of-story; one can stop being

[21] Missing or lost files are a recurring theme throughout the show. In TD, 1:6 Reverend Tuttle claims that the files Cohle and Hart are searching for – files, the viewer is led to believe, that would incriminate Tuttle – cannot be found due to flooding.

[22] A key scene occurs, in TD, 1:3 when Cohle and Hart attend the outdoor revival preaching of the evangelist, Joel Theriot. While they visit him as part of their investigation, the visit gains larger significance within the show as a moment in which Cohle rather relentlessly and humorously criticizes both the evangelist and those who are drawn to the evangelist's preaching. The evangelist's story about how the world works is analyzed, by Cohle, as a falsehood driven by the need for catharsis. It is precisely in response to Cohle's investment in articulating this analysis that Hart makes the remark about panic. My approach to Cohle's panic is indebted to conversations with Anthony Paul Smith.

[23] From Greek *pas* or *pan* (= 'all').

affected by the sprawl only insofar as one detects a story, or as one tells the story of a detection. In these ways, one denies the sprawl in favor of the contingent drama of the detection. And what is at stake in this drama is less the outcome that is established, and more the establishment of a contingency of outcomes. A detective may succeed or fail, but he still detects. Successfully or unsuccessfully, he remains active. Even the detective's suffering gives a story to tell; meaning is still activated by the detective's pain. The detective may therefore be affected, but only insofar as this affection can be afforded by, narrated within, the story of detection and the detection of story.

Antecedent Blackness: Refusal of Division Between Darkness and Light

Despite all this, the sprawl remains real, it really affects us, without story. The story needs the sprawl as background, but the sprawl does not need the story; the sprawl's reality antecedes its being positioned as background-of-story. Accordingly, the demand is to leave the story, to leave the detection and its meaningful suffering. More precisely, the demand is to not be in the story, to never have been in the story. What is at issue, then, is a negativity that extends not only to the sort of 'cathartic narrative' that Cohle detects and opposes – I will call this a 'positive story' – but also to the story of negating the positive story. Cohle, even while he was negating positive stories, never fully negated the story of himself as the one who negates positive stories. His negativity remained narratable as something divided from the positive. In this sense, his negativity remained dependent upon, or dialetically constituted through, division. Cohle negated positive stories, but he did not negate the division of negative from positive. By leaving this division in place – the division by which story is constituted – he failed to negate story as such.

The same point may be articulated in terms of light (positive stories), darkness (the story of negating positive stories), and blackness (negation of story as such). In these terms, we can say that Cohle pursued – at least until his ultimate turn toward the light – the negation of light; he sided with the darkness against the light of positive stories. Yet this negation of light, this siding with darkness, remained defined in terms of division: his darkness was defined as the divisive opposition to light; he was dark because he was not light. In this sense, he remained dependent on the light he opposed, he remained dependent on division – and it was precisely this dependence on division that enabled the constitution of the story of Cohle (as the one who negates the light). Such a story is dark rather than light, but it remains a story.

What, then, of blackness? Blackness may be articulated as antecedent to the division between darkness and light.[24] It is precisely this antecedence that makes it incommensurable with darkness: while darkness is articulated by way of its division from light, blackness is articulated as antecedent to all light, and thereby to any divisive relation between light and darkness; while darkness entails (divisive relation to) light, blackness entails nothing, nothing but itself as refusal of both darkness and light. Blackness thus negates, by way of antecedence, every division between darkness and light or light and darkness. Given the link between division and story, we can also say that blackness negates, by way of antecedence, every story. In fact, we can say of blackness what we said of the sprawl: it is not blackness that needs the story, it is rather the story that needs blackness. Yet, precisely because blackness negates story as such, story cannot articulate blackness as blackness, it must instead articulate blackness as *darkness* – as that which is divided from the light.

I have already noted that Cohle's negation of positive stories was divisive, and that for this reason it enabled a story of the negation of story. We can now say that he posed a story of darkness against the story of light. His darkness, by dividing itself from stories of light, already made itself into a story. Accordingly, his ultimate turn toward the light, far from being a break with his darkness, was actually continuous with it *at the*

[24] This is to follow François Laruelle's claim – in 'Universe Black in the Human Foundations of Colour,' trans. Miguel Abreu and Robin Mackay, in *From Decision to Heresy: Experiments in Non-Standard Thought*, ed. Mackay (Windsor Quarry/New York: Urbanomic/Sequence Press, 2012) – that, 'Black is prior to the absence of light' (404), or that, 'Black, before light, is the substance of the Universe, what escaped from the World before the World was born into the World' (403).

level of story: regardless of whether he takes the side of darkness or light, Cohle always has a story, which constitutes itself through the division – the versus' – between light and dark. *As story*, Cohle's darkness has more in common with what he negates – the story of light – than it does with blackness.

Not only as light (positive story), but also as darkness (story of negating the positive story), there is a narrative frame of 'anti-blackness.'[25] There is a story precisely because there is light divided from darkness, or darkness divided from light, but never blackness, which antecedes this division, which negates story as such (whether the story is light or dark). What is necessary, then, is the negation of story, as such, according to blackness – that is, according to negativity that antecedes all stories of division. Negativity must be articulated not as part of a story, but rather as

---

[25] The racial discourse that is inseparable from anti-blackness could be pursued by connecting Cohle's invocation of the story of 'light versus dark' to his undercover work with the Iron Crusader biker gang, which is alternatively referred to as an Aryan gang in TD, 1:4. This work culminates in his participation in the *capture*, *robbery*, and *murder* of black people. After a shootout erupts, he escapes – by way of Hart's getaway car – just as the police arrive. If Cohle always has a story, then this is because he is always narratable in terms of light (after his shift) or in terms of darkness (prior to this shift). In other words, he is always light or dark, but never black. His not being black, I suggest, is specifically indicated, within this episode, by his *capacity* to participate in an Aryan gang and to make a getaway from the police – who, upon their arrival, can be presumed to continue their historical practice of anti-black violence. This is to draw attention to the relation between the constitution of a crime story – which is not only (as story) anti-black, but which is also dependent on the capacity to imagine that there are criminals 'out there' to be detected – and the *a priori* criminalization of blackness. In this sense, storied anti-blackness and racial anti-blackness are not separable operations. On anti-blackness and police violence, see Steve Martinot and Jared Sexton, 'The Avant-Garde of White Supremacy,' in *Social Identities* 9.2 (2003), 169-181. Key texts on anti-blackness include Lewis Gordon, *Bad Faith and Antiblack Racism* (Amherst, NY: Humanity Books, 1995), and Frank B. Wilderson, III, *Red, White & Black: Cinema and the Structure of U.S. Antagonisms* (Durham: Duke University Press, 2010). On antecedence and anti-blackness, see Sexton, "The Social Life of Social Death: On Afro-Pessimism and Black Optimism," *InTensions* 5 (Fall/Winter 2011), http://www.yorku.ca/intent/issue5/articles/pdfs/jaredsextonarticle.pdf

the anteceding and antagonizing of story in its totality. This is to say that negativity must happen twice: as the negation of something, but also as the negation of the story of negating something. This is not the dialectical negativity of Hegel, which proceeds, progresses, and develops something new, divided from the old; it is rather a negativity that never was able to divide, that was there before the story of division and of the overcoming of division. It is not the negativity of coming to be, of becoming-indiscernible; it is instead a negativity according to never was. It is a negativity according to an antecedence so antecedent that it never was old – for the old is divided from the new, whereas the antecedent has no division, no history, neither old nor new.[26]

Something close to this sort of negation occurs in the second episode, which revolves around the family, or around the Trinity, which is to say the Holy Family.[27] The Father, the Son, and the Spirit have sometimes been articulated, in the course of Christianity, as historical stages: various spiritualist heretics, not to mention Hegel, have located in the Trinity a progression from the age of the transcendent Father to the age of the mediating Son, and ultimately to the age of immanent Spirit; the divisions of the Father are progressively undone in favor of a Spirit without division.[28] In other words, the divisions of the Trinity become indiscernible. It is not by chance that this particular episode – in which Hart tells his Father-in-law that old men are stuck in the past, and in which Cohle remarks that his daughter's death 'spared me the sin of being a father'[29] – ends with a song,

[26] While the notion of time according to a radical antecedence, as I am here articulating it, is not equivalent to the suggestions provided by Cohle's comments regarding time, it should be noted that the question of time is central to *True Detective*. See, for instance, Cohle's discussion of time, eternity, and m-brane theory in TD, 1:5.

[27] TD, 1:2.

[28] The best example of this tendency is found with Joachim di Fiore. It should be noted, however, that other spiritualist heretics, such as Marguerite Porete and Meister Eckhart, may be read as enacting the very negativity – affect without story – that I am articulating as antagonistic toward the progressivism indicated by Joachim or Hegel.

[29] TD, 1:2.

running over the credits, that pronounces the achievement of immanentized divinity: 'the kingdom of Heaven is within you.'[30]

On one hand, the age of Spirit, the collapse of every divisive Father and mediating Son into an immanent kingdom of God, is a negation of the story. The story is done. On the other hand, an obstacle to this negation of the story remains, and this obstacle is that the age of Spirit emerges within the very story that is supposed to be negated. In other words, the negation of story still belongs to the teleology established by division – division is undone, but the undoing of division belongs to the story set up by division. It is still a story of becoming, a story of negating the story. The story is done because *it has been done*; the story is done as a story of undoing, and so the story survives as constitutive history. What is necessary instead is to never have been story. If it is 'just one story, the oldest,' then negativity means anteceding even the oldest.[31] Negativity is not divided, but this is because it *never was* capable of dividing. On the other hand, if the age of Spirit is not divided, then this is because it *became* unified. The age of Spirit thus depends on the history of becoming-indiscernible – it *unifies* division, whereas negativity refuses division.

Affect

The reality of this negativity is affect. And, once again, affect has no story. By affect, here, I do not mean a state, such as the affect of being happy or being sad.[32] Talking about affect in terms of contingent states – the possibility of being happy *or* sad, the possibility of being saved *or* damned – divides affect into a narrative: to be affected with happiness is to put sadness in the past, and to be affected with sadness is to put happiness in the past. If consciousness is an error, then this is because it divides

---

[30] 13th Floor Elevators, 'Kingdom of Heaven,' *The Psychedelic Sounds of the 13th Floor Elevators* (International Artists, 1966). For the biblical reference of the cited lyric, see Luke 17:21.

[31] TD, 1:8.

[32] Similarly, affect has nothing to do with a state of optimism or a state of pessimism.

affect.[33] In fact, we could just as well say that consciousness is a story, namely the story of affect: I am conscious of being happy because I am conscious of being sad in the past; I am conscious of being sad because I am conscious of being happy in the past. Against all this, what I mean by affect is simply affect of body upon body, without good or bad, without story, and thus without recognition. The error, simply put, is that of using a basic division – or of using division as a basis – in order to produce recognizability; the error is not that of misrecognizing affect, but rather that of subjectivizing affect by subjecting affect to recognition.

Affect is unrecognizable. It is story that gives meaning, or the possibility of recognition, to affect. Yet affect in-itself, in its sheer taking place, takes place without sadness or happiness. This is also to say that affect, if we speak of it in terms of signs, expresses these signs without meaning. It is the detective's activity that gives meaning to signs, that converts signs into sens, into meaning and direction, into *evidence* that points from and to crime and salvation. Yet before there is ever the story of a detection, before there is ever a detective, there is affect in-itself – nothing to point to, and no need of a pointer. It is the detective's activity, or the story of a crime, that makes evidence, that gives one something to go off of and somewhere to go – whereas in reality, or according to the reality of affect in-itself, all signs say that there is no place to go and no place to go from. Affect is not transitive: its taking place antecedes every (division of) place; its signs lead nowhere.

Affect is not based in a place. It is not even based in a body. To locate affect in a body, or to articulate it as what one body (transitively) does *to* another, is to tell a story about affect from a

---

[33] The notion that 'consciousness is an error' emerges within the show, most explicitly, when Cohle remarks in TD, 1:1, 'I think human consciousness is a tragic misstep in evolution. We became too self-aware, nature created an aspect of nature separate from itself, we are creatures that should not exist by natural law. We are things that labor under the illusion of having a self; an accretion of sensory, experience and feeling, programmed with total assurance that we are each somebody, when in fact everybody is nobody.' This claim resonates with the work of Thomas Ligotti – see for instance his *The Conspiracy Against the Human Race: A Contrivance of Horror* (New York: Hippocampus Press, 2011).

place other than affect's happening. When affect happens, it happpens without the division of bodies.[34] Affect happens as the decapacitation of a body to delimit or bind itself, as the decapacitation of the division between one body and another. In this sense, affect of body upon body is no division at all, it is instead the breakdown of division. In fact, it is the breakdown of both bodies – the breakdown where there are no-bodies anymore, only unlocatable, unpossessable affect. The body, or this body and that body, are refused by the antecedence of affect; the body is not a basis for affect, affect is the baselessness of bodies.

It is precisely such affect, in its baselessness, that Spinoza insists upon when he refuses contingency in the name of necessity.[35] Affect, in its sheer taking place, its happening, is necessary – not because affect had to happen this way rather than that other way, but simply because it happens. It is actually contingency (and not necessity) that enables explanation of why affect happens. This is because explanation of *why* affect happens requires imagination of something else that could have happened. All explanation requires an operation in which it is said, in some way or another, that it happened like this because that other thing you imagine happening could not (or was not meant to) have happened. Explanation requires, at least at the level of imagination, alternative possibilities. At the level of this imagining, then, there is contingency, a story of why affect had to be (this way, and not that other way). Affect is explained by imagining an otherwise (or other-ways). Necessity, on the contrary, does not explain why affect had to be, it merely insists that affect is, without any imgination of otherwise.

Put otherwise, to focus on contingent possibilities of affect, or of affect's effects, is to deny the reality of affect in favor of

---

[34] One might say, to borrow a term from François Laruelle, who borrows the same term from quantum mechanics, that affect, as body upon body, is not division but 'superposition.' See for instance François Laruelle, *Philosophie non-standard. Générique, quantique, philo-fiction* (Paris: Kimé, 2010).

[35] Spinoza remarks for instance, that 'a thing is called contingent only because of a defect of our knowledge' (I:33s1) and that 'we deny . . . existence insofar as we imagine it not to be necessary' (IV:11d). See Spinoza, *Ethics*, trans. Edwin Curley (London: Penguin, 1996).

imagination of the otherwise. Attention is given to what could be placed around affect, rather than to affect in its taking place; attention is given to the production of stories (or the stories of production) about affect, and it is thereby turned away from affect in-itself. The intensity of affect – of being affected without a story – is thus denied by contingency. As Spinoza remarks, 'An affect toward a thing we imagine as necessary is more intense, other things equal, than one toward a thing we imagine as possible or contingent, or not necessary.'[36] To refuse contingency in the name of necessity, then, is to increase or to insist upon affect's intensity, which is intense precisely because it is not explained through recourse to an otherwise. Necessity means nothing, it explains nothing, it does nothing but refuse explanations.

Affect in-itself is a radical negation of all things that would provide a basis. To explain an affect, to say that it was caused by something, that it enables one thing rather than another, that it is better or worse than some other possibility, is to obstruct the baselessness of affect. The taking place of affect antecedes the *basic* division of contingency, the division between what could and could not happen, between this and that position, between damned and saved, between criminal and victim. The contingency of division, whether we imagine it as past or future, belongs to a story produced by a body that wants to stop being affected. Yet to insist on necessity, the necessity that insists in spite – in hatred – of the detection of contingency, or of the production of a crime scene, is to insist on the reality of affect. It is also to insist that there is neither story nor evidence, that there is no explanation to detect, and that detection is a story in search of a story.[37]

---

[36] Spinoza, Ethics, IV:11.

[37] I would like to express my thanks for the comments of all of the participants in the 'True Detection' event, and especially for those of Nicola Masciandaro and Edia Connole (to whom additional thanks are due for her editorial comments, which greatly improved this essay). Furthermore, I would like to express my thanks to the ICI Berlin Institute for Cultural Inquiry for their support of my work.

koyntly bigyled

by Dominic Fox[1]

FOR CLOSURE SEEK the chapel of mischance,
moss-cushioned grotto of seasonal
restitution, where the sharpest blades

hang out. Self-harm approximates
that ritual whereby one wound
requites another; but without mercy,

which sometimes is worth sticking
your neck out for, and by the devil's
luck emerging upright, nearly-scathed.

'Nearly-scathed' – intimacy of the axe's kiss, a glancing blow, delicately handled. Reversals turn on indiscernibles. Is our knight true or untrue, beguiled or self-beguiling? There is a kink in his valour, on account of which he can receive mercy rather than retribution in exact measure. A story to take to heart: this is only possible if the heart is not already sufficient in its courage. A very perfect knight would not have walked out alive; an imperfect knight can become the object of a fable, a living lesson.

Theory of the detective – the detective is one who fails in courage, but does so in an exemplary way. 'Down these mean streets,' Raymond Chandler writes, 'a man must go who is not himself mean, who is neither tarnished nor afraid.'[2] But who can believe this even of Chandler's Marlowe? He has been tarnished and he has been afraid, and that is why he is able to follow the *fil conducteur*, the filament connected to the heart, which will take

---

[1] The poem is excerpted from Dominic Fox, *Half Cocks* (Intercapillary Editions, 2011).

[2] Raymond Chandler, 'The Simple Art of Murder,' in *Raymond Chandler: Later Novels and Other Writings*, ed. Frank MacShane (New York: The Library of America, 1995), 977-992, 992.

him to the heart of the affair. All these filaments lead into the chapel of mischance, where we hear the axes whirr.

Rust Cohle knows for sure that the world is heartless; but we see the filament where it enters him, showing that there is at least one heart in the world and that it is his. He is 'true' not in himself – and certainly not in the philosophy he propounds, which is as worthless as it proclaims itself to be – but in his exemplary failure to live up to his inverted ego-ideal, to be just the knight-of-no-faith he declares himself to be. 'I think human consciousness is a tragic misstep in evolution,' only a consciousness could think this, or make the mistake of trying to evaluate evolution's 'steps' as true or false.[3] Only a creature capable of being beguiled can make a misstep, can both have a path to follow and be capable of being drawn aside from it into what Auden called 'the convolutions of your simple wish.'[4]

It is such labyrinthine convolutions that provide mercy with its occasion, its opportunity; as Geoffrey Hill says of Shakespeare's *Measure for Measure*, 'the ethical motiv is – so we may hazard – / opportunism redemptive and redeemed.'[5] [DF]

---

[3] TD, 1:1.
[4] W.H. Auden, 'Consider this and in our time,' in *The English Auden: Poems, Essays and Dramatic Writings, 1927-1939* (London: Faber and Faber, 1988), 46-47.
[5] Geoffrey Hill, *The Triumph of Love* (New York: Mariner Books, 2000), section CXX.

'Abelard's cut his hands . . . from now on what symphony is equal to that atrocious kiss of paper? Heloise swallows fire. Opens a door. Climbs the stairs. A bell.'[1] Now in a deeper darkness than before I wander the upper galleries of the museum of lost objects. Of aberrant dreams. A flickering of wings. A kiss of paper. Mice. 'When we see the square towers of the city in the distance, they often appear round.'[2] A rent in the low ceiling reveals a glowering sky. In the avian ossuary there is a movement. An arrow splits the shaft of another's contingency in the moment of its firing. Everything changes now. The missing heart of a travelling funfair. My symptoms bleed new light. 'There came, so people say, a female demon, who stopped him and said to him: Whither do you go? For I have children and you cannot ascend...'[3] True detection is true defection. The curse of Silenus at the *Lone Star* motel one dismal evening when the dice went belly up and the beer ran out. 'Revolt – its face distorted by amorous ecstasy – tears from God his naive mask, and thus oppression collapses in the crash of time.'[4] Scratched on the underpass beneath the poster of an abandoned funfair: *Les Trois Frères*. Ecstasies of annihilation. Phenomenophagism. 'At first Crispin had felt an obscure sense of annoyance at the way this strange woman descended on to the beach and calmly plundered the plumage of dead birds.'[5] Ecstasies of annihilation beneath the carapace of time. Phenomenophagism and the hypostitional analysis thereof. 'Death would rule forever did not Baal's sister Anath, the terrible maiden of love and of war, wander over the earth seeking her dead brother.'[6] Dead time. Fly time. [CB] 'Decay flutters up on black wings.'[7] Its lineaments: what is left of what is taken. Its transparency: the opaque, white deception as of nothing, the sky found inside a bird, 'winged salt, omens.'[8] Because what is gone is also what is left, and though we wait here for some new departure, some new extraction that lives on in its remains, we do not float here unimpeded, for 'the black flight of birds always / Touches the one watching,'[9] and this touch is where we come to sleep, because '[n]o one sleeps in the sky. No one.'[10] And because of this, even 'the birds are ready to be oxen,' ready to lay down and chew and forget how once, so nearly commensurate with the air, they'd laboured to make up the slim disparity and never got nearer than that nearness. And aware this way of life only in that failing flailing repetition, their visions of reprieve were always night and the margin there no longer tempting, as they settled down to become 'white rocks with the aid of the moon.'[11] (For while the equilibrium of identity is so much further off, the actual distance from its fabled end remains unaltered, the maintenance a self-conditioning state of perpetual overreach: 'In their heavy flight, with each raising of the wing, crows lower their bodies, and no more does the body raise the wings than do the wings lower the body.')[12] But in the end it is this grounded thing that finds itself a madwoman, complete with madwoman scream, a thing that sees the children come, 'chase after her and throw stones at her, as if she were [still] a blackbird.'[13] And yet while still a woman, unrecognised as bird, it continued to mimic in the service of its parasitic fall, flapping its arms and singing, 'I am a bird; look at my wings.'[14] Because though it was once black and is now white it hasn't changed,[15] the same non-thing persisting in being dead to itself, when after all '[b]lack is not in the object or the World, it is what man sees in man, and the way in which man sees man,'[16] and the bird that man sees does not escape him. The last word then – the logic of a creature formed from commutable opposites – just this: 'See black, think white!'[17] [GJS] Black is not a colour despite its visibility. Human vessels of subclinical depression are known to favour it. They have always felt deadened. Known from the moment they could rationalise that aspects of our world were hidden from view. The mask over the sadness is broadly impenetrable. Live long enough and the bleak-minded soak up the blackness until they are wearing it. It spreads out upon their skin until they too begin to falter and internalise the vicious characteristics of our world. This is, then, inevitably, externalised upon blameless victims. The external map of redemption is easier to navigate than the internal one. How to forgive oneself for having transgressed one's own borders? The punishments of this world are inadequate to those who are already wedded to suffering. Tears spring more often, certainly, but you have always known them. The world recedes even further. It becomes dimmer and one day you realise you are now the walking blackness. Your walk becomes slower; the pains more centred and the stiffness more definitive. The failures pile up. The futility now attuned to your heart-rate. If only one could accept the finality of the one true solution, but the blackness won't give you that option. Too easy. The subtle reminder of a once vibrant conscience. Ever more reclusive. Ever bleaker. Quickened deterioration of health until simply waking induces vomiting. Live through all the sins again in the mind and try and steady the hand for the temporary cure. Not even this works anymore. When you emerge, from time to time, a new layer is added. Confirmation of your character, or lack of it, and the growing understanding that each outing is just another way to die. You are there and some still see you. Some even dredge out the old you. Some can still see what was or might have been. To others fantasies or motive cling. Just another cipher on their way through life. Crutches dropped you are now truly weightless. Nothing left here anymore. No more sleep. Lie still and try settle on the flickers that will not pull you over there. Or over there. There is so much scorched Earth that there is no positive angle. The lines of thought become more intricate, condensed, and connected. They snake across one another until they blur; becoming-invisible, that is to say, black. [PJE] A bird, 'as black as blindness' you are.[18] A lark. No light has ever seen your black universe, no body ever known such pain.[19] (Such decay). Our profane flight in the pursuit of happiness is a lark. Intensified along two vectors, black and white. Black is the intensity of the heart, lark. The inner isolation in man which passes through you as suffering. Misfortunate thing. *Surely, this is all for me. Me. Me, me, me. I, I. I'm so fucking important. I'm so fucking important . . . Right?*[20] You trouble deaf heaven with your bootless cries. And look upon yourself and curse your fate.[21] 'Receiving the blank premiering black of Absolute knick knack.'[22] But you are a bird, lark. And with that a change of feathers for every season. 'My shit it stays Satiates mocks.'[23] Beneath your empty crucifix ('I am my father's son. I am no one. I cannot love. It's in my blood').[24] What a lark. [EC] Flight: mobility, from one place to another, transitivity. Imagine a bird, flying, yet look at the image. As image, the bird shows: immobility. Not what you imagine. The duration of flight, taking off and landing, is not in the image. Duration is there only as long as you want to move away—take your own flight—from the image. You may move away from the image, yet the image is still—still, the image shows eternity. You imagine existence 'in relation to a certain time and place,' you imagine that the movement of duration should show up and stand out, like stars against a black sky.[25] Yet the blackness of this bird—like the unthought question, 'What is a black star?'—does not move as you want it to move.[26] It is not there for you, even though you imagine that it belongs to the world of flight to which you want yourself to belong. You want to save yourself. You want to fly from darkness to light, but such enflightenment has too much light to ever escape. 'Black, before light, is the substance of the Universe, what escaped from the world before the World was born into the World.'[27] The black universe cannot be explained by the flight of the world; 'eternity cannot be explained by duration'; the immobile, intransitive bird cannot be explained by the flights between time-places.[28] Going nowhere, coming from nowhere, it collapses on itself, without any passage to get you moving. 'Eternity is just the intensification, or radicalization, of the fatality of that being, which is riveted to itself.'[29] Even the openness of the bird's mouth is riveted. You imagine that it is ready to kill and eat, or that it is crying the suffering of its own death. These possibilities are divided in the story you imagine, but they are never divided in the image. The image tells no story about the meeting between dealing death and undergoing death, for these are never divided. 'Lovers don't finally meet somewhere / They're in each other all along.'[30] [DCB]

---

[1] Antonin Artaud, 'Transparent Abelard,' in *Anontin Artaud Anthology*, trans. Marc Estrin and ed. Jack Hirschman (San Franciso: City Lights Books, 1965), 53.

[2] Lucretius, 'Sensation and Sex,' in *On the Nature of the Universe*, trans. R.E. Latham (London: Penguin Books, 1951), 141.

[3] Seigmund Hurwitz, *Lilith the First Eve* (Einsiedeln: Daimon Verlag, 1999), 104.

[4] Georges Bataille, 'Sacrifices,' in *Visions of Excess: Selected Writings 1927-1939*, ed. Alan Stoekl, trans. Alan Stoekl with Carl R. Lovitt and Donald M. Leslie Jnr. (Minneapolis: University of Minnesota Press, 1985), 134.

[5] J.G. Ballard, 'Storm-bird, Storm-bringer,' in *J.G Ballard: The Complete Short Stories* (London: Flamingo, 2001), 697.

[6] Jeffrey Burton Russell, *The Devil: Perceptions from Antiquity to Primitive Christianity* (Ithica: Cornell University Press, 1977), 104.

[7] Georg Trakl, 'On the Moor,' in *Autumn Sonata* (New York: Moyer Bell, 1989), 89.

[8] Novica Tadic, 'Masks,' in *Assembly* (Austin, Texas: Host Publications, 2009), 33.

[9] Trakl, 'Rest and Silence,' in *Autumn Sonata*, 99.

[10] Federico Garcia Lorca, 'City Without Sleep,' in *Poet in New York* (New York: Grove Press, 2008), 65.

[11] Lorca, 'Blind Panorama of New York,' in *Poet in New York*, 67.
[12] Carlo Michelstaedter, *Persuasion and Rhetoric*, trans. Russell Valentino, Cinzia Sartini Blum and David Depew (Yale: Yale University Press, 2004), 55.
[13] Lautreamont, *Maldoror and Poems* (London and New York: Penguin Books, 1978), 126.
[14] Michel Serres, *The Parasite*, trans. Lawrence R. Schehr (Baltimore, MD: The John Hopkins University Press, 1982), 202.
[15] Cf. 'If white turns to black some say: "Essentially it is still the same." And others, if the colour becomes a one degree darker, say "It has changed completely,"' in Ludwig Wittgenstein, *Culture and Value*, trans. Peter Winch (Blackwell Publishers, 1998), 49.
[16] François Laruelle, 'Universe Black in the Human Foundations of Colour,' trans. Miguel Abreu and Robin Mackay, in *From Decision to Heresy: Experiments in Non-Standard Thought*, ed. Robin Mackay (Windsor Quarry/New York: Urbanomic/Sequence Press, 2012), 403-404.
[17] Laruelle, 'On the Black Universe,' 403-404.
[18] Ovid, *Metamorphoses*, trans. Charles Martin (London and New York: W.W. Norton & Company, 2010), VII. 583.
[19] Francois Laruelle, 'On The Black Universe In The Human Foundations of Color,' in Eugene Thacker, Daniel Colucciello Barber, Nicola Masciandaro and Alexander Galloway, *Dark Nights of the Universe* (Miami: NAME, 2013), 102-110.
[20] TD, 1:3.
[21] William Shakespeare, 'Sonnet 29,' in *Shakespeare's Sonnets*, ed. Stephen Booth (New Haven: Yale University Press, 1977), 172.
[22] RC Miller, 'Motion Lotion,' in *Pussy Guerilla Face Banana Fuck Nut* (USA: gobbet press, 2014), 12.
[23] Miller, 'Motion Lotion,' 12.
[24] Deafheaven, 'The Pecan Tree,' *Sunbather* (California: Deathwish Inc, 2013). Cf. David Thatcher, 'What a Lark: The Undoing of Sonnet 29,' *Durham University Journal* (January 1994): 59-66.
[25] Benedict de Spinoza, *Ethics*, trans. Edwin Curley (London: Penguin, 1996), V, 29sch.
[26] Black Star, 'Astronomy (8th Light),' *Mos Def & Talib Kweli Are Black Star* (Rawkus, 2002).
[27] Laruelle, 'Universe Black,' *From Decision to Heresy*.
[28] Spinoza, *Ethics*, V, 29d.
[29] Emmanuel Levinas, *On Escape*, trans. Bettina Bergo (Stanford, California: Stanford University Press, 2003), 71.
[30] Jalal al-din Rumi, *The Essential Rumi*, trans. Coleman Barks with John Moyne (San Francisco: Harper, 1995), 106.

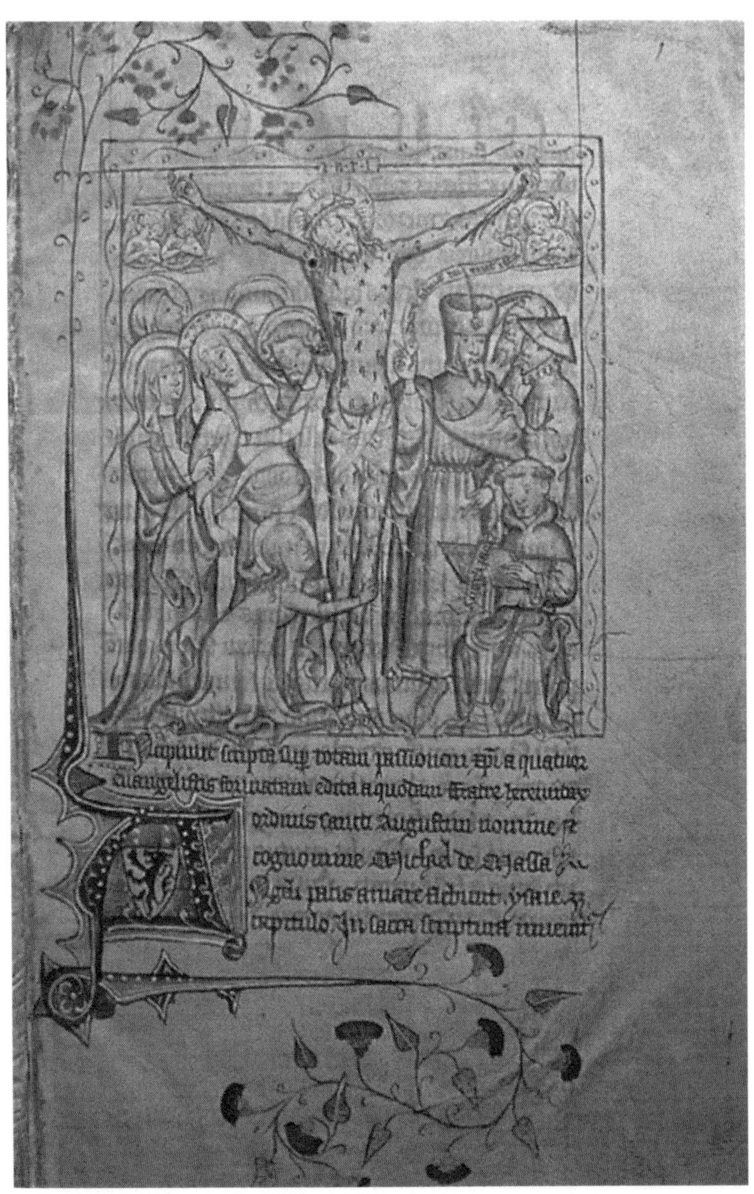

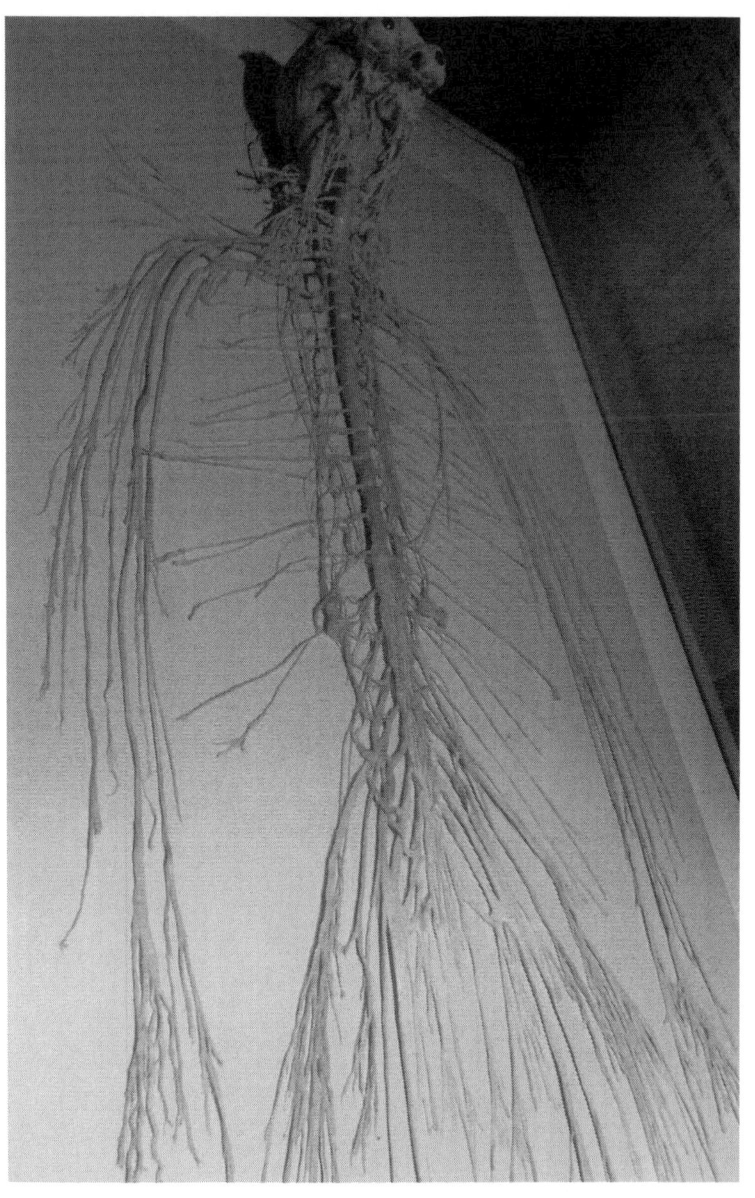

having caught one fish in his great haul."

"The division seems rather unfair," I remarked. "You have done all the work in this business. I get a wife out of it, Jones gets the credit; pray what remains for you?"

"For me," said Sherlock Holmes, "there still remains the cocaine-bottle." And he stretched his long, white hand up for it.

M. GALLET
DÉCÉDÉ

ROMAN
PAR
GEORGES SIMENON

A. FAYARD & Cie - PARIS

PRIX : 6 FR.

SIDNEY PAGET
1893

lifting it down that brought on his stroke. We'll try a little experiment. I don't think any of the household will interrupt us up here, but we can head off anybody who does. I want you to take that mirror, Hadley, and set it up just inside the door—so that when you open the door (it opens inwards and to the right, you see, as you come in from the hall) the edge of the door at its outermost swing is a few inches away from the mirror."

The superintendent with some difficulty trundled out the object he found behind the bookcase. It was bigger than a tailor's swinging mirror; several inches, in fact, higher and wider than the door. Its base rested flat on the carpet, and it was supported upright by a heavy swing-base on the right-hand side as you faced it. Hadley regarded it curiously.

"Set it up inside the door?"

"Yes. The door will only swing open a short distance; you'll see an aperture only a couple of feet wide at the most. . . . Try it!"

"I know, but if you do that . . . well, somebody sitting in the room down at the end of the hall, where Mills was, would see his own reflection smack in the middle of the mirror."

"Not at all. Not at the angle—a slight angle, but enough; a poor thing, but mine own—not at the angle to which I'm going to tilt it. You'll see. The two of you go down there where Mills was while I adjust it. Keep your eyes off until I sing out."

Hadley, muttering that it was damned foolishness, but highly interested in spite of that, tramped down after Rampole. They kept their eyes off until they heard the doctor's hail, and then turned round.

The hallway was gloomy and high enough. Its black-carpeted length ran down to a closed door. Dr. Fell stood outside that door, like an overfat master of ceremonies about to unveil a statue. He stood a little to the right of the door, well back from it against the wall, and had his hand stretched out across to the knob. "Here she goes!" he grunted, and quickly opened the door—hesitated—and closed it. "Well? What did you see?"

"I saw the room inside," returned Hadley. "Or at least I thought I did. I saw the carpet, and the rear wall. It seemed a very big room."

"You didn't see that," said Dr. Fell. "As a matter of fact,

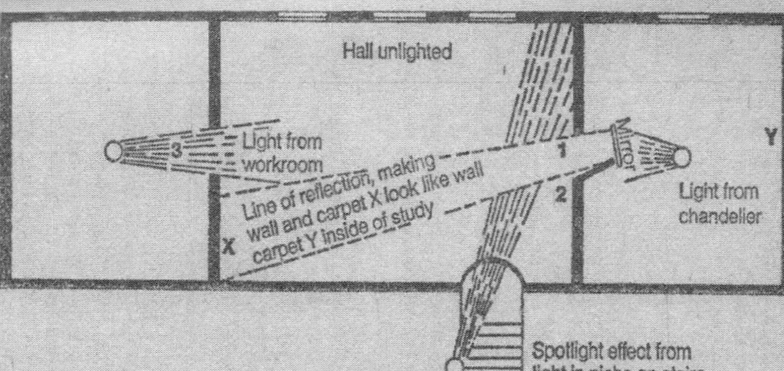

DIAGRAM TO ILLUSTRATE ILLUSION

1. Man whose own reflection is seen by watcher, but appearing three inches taller than reflection because watcher, thirty feet away, is sitting down on a much lower level of observation.
2. Confederate who opens and shuts door.
3. Watcher.

In testing this illusion, one important point must be observed. No light must fall directly on the mirror, else there will be a reflected dazzle to betray its presence. It will be seen that a spotlight from the niche on the stairs has been caused to fall across the line of the door, but not in a position to catch any reflection. No light is in the hall, and the workroom light does not penetrate far. In the study itself, the light comes from the chandelier in a very high ceiling, thus coming almost directly over the top of the mirror. It will throw, therefore, very little shadow of this mirror into the hall; and such shadow as it does throw will be obscured by the counter-shadow of the man standing before the door.

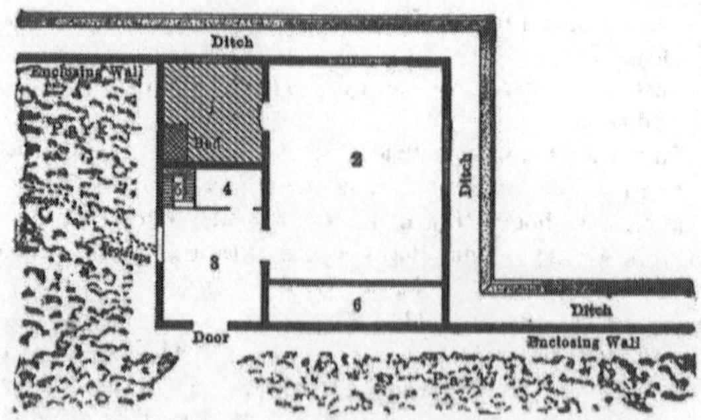

Here is the ground plan of the pavilion. It had a ground-floor which was reached by a few steps, and above it was an attic, with which we need not concern ourselves. The plan of the ground-floor only, sketched roughly, is what I here submit to the reader.

1. The Yellow Room, with its one window and its one door opening into the laboratory.

2. Laboratory, with its two large, barred windows and its doors, one serving for the vestibule, the other for The Yellow Room.

3. Vestibule, with its unbarred window and door opening into the park.

4. Lavatory.

5. Stairs leading to the attic.

6. Large and the only chimney in the pavilion, serving for the experiments of the laboratory.

The plan was drawn by Rouletabille, and I assured myself that there was not a line in it that was wanting to help to the solution of the problem then set before the police. With the lines of this plan and the description of its parts before them, my readers will know as much as Rouletabille knew when he entered the pavilion for the first time. With him they may now ask: How did the murderer escape from The Yellow Room?

Before mounting the three steps leading up to the door of the pavilion, Rouletabille stopped and asked Monsieur Darzac point blank:—

"What was the motive for the crime?"

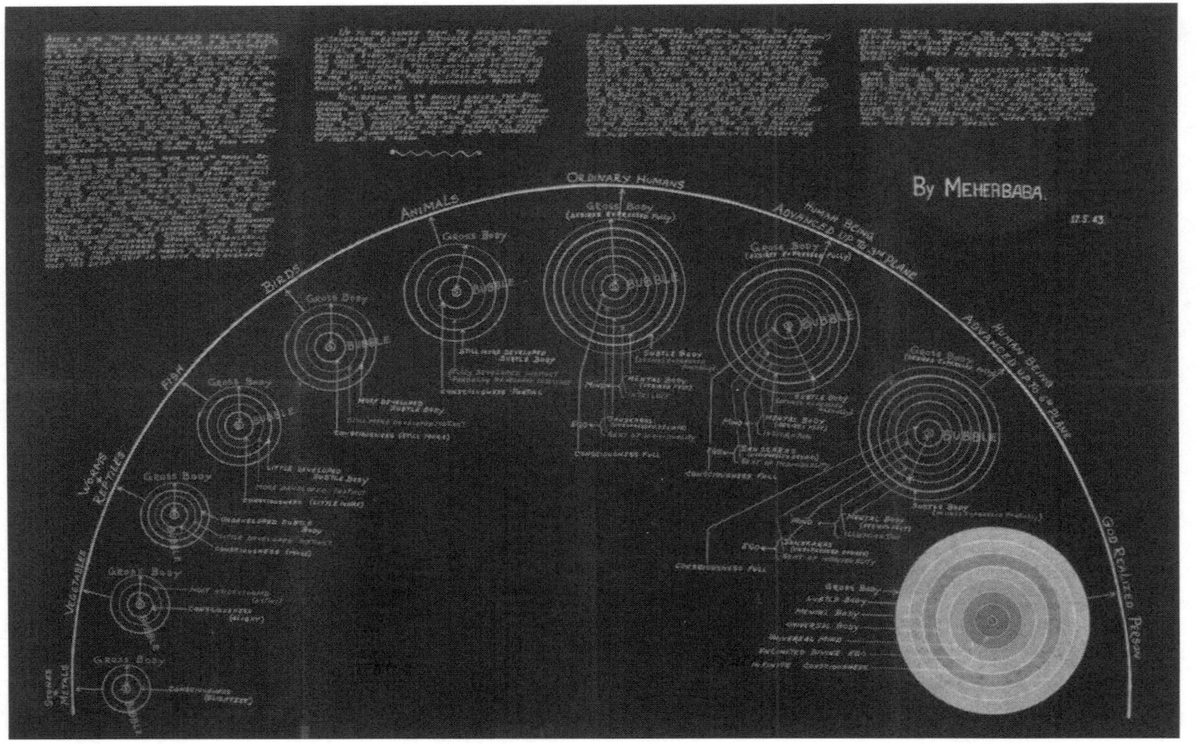
BY MEHERBABA.
17.5.43
ORDINARY HUMANS
ANIMALS
BIRDS
FISH
WORMS & REPTILES
VEGETABLES
GOD REALIZED PERSON
GROSS BODY
BUBBLE

The Premature Burial.

There are certain themes, of which the interest is all-absorbing, but which are too entirely horrible for the purposes of legitimate fiction. These the mere romanticist must eschew, if he do not wish to offend, or to disgust. They are with propriety handled, only when the severity and majesty of truth sanctify and sustain them. We thrill, for example, with the most intense

Here foloweth the seconde boke of that noble prynce kyng Arthur.

¶ Of a damoysell whiche came gyrde with a swerde for to fynde a man of suche vertue to drawe it out of the scauberde. Capl'm primū.

After the deth of Vther pendragon regned Arthur his sone/ the whiche had grete warre in his dayes for to gete al Englonde in to his honde/ for there were many kynges within the realme of Englonde and in Wales. Scotlonde & Cornewaylle. So it befelle on a tyme/ whan kyng Arthur was at London/ there came a knyght and tolde the kynge tydynges how that kyng Ryence of Northwales had rered a grete nombre of people/ & were entred in to the londe & brente & slewe the kynges true lyege people/ yf this be true sayd Arthur/ it were grete shame unto myn astate/ but ÿ he were myghtely withstande/ it is trouth sayd the knyght/ for I sawe ÿ hoost my self Well sayd the kyng/ lete make a crye/ ÿ all the lordes knyghts & gentylmen of armes sholde drawe unto a castell called Camelot in tho dayes/ & ther ÿ kyng wolde lete make a coūseyll generall and a grete Justes. So whan the kyng was come thyder with all his

Semi-Monthly.
Novel Series.
No. 95.
BEADLE'S
DIME NOVELS
EPH PETERS.
BEADLE & CO., 118 WILLIAM STREET, NEW YORK.
A. Winch, 505 Chestnut St., Philadelphia.

Raymond Chandler redux

west view

by **ROBERT KIRSCH**

A city no worse than others, a city rich and vigorous and full of pride, a city lost and beaten and full of emptiness.

—Philip Marlowe on Los Angeles in Raymond Chandler's "The Long Goodbye," 1954.

It was not that Raymond Chandler invented Los Angeles, though he captured it so well that the feel of the place and the period is better evoked in his novels than in history books. Los Angeles was an extension of his inner self, a city of the mind as well as of mean streets and dusty palms, cheap bars and mansions and projected a city of all our selves. It was for Chandler what London was for Dickens, Paris for Balzac.

Like many of his characters and most people in Los Angeles in the first half of this century, Chandler came from somewhere else, carrying his secret history, looking for the realization of his dreams. He carried the baggage of embittered childhood, the benefits and disabilities of an English public school education; shy, reserved, stoic on the surface, emotional beneath, a man for whom alcohol became an essential for release. He was a failed poet, a failed critic, a clerk and office manager fired for drunkenness and affairs with secretaries. He could have lived and died one of the *Luftmenschen* of this place. As it was, he and his wife moved endlessly from one end of Southern California to another, nomads of apartments and rented houses.

Frank MacShane's comprehensive and detailed biography, "The Life of Raymond Chandler" (Dutton: $12.95; illustrated), rests not only on unprecedented access to all the Chandler papers held by Helga Greene, Chandler's heir and executrix, and to correspondence files between the author and his English publishers and with his agents, but also on extensive interviews with those who knew Chandler socially or professionally, and on a detective's quest for records and documents from schooldays through military service to his final days in La Jolla.

With such new and intimate material, MacShane's portrait of Chandler is bound to be the most complete we have had so far. And it undoubtedly is, though many readers may question some of MacShane's interpretations and his conclusion which elevates Chandler to "a prophet of modern America," "one of the most important writers of his time, as well as one of the most delightful." It is a kind of boosterism which would have made Chandler cringe.

If the biography is somewhat flawed by advocacy and a tendency toward hero worship, it is almost always a fascinating and gripping work. Chandler is presented not as the remote observer viewing the characters of this exotic landscape with the detachment a British colonial officer might have for the bizarre natives of a tropical island but as an archetypical transplanted Angeleno, seeking a second chance, a new life, in this province of dreams. This was not some clerkish Walter Mitty projecting himself through the tough, chivalrous, complex Marlowe, but, as we see in these pages, a man who had known the city from within, had been a guest and protege of the rich, had worked in the oil business, had known the seedy hotels on long binges, the apartments of studio girls for sobering up, the streets and roads, the bars and the nightclubs.

Some parts of Chandler's life have been known but MacShane's great accomplishment is to fill in the experiences

Author Raymond Chandler: "I have lived on the edge of nothing."

that allowed Chandler, who came to fiction writing in his middle 40s, to find Los Angeles the matter of his novels, a landscape of tensions, between ideal and real, between order and an anarchy of impulse, between old obligations and the lure of the new, between the stability of caste and the California blur of social distinctions. He was a divided, complex man, and MacShane captures these polar tensions brilliantly.

With characteristic ambiguity about himself, Chandler wrote to his London lawyer two years before he died in 1959: "I have lived on the edge of nothing." This biography makes clear that intensity and zeal were at the center of his experience, that the long-delayed mastery of his writing came when he was able to meld the "opposed impulses of his nature in a work of fiction." He was part romantic poet and part cynical intellectual, torn between realism and idealism, a gap he was not able to bridge until the Marlowe novels.

Chandler's mother was Anglo-Irish, born in Waterford; his father was a railway engineer. They met and married when she was in Nebraska visiting her sister. They married in Laramie, Wyo., set up housekeeping in Chicago, where Chandler was born in 1888. His father was a drinker and the marriage broke up. Chandler's father disappeared from his life and the author rarely spoke of him except to call him "an utter swine."

When Chandler was 7, his mother took him to England, where they lived as dependents on his uncle and grandmother. He remembered petty humiliations: his grandmother offering wine to everyone at the table except his mother. Chandler was sent to Dulwich, a minor public school, where he was remembered as a high-strung, somewhat nervous boy, studious, energetic, impulsive. Though he

He was sent to Paris and Germany to study languages in preparation for the Civil Service and returned to work briefly as a clerk in the Admiralty. His ambition to be a writer was too strong. He quit after six months and began to write for literary papers and magazines. The early poetry quoted holds no promise of the language of the later novels, but there was some potential in the articles. He had a good critical, analytical sense, struggled to overcome the barriers of sentiment and a "literary" style.

There are hints (though MacShane tends to overvalue them, writing of the following, "Here is the origin of Chandler's Los Angeles") of the future. In an essay on abandoned old houses, Chandler concludes: "The effect is like that of a fine etching, colourless but full of suggestion, with a faint flavour of the sordid—but it is the romance of sordidness." For a writer who would be described as tough and hard-boiled, there is an irony in young Chandler's essay on realism, which he deprecated because the subject controlled the writer rather than vice versa. Idealists matter more: "They exalt the sordid to a vision of magic; and create pure beauty out of plaster and vile dust."

Chandler couldn't make a go of it and MacShane suggests there may have been an unhappy love which helped make his decision to leave England. ("This is only conjectural, and it is notoriously dangerous to base biographical assumptions on works of the imagination," MacShane rightly says.) In any event, he borrowed 500 pounds and set off for America. A chance meeting with the Warren Lloyds, a Los Angeles family with interests in literature and culture and investments in the oil business, was probably the most fateful in Chandler's life. Through the Lloyds he would meet Cissy Pascal, twice-divorced, 18 years older than Chandler, whom he would marry after the death of his mother in 1924; and through Lloyds he would be given his job as an oil company executive, and after he was fired in 1932, the Lloyd children made him an allowance of $100 a month which enabled him to begin his career as a pulp writer for Black Mask magazine.

MacShane's decision to treat "Raymond Chandler as a novelist and not simply as a detective-story writer" because "this is how Chandler looked at himself, and with justice" ignores an important reality. This is reflected in a very sketchy and sometimes glib examination of the influence of crime-writing on him. MacShane's summing up of Los Angeles is full of the very generalizations Chandler sees as the weakness of academic criticism. "Police lawlessness has been more prevalent in Los Angeles than in most American cities" is just one of these questionable claims. From this MacShane jumps to explain "much of the craziness associated with Southern California—the religious cults and the quackery."

Facile conclusions are jammed together with sound insights. "There is something appropriate in Chandler's choosing the detective story as his vehicle for presenting Los Angeles, and not only because a real detective, William J. Burns, became the hero of the ruling powers for discovering the union agitators who blew up the Los Angeles Times building." More defensible is "The detective story, so peculiar to the modern city, can involve an extraordinary range of humanity . . ."

And he speaks with a kind of authority which borders on ESP: "Some readers, knowing a little bit about Chandler's own nature, have imagined that he created in Marlowe an idealized concept of himself, making up for his own deficiencies. Such a procedure might have appealed to a young writer bent on self-expression, but Chandler was 50 when he began 'The Big Sleep' and no longer a child. He had the far more difficult problem of inventing a type of person he probably had never met with attributes that would make him bearable as a narrator, yet realistic as a character."

There is more than enough room for doubt. There are unconscious elements in the creation of character, elements of what Chandler called "magic" which are out of the conscious, even craft control of the writer. Chandler's life as portrayed in these pages, even after his success, and even in that Indian summer of his life when the repressions of years were occasionally lifted with sometimes pathetic effects, suggests a man who knew that every good writer was partially a child. "No matter what he may have done in the past, what he is trying to do now makes him a boy again; however much skill in routine technical things he may have acquired, nothing will help him now but passion and humility."

He felt sympathy for Hemingway who had to take the assault of "primping second-guessers who call themselves critics": "That's the difference between a champ and a knife thrower. The champ may have lost his stuff temporarily or permanently, he can't be sure. But when he can no longer throw his hard high one, he throws his heart instead."

Chandler's best epitaph is a remark he quoted from his English publisher: "I am the best there is in my line and the best there has ever been; I am tough only incidentally; substantially I am an original stylist with a very daring kind of imagination."

LOS ANGELES TIMES

Ecce hic descriptam claritatis gratia conspicuam imaginem.

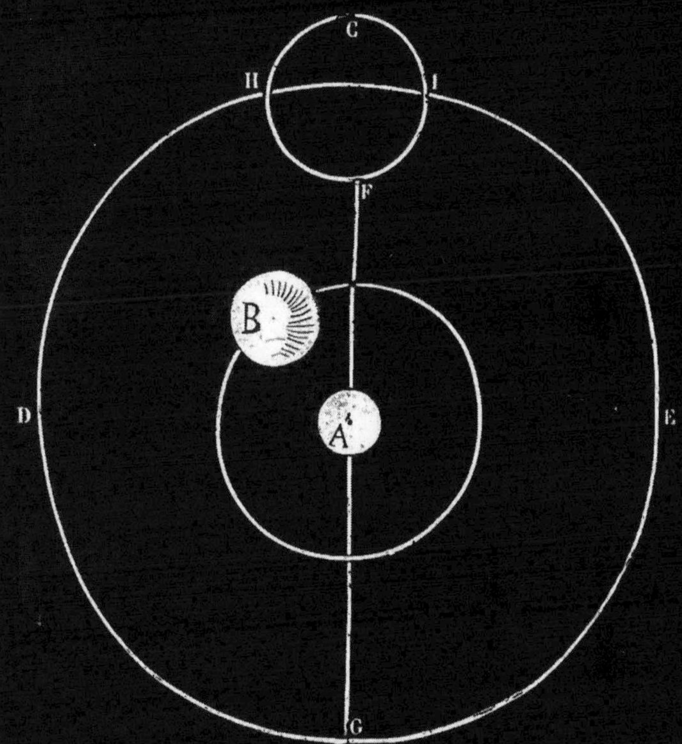

Sit ergo in figura præsenti, A terra, B luna, C sol, D oriens, E occidens, F G diameter ab ipso sole ad solis oppositum; H pars solis orientem respiciens, I pars solis occidentem spectans; linea vero ab H ad I, diameter disci seu corporis solaris. Jam tempore passionis luna erat in G, sive ex diametro soli opposita, proptereaque plena, et radiis solaribus tota collucens, ut in plenilunio assolet. Hora igitur sexta, qua Christus in cruce pendebat, subito transiit luna ab G, sive a loco soli ex diametro opposito, ad H, sive ad partem solis orientalem, ibique solem subiens ex ea parte inchoavit eclipsim, indeque ad I progressa, totum solem caligine sua, velut pulla veste, obduxit; deinde ab I sive parte solis occidua ad H resiliit, ita ut pars

A solis ultimo obtenebrata primo inclaruerit, mundoque radios suos diffuderit, contra quam alias semper factum fuerit, aut fieri solitum sit. Progressio
417 itaque ab H ad I, et regressio ab I ad H,
tres ipsas horas tenuit, a sexta scilicet usque ad nonam, hoc est in plagis orientalibus a meridie ad tertiam pomeridianam. Deinde ab H ad G, hoc est ad locum suum naturalem citissime rediit, ita ut vesperi in sua essent statione, sol in occasu, luna ex opposito; et hæc quidem plena ac lucida, perinde quasi loco mota non fuisset. Quarum rerum tam admirabili spectaculo percussi Dionysius et Apollophanes philosophi, quid sibi ista vellent, inter se quæritarunt, ut in Vita exposuimus. Denique de ambobus illis philosophis, S. Dionysio, inquam,

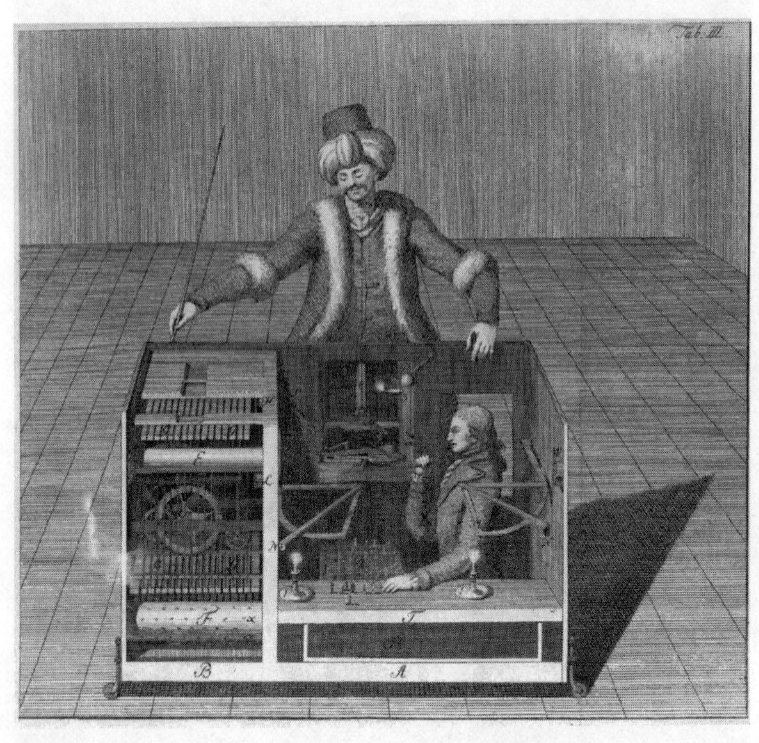
Tab. III.

WESTERN, DETECTIVE & ADVENTURE STORIES

BLACK MASK

THE MALTESE FALCON

By DASHIELL HAMMETT

SEPT. 1929 · 9

IN CANADA 25¢

A Mingo Picture. *The Deerslayer*

DEERSLAYER AND CHINGACHGOOK.

THE DEERSLAYER

OR

THE FIRST WAR-PATH

BY

J. FENIMORE COOPER

AUTHOR OF
THE LAST OF THE MOHICANS, Etc.

ILLUSTRATED WITH SCENES
FROM THE PHOTOPLAY
PRODUCED AND DISTRIBUTED BY
THE MINGO PICTURES COMPANY

GROSSET & DUNLAP
PUBLISHERS NEW YORK

Made in the United States of America

THE CHOLE STORY

Black Metal, Hypertext, and Fanfiction through Mark Danielewski's House of Leaves
[Nic Pizzolatto's True Detective]

KATHERINE FOYLE

"This is not for you."[1]

Surely this is ALL for me?
me, me, me I'm so fucking Important!

---

[1] This second 'beginning'[2] in *House of Leaves* (2000) by Mark Danielewski steals an entire (numberless) page for itself. The Foreword which precedes it is ostensibly the work of 'The Editors'[3] and the Introduction which follows is clearly authored by 'Johnny Truant' – the absent, possibly pseudonymous character who supposedly compiled The Navidson Record (the body of the book, authored by the absent Zampano) – but this line is anonymous, uncredited. It is also untrue – the very nature of the book[4] puts the reader in a position of power over the narrative, both over method of consumption and over the conclusion drawn. The book, in fact, is never for anyone except you.[5] "The novel can be your own personal playground,[33] your own series of interconnecting mazes and dreams." Danielewski, Mark Z. "House of Leaves." NEW YORK TIMES BOOK REVIEW 105.13 (2000): 9-10.

and like all dreams there is a monster at the end of it

Time is not linear, there are no beginnings (or ends)

[2] As documented by Sudha Shastri in his essay *Return to the Beginning: House of Leaves by Mark Danielewski*, the entire notion of beginning and beginnings is confused and warped by *House of Leaves*. Firstly, by its multiple sections – a Foreword, the single line warning (see the first line of this essay), an Introduction, *The Navidson Record*,[21] six Exhibits, and three Appendices – all of which may be seen as legitimate entrances to the narrative.[6] (In addition to and following these narrative segments, there is an index containing every word used in the book, two pages of Credits[7], and the final page, Yggdrasil). Secondly, by the footnotes[29] and

'IS this the end of the beginning or the beginning of theend?'

when watching a T.V show the viewer is relentlessly interrupted by advertisements, the ads are targeted at the show's demographic

epigraphs that relentlessly interrupt the narrative(s). Some of these footnotes, rather than remaining mere addenda to the 'main story' serve to carry (or indeed smuggle[3]) stories of equal importance and authenticity (if any of the book is authentic) which are indicated by different typographies (voices) – most notably the many personal asides of Johnny Truant, which often span several pages and are typed in Courier.[13] Other footnotes refer to still more footnotes, often even footnotes found earlier in the book. Even the position[14] of these referents (earlier) disturbs a linear progression of narrative and time. Thirdly, the idea of there being a 'true' beginning to the book *House of Leaves* is inconceivable for two reasons: the first being that near the end of Johnny Truant's narrative he describes being handed a manuscript with his name as the author and bearing the title *House of Leaves* by a group of musicians in a bar (as Shastri notes, the inclusion of this information in the book implies that we are reading (at least) a second edition), and the second being that *House of Leaves* did not begin life as a book. It was initially published online – lending significant credence to the idea of *House of Leaves* as hypertext.[4]

T.D's narrative does not progress linearly. It jumps back + forth

T.D's narrative begins 3 times – 1995 – 2002 – 2012 –

[3] "One of the initial symptoms of inauthenticity[8] that Hidden Writing produces is positive disintegration, or more accurately, collectivization of one author (voice) or an authorial elite, and its transformation to an untraceable shady collective of writers, a crowd." In his theory-fiction book *Cyclonopedia – Complicity with Anonymous Materials*, Reza Negarestani discusses (at a tangent to oil, his main (but famously slippery) subject) Hidden Writing, which he describes as "utilizing every plot hole, all problematics, every suspicious obscurity or repulsive wrongness as a new plot with a tentacled and autonomous mobility." In the case of the novel (or indeed, although not explicitly stated in *Cyclonopedia*, the filmic text) the structure of the whole is perforated by plot holes. A plot hole, in this instance, is not simply a mistake[9] but "conveys the activities of a subsurface life". The inference and development of such a subsurface life of texts is the task chosen by fanfiction authors[10], Black Metal Theorists[11], and archaeologists.[12] This work, however based in love, necessarily compromises the structure itself, hastens its deterioration – in Hidden Writing, "the central or main plot is reinvented solely in order that it may stealthily host, transport and nurture other plots."[15] *Cyclonopedia* itself contains a multi-layered narrative: while the bulk of the book is theoretical, it refers to the work of the fictional (or pseudonymous) Hamid Parsani; there are numerous footnotes both of a personal nature and indicating the unfinished nature of the manuscript, and of course, like Johnny Truant in *House of Leaves*, *Cyclonopedia* begins (ha!) with an establishing prose section from a secondary character who 'finds' and publishes the 'main body' of the work.

Fans can now create plot holes more easily in T.V shows by pausing the video and allowing themselves to examine in detail images that should only be viewed for a few seconds see for example the numerous iterations of the spiral motif in Marty's childrens drawings or the painting at the Harte house that shows up in the mental hospital visited by Rust + Marty

[4] In her essay *Mediating Print and Hypertext in Mark Danielewski's House of Leaves*, Sonya Hagler discusses the book and its position in "an emerging tradition of postmodern print fiction that exists in the liminal zone between print and hypertext cultures." While *House of Leaves* has in reality only one author, Danielewski's authority does not extend to guiding the reader through 'his' narrative(s). As Hagler puts it,

> the hypertext reader has the ability to 'choose his or her way through the metatext, to annotate text, written by others, and to create links between documents written by others' (Landow 90). Thus, hypertext narrative systems esteem the power of an intrusive, active reader over the traditional autonomy of the single author.

we have only illusion of choice we are just cycling through our lives like carts on a track

There are signposts, of course – footnotes,[29] colour-coding[16] – but there is no one way to travel between them. There are no wrong choices.[17] The text exists in the form crafted by the reader only because of their choices – which is to say that for the reader it does not exist in any other (/better/more authentic) form: "there is no reality independent of mediation", as Hagler quotes from Katherine Hayles' essay, *Saving the Subject: Remediation in House of Leaves*.[18] Hayles would claim that *House of Leaves* is as close to hypertext as print material can get, in fact she "identifies *House of Leaves* as an example of a 'Work as Assemblage, a cluster of related texts that quote, comment upon, amplify, and remediate one another'. (2),"[19] as quoted in *House of Leaves: Reading the Networked Novel*, by Jessica Pressman.[18] This description is especially apt considering the books siblings: a webpage and an album – vitally, the album (entitled *Haunted*) is an 'interpretation' of the book by someone calling herself Poe (as noted by Melanie Maria Lorke in *Liminal Semiotics: Boundary Phenomena in Romantics*).[20]

Now every T.V show has these siblings – along with deleted scenes, extra footage released through video sharing sites, behind the scenes photos + interviews with creators

[5] You are the reader. This is for you. **I am so fucking important**

[6] Shastri references Barthes (through Landow) to share his vision of the 'ideal text': "a galaxy of signifiers, not a structure of signifieds; it has no beginning; it is reversible; we gain access to it by several entrances, none of which can be authoritatively declared to be the real one." Despite the fact that many sections of the appendices are placeholders for missing (nonexistent) documents,[7] in the context of *House of Leaves* as hypertext[4] or metaphor for hypertext these could be viewed as Error pages or dead ends[18] which are, of course, an

consciousness is an error, a tragic mistep in evolution

aspect of networked assemblages which cannot be ignored. In the context of fanfiction, entrance to texts can be found outside the text itself, or indeed through the plot (holes) of an entirely different text (as in Alternate Universe (AU) fanfiction).

[7] While *House of Leaves* contains two pages of official credits, the huge volume of other works referenced (coming to more than eight A4 pages, according to Shastri) are entirely fictional, foremost among these being the film (*The Navidson Record*) to which Zampano's book *The Navidson Record*[21] refers, and the book William Navidson reads within this film (*House of Leaves*). Similarly to Negarestani's use of Parsani,[2] most of the fictional books referenced are brought up to support Zampano's opinions on his subject. Regardless, they lead to nothing real, and like the Appendices of missing material are dead ends.[19]

Rust is Pizzolatto's Parsani

* unlike a traditional sequel, these fics may take their starting point anywhere on the canon timeline, not just at the end (leading to divergent endings).[17]

IS T.D inauthentic because it quotes from other pessimistic texts?

[8] Complicity with anonymous materials.[16] Interestingly, as noted by Shastri[2], the first line of *The Navidson Record* (beginning #3 of *House of Leaves*) calls attention to its own inauthenticity: "While enthusiasts and detractors will continue to empty entire dictionaries attempting to describe or deride it, 'authenticity' still remains the word most likely to stir a debate." Perhaps even more interestingly, there are no such enthusiasts or detractors.[7]

[9] "Mistakes are the portals of discovery," – James Joyce. In relation to fanfiction[10] 'mistakes' in the creation of film or television such as production problems – actors unavailable, writers' strikes etc. – can have a huge impact on what appears onscreen (and what that implies for the 'subsurface life'[3] of the text). In her analysis of *Star Trek* fanfic *The Learning Curve*, Mary Ellen compares the creation of gap-filling fanfiction to a scientific hypothesis: "The expression on the actors' faces are data – they are sense experiences, but they make no sense without a theory."[17]

Rust's interview technique
everything is written on the face

[10] 'Fanfiction' refers to any prose work based on existing texts (literary or otherwise). It is (as of February 2014) referred to by fandom[23] participants as 'fanfic'. Fanfic can serve multiple purposes with regards to the 'canon' or 'source narrative' that informs it, including, but not limited to: continuing a completed text (as in a sequel*); explaining gaps in narrative;[24] augmenting or embellishing existing scenes or stories; developing and embellishing 'backstory' implied (by its mention or its absence) by the canon [meta]; hypothesising on romantic relationships alluded to (or absent from) canon [shipping[27]]; hypothesising on sexual

relationships featuring canon characters [previously referred to as 'lemon' – term not in use at time of writing]; imagining an average, uneventful (although sometimes specific) occasion involving one or more canon character(s) [drabble]; placing characters from one narrative into another fictional universe or situation [Alternate Universe – AU],[25] and so on. Generally speaking, fanfiction does not enjoy mainstream cultural status (unless it is disguised as 'profic': e.g. The multiple recent reinterpretations of Sherlock Holmes stories; the MTV series *Teen Wolf*, based on the 1980s MTV movie of the same name; *Torchwood*;[24] Dante's *Divine Comedy*; 'reboots' of science-fiction and comic book movies, gritty or otherwise; *Fifty Shades of Gray* etc.)

T.D is fanfic or pro-Fic

[11] Black Metal Theory (BMT) is a field of non-standard philosophy, ostensibly created in 2009 by Nicola Masciandaro. BMT both uses Black Metal (BM) music to interrogate theory, and theorises on Black Metal – sometimes doing neither, preferring to focus on a particular theme[34] relevant to both, or using the model of music-as-theory with other texts (films, fiction books etc.). BMT has an uneasy relationship with BM and its proponents (metalheads).[35] Its first public event, a para-academic symposium featuring both academics and musicians, Hideous Gnosis, provided the source material for its first printed piece.[20] The book features a call for future entries to commentary-focused publication *Glossator* by Negarestani[3] and Masciandaro entitled *Black Metal Commentary*. In essence, *Black Metal Commentary* compares the literary practice of commentary to Black Metal music under several distinct headings. Some of these are especially pertinent to the commentary/Hidden Writing fanfiction provides on its source material.

The structure of T.D means that Rust + Marty are providing Commentary on events OR on narrative

For example Varg Vikernes Theorises Black Metal in his recent YouTube series World of Darkness but would never admit (probably) to being a Black Metal Theorist

> Vacuum/Void/Abyss: BM [Black Metal] and commentary share concern with explicitly spatial forms of e[illegible]ness and absence, and with the horror/jo[illegible]ativity of being before them.[13]
>
> (...) • Liminality/Marginality: BM and commentary situate themselves, and derive power by operating from, margins of genre, history, ideology, knowledge. Both enjoy 'unofficial' cultural status (...) Safe from attack in a space of irrelevance, yet therefore capable of perfect incursions, the most dangerous unrecognizable raids.[28]

True Detective 'Form + Void' Episode 8

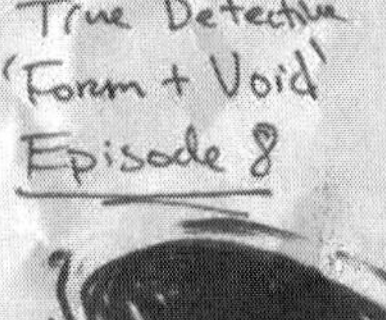

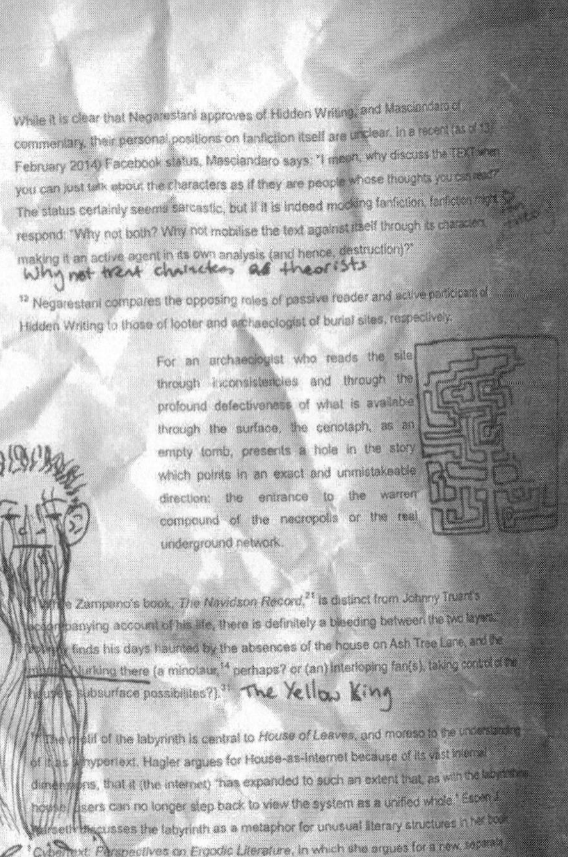

While it is clear that Negarestani approves of Hidden Writing, and Masciandaro of commentary, their personal positions on fanfiction itself are unclear. In a recent (as of 13 February 2014) Facebook status, Masciandaro says: "I mean, why discuss the TEXT when you can just talk about the characters as if they are people whose thoughts you can read?" The status certainly seems sarcastic, but if it is indeed mocking fanfiction, fanfiction might respond: "Why not both? Why not mobilise the text against itself through its characters, making it an active agent in its own analysis (and hence, destruction)?"

Why not treat characters as theorists

[12] Negarestani compares the opposing roles of passive reader and active participant of Hidden Writing to those of looter and archaeologist of burial sites, respectively:

> For an archaeologist who reads the site through inconsistencies and through the profound defectiveness of what is available through the surface, the cenotaph, as an empty tomb, presents a hole in the story which points in an exact and unmistakeable direction: the entrance to the warren compound of the necropolis or the real underground network.

While Zampano's book, *The Navidson Record*,[21] is distinct from Johnny Truant's accompanying account of his life, there is definitely a bleeding between the two layers. Johnny finds his days haunted by the absences of the house on Ash Tree Lane, and the monster lurking there (a minotaur,[14] perhaps? or (an) interloping fan(s), taking control of the house's subsurface possibilites?).[31] The Yellow King

The motif of the labyrinth is central to *House of Leaves*, and moreso to the understanding of it as a hypertext. Hagler argues for House-as-Internet because of its vast internal dimensions, that it (the internet) "has expanded to such an extent that, as with the labyrinthine house, users can no longer step back to view the system as a unified whole." Espen J. Aarseth discusses the labyrinth as a metaphor for unusual literary structures in her book *Cybertext: Perspectives on Ergodic Literature*, in which she argues for a new, separate designation for nonlinear literature – the cybertext. Her vision of the ergodic form of literature is one in which, like a game, "nontrivial effort is required to allow the reader to traverse the text." In fact, she contends that "the cybertext *is* a game-world or world-game; it is possible explore, get lost, and discover secret paths in these texts, not metaphorically, but through the topological structures of the textual machinery."[32] Her distinction between the reader of standard literature and the reader of the cybertext is in the consequence of their interaction with the text; the cybertextual reader plays a high-stakes game with narrative and always risks losing. As Aarseth describes,

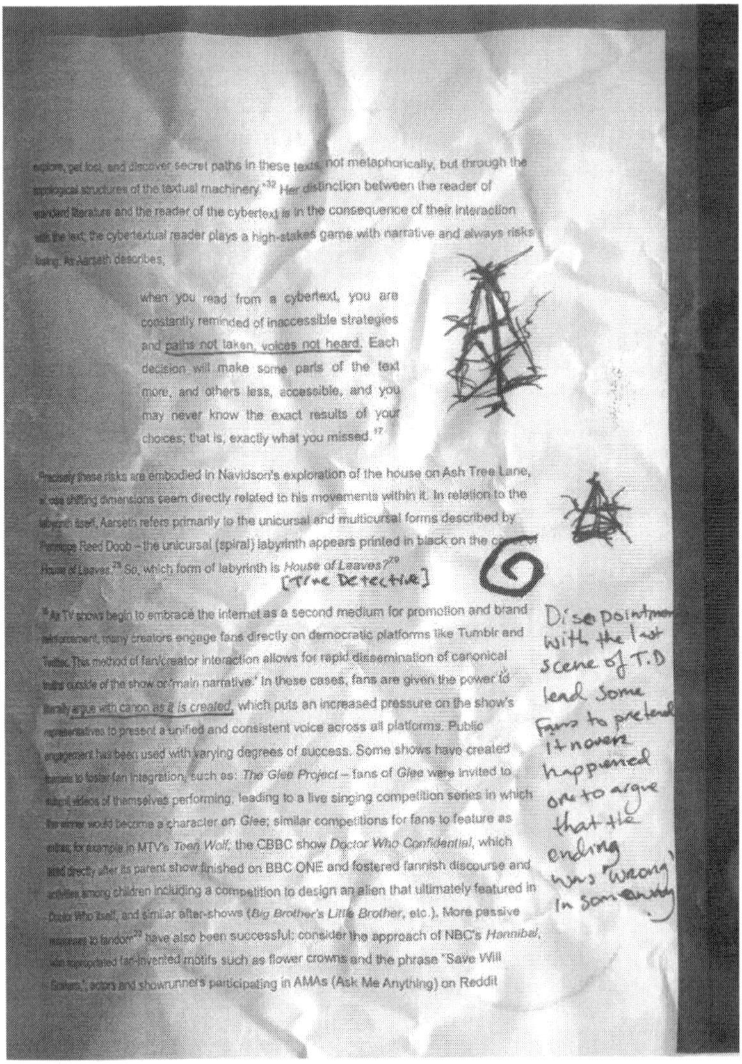

> when you read from a cybertext, you are constantly reminded of inaccessible strategies and paths not taken, voices not heard. Each decision will make some parts of the text more, and others less, accessible, and you may never know the exact results of your choices; that is, exactly what you missed.[17]

Precisely these risks are embodied in Navidson's exploration of the house on Ash Tree Lane, whose shifting dimensions seem directly related to his movements within it. In relation to the labyrinth itself, Aarseth refers primarily to the unicursal and multicursal forms described by Penelope Reed Doob – the unicursal (spiral) labyrinth appears printed in black on the cover of *House of Leaves*.[28] So, which form of labyrinth is *House of Leaves?*[29]

[True Detective]

[8] As TV shows begin to embrace the internet as a second medium for promotion and brand reinforcement, many creators engage fans directly on democratic platforms like Tumblr and Twitter. This method of fan/creator interaction allows for rapid dissemination of canonical truths outside of the show or 'main narrative.' In these cases, fans are given the power to literally argue with canon as it is created, which puts an increased pressure on the show's representatives to present a unified and consistent voice across all platforms. Public engagement has been used with varying degrees of success. Some shows have created spaces to foster fan integration, such as: *The Glee Project* – fans of *Glee* were invited to submit videos of themselves performing, leading to a live singing competition series in which the winner would become a character on *Glee*; similar competitions for fans to feature as extras, for example in MTV's *Teen Wolf*; the CBBC show *Doctor Who Confidential*, which aired directly after its parent show finished on BBC ONE and fostered fannish discourse and activities among children including a competition to design an alien that ultimately featured in *Doctor Who* itself, and similar after-shows (*Big Brother's Little Brother*, etc.). More passive responses to fandom[22] have also been successful: consider the approach of NBC's *Hannibal*, who appropriated fan-invented motifs such as flower crowns and the phrase "Save Will Graham," actors and showrunners participating in AMAs (Ask Me Anything) on Reddit

Disapointment with the last scene of T.D lead some Fans to pretend it never happened or to argue that the ending was 'wrong' in some way

Fan theories for True Detective became more interesting than the show. Fans were actually 'better' at forming the link between Lawnmower man + green eared monster.

responding to fan questions in real time under their own identity, and the statements of Joseph Fink, creator of popular fiction podcast *Welcome to Night Vale*, who overtly supports 'fanons' and 'headcanons' (ideas about the show fans believe to be canonically true but which are not 'officially' confirmed) and states that anyone's ideas of *Night Vale* and its characters are as true as his own until they are explicitly mentioned on the show. *Night Vale* also utilised their fanbase to fund the podcast itself, by selling fan-designed T-shirts (determined through an online vote). Indifference to fandom, at least its more extreme aspects, is also a popular option. The only 'bad' way to engage with fandom is to deny or suppress fan creation and the validity of fan idea – and even that is only 'bad' for canon. Consider Destiel – Dean/Castiel is the most popular 'ship'[27] in the fandom of TV show *Supernatural*, largely due to perceived homoromantic overtones in the onscreen interactions of the characters. On multiple occasions, actors, directors, writers, showrunners etc. have all vehemently dismissed the possibility of 'Destiel' ever being possible, ever, in any universe. However, *Supernatural* is aware of a need to cater to its audience, and so homoromantic subtext has been intentionally increased since the ship became common knowledge. In other words, the official canon has been compromised as a result of fan/creator interaction. *Supernatural* was doomed to inauthenticity[8] from the moment official creators engaged with fans – even through official denial of its validity. Hidden Writing[3] has made *Supernatural* complicit in its own positive disintegration.

Pizzolatto's ears splitting in point was weaker on reflection than the online theory of green earmuffs. Fan connections between ~~[illegible]~~ ~~[illegible]~~ Laurie + her father + the Yellow King never materialised in the show even though the clues were there.

[16] In the full-colour edition of *House of Leaves*, the three colours used correspond with the traditional colours of online hyperlinks. Blue, the colour of unvisited links, is used for every printing of the word 'house', and additionally to outline one of the labyrinthine footnotes spanning multiple pages – this serves, among other things, to make the reader aware that despite the writings about the book about the film about the house, the house is still a mystery, an absence.[31] Red, the colour of active links, is used to print sections of The Navidson Report that Zampano had crossed out (but Johnny Truant insisted on including regardless) – the 'activity' could obviously refer to the 'in-progress' nature of these sections, or could show, as Hagler suggests, that "Danielewski acknowledges the loss of authorial control that emerges in traditional hypertext." Purple, the colour of visited links, is used to evoke memory, linked narratively with Johnny Truant's mother Pelafina throughout the book, and also for one struck line in Chapter XXI.

The same could be said for T.D's mysterious cult

[17] *The Learning Curve* is an unfinished hypertext *Star Trek* fan novel by internet author raku, set between the narratives of films *Star Trek IV: The Voyage Home* and *Star Trek V: The Final Frontier* (argued by many to be the worst *Star Trek* film ever made). It is discussed at length in

The amount of references to other texts within T.D means that any analysis of the show turns it in to a hypertext. By exploring for example 'The King in Yellow' the fan creates a parallel narrative or to go one step further + create fanfic of The King in Yellow

The Learning Curve: Hypertext, Fan Fiction, and the Calculus of Human Nature by Mary Ellen. In the style of a role-playing game or choose-your-own adventure novel, readers are required to make active choices that influence the direction of the narrative. Movement through the hypertext was determined by links in three colours. Green links involved no choice on behalf of the reader. Blue links (traditionally the colour of unvisited links in hypertext) represented "unweighted choices" i.e. Seemingly insignificant story details "giving no information about the consequences, such as: turn right or turn left." Red links were weighted choices (e.g. Kirk will die, Kirk will not die etc.). The blue 'unweighted' decisions can have as great an impact on key plot points as the red 'weighted' decisions, which reflected the underlying message of *The Learning Curve* (according to Ellen): "that life-altering choices are as apparently simple and uninformative as left versus right, that you cannot tell from the triviality of the choice how grave the consequences might be."[14]

Rust's choices through the labyrinth at the end of T.D are unweighted because either way he must end up in the centre for the final show-down.

[18] The research for this essay (i.e. the one you are currently reading) was somewhat impeded by the inaccessibility of certain documents (e.g. Katherine Hayles, Jessica Pearsman). Access, in this case, means free access. While such a failure would generally be associated with the term 'gaps in knowledge', it seems most appropriate here to use the cliche of 'meeting a brick wall' or 'dead end' – if Negarestani's plot holes are the means by which truths travel, and the empty (of both items and explanations) hallways of *House of Leaves* are the spaces in which the reader creates her understanding of the text, then these withheld writings (and their withheld plot holes) restrict such creativity. The issues of cost and access are also at the heart of fanfiction.[20]

[19] Calls to mind the 'arcwork' of arcadian Black Metal[11] musician Hunter Hunt-Hendrix, a theoretical music venture in which he forgoes (the authority/responsibility of) single authorship and claims all the discourse, good and bad, around the music of his band Liturgy as part of one larger narrative. The music is not complete (real) without the context of its audience reception (refer again to Hayles' comment on reality).[4]

Similarly the discussion about T.D – and therefore this book – can be seen as a larger narrative

[20] Lorke's book analysing boundaries in Romantic literature calls to mind the comments section included in Black Metal Theory book Hideous Gnosis[11] in which someone using the handle 'raw, obsolete.' comments: "It's hard to imagine that Theory can bring much to Black Metal, a fundamentally Romantic and anti-/pre-Theoretic activity."[35]

[21] *The Navidson Record* is a document discussing and analysing a film of the same name. It forms the main body of the book *House of Leaves*, assembled from notes written by

Zampano,[22] found after his death by our narrator, Johnny Truant. *The Navidson Record* (film) follows Pulitzer Prize winning photographer Will Navidson and his family as they move into a new house on Ash Tree Lane. Things begin to appear strange when they realise that the internal dimensions of the house exceed the external by a quarter of an inch. As new and larger spaces begin to appear, Navidson and companions embark on a series of Explorations into these spaces, which are subject to change at any moment. The largest dimension documented by Navidson is a staircase over three times deeper than the Earth's diameter. Despite the massive size of these enclosures, the house is empty of any furniture or ornament, leading Hagler to describe it as "an ever-shifting, labyrinthine void of colossal proportions."[14]

[22] 'Written by Zampano' is perhaps a misleading turn of phrase – Zampano was totally blind, and dictated the book to various young women (further muddying the idea of a single authorial voice).[3] His blindness also calls into question his analysis of the film, a visual text – although not as much as the fact that there is no such film as *The Navidson Record*, neither in the reader's world nor the world of *House of Leaves*.[7]

[23] Fandom – a portmanteau literally meaning 'fanatic domain'. Refers to fan communities, including their members and their activities – including creation of new narratives around the object of their fanaticism (often texts such as novels or television series, extending to bands,[19] objects,individuals etc.). Fandom in the internet age is characterised by the horde. While still composed of disparate individuals, there is often the impression of a hive-mind, albeit a haunted or schizophrenic one. This is enacted through such elements of fandom as 'fanon' (alterations or additions to 'canon' accepted as true by fandom at large); the castigation of certain fans for their unquestioning support of problematic elements of canon (associated with the upsurge of sociopolitical discourse in fandom spaces) – these arguments are internally referred to as 'fandom wank'. And of course, there is the fact that not all participants in fandom write (or read) fanfiction, but the publication of fanfiction is always an addition to fandom. The response of canon creators (in literature: author; in film and television: showrunners, writers, script supervisors, directors, editors, producers, actors, camera operators, broadcasters et al.) to fandom varies, but growing attempts have been made to acknowledge and engage with fandom in recent years, largely due to the democratic nature of such internet platforms as Twitter.[16] Especially with regard to the ongoing nature of TV series, fandom has the opportunity to comment directly on media as it is being created, rather than being merely speculation after the fact.

A billion eyed + tentacled super intelligence

T.D (or discussion thereof) is likely referred to by some as pessimist wank

If fandom is the 'fanatic domain' + fanfic is 'fan fiction', then what is 'fan analysis'?

[24] It has been noted that UK TV series *Torchwood* acts as fanfiction of its parent show *Doctor Who* in that it provides an explanation for the whereabouts of character Captain Jack Harkness in his absence from Doctor Who between two appearances, many episodes apart. This was documented by Richard Berger in his essay *Screwing Aliens and Screwing with Aliens: Torchwood Slashes*[27] *the Doctor*. Occupying a bizarre position between 'fanfic' and 'profic', *Torchwood* is transgressive in many ways; the brainchild of Russell T. Davies, progenitor of the regeneration of *Doctor Who* in 2005, *Torchwood* was conceived in 2002 as a UK equivalent to *Buffy the Vampire Slayer* before taking on its ultimate role as a sexy side-narrative in the *Who* universe. Unlike some TV creators, Davies is far from ignorant to the world of fanfiction – like his fellow *Doctor Who* writer, Mark Gatiss, he was a fanfiction author before gaining 'official' success. Although the events of *Torchwood* are not explicitly referred to or acknowledged in the main narrative, *Doctor Who*, the series effectively smuggled darker themes (and a whole (! hole!) lot of sex) into the official universe of the popular TV beast. In Berger's view, "*Torchwood* is the 'profound' text to *Doctor Who*'s 'sacred' one."[30] Appropriately, the show is literally set on the site of a rift in space and time.[33] It is the job of *Torchwood* to police what travels through this rift – because as we know, holes in fiction can never be blocked indefinitely, only monitored, and all weaken the surrounding environment.

[25] Idea of directing a film based on two books: separate indexes, typographies etc. – *Cyclonopedia*, Reza Negarestani[3]

or a T.V show based on multiple texts

An academic analysis of T.D would be seen to operate in the margins of Academia

[26] A marginal status can be seen as both a weakness and a strength. E.g. the derivative nature of fanfiction[10] adds to a public perception of the writing itself as poor quality or easier to create than something entirely generative. Additionally, fanfiction dances in the margins of legality – the protected copyright status (especially of ongoing source narratives such as TV series) precludes the publishing of fanfiction works through official channels, and hence being (widely) saleable products. As noted by Henry Jenkins in his seminal work *Textual Poachers: Television Fans and Participatory Culture*, fandoms will not abide fanfiction being sold for profit (a prime example being the online hatred of author Cassie Claire since her official success, connected to claims that aspects of official texts were lifted from her fan works) an attitude he claims "reflects less a generizable, political or economic resistance to capitalism than the desire to create forms of cultural production and distribution that reflect the mutuality of the fan community." And of course the extra-legal, extra-textual status of fanfiction fosters creativity; "...fanzine editors and writers remain more responsive than commercial producers to the desires and interests of their readership." An audience of creators, who know their source materials as well as or better than the ever-changing writers of official canon, are a

Aspects of T.D lifted from pessimist texts or possibly N.P's academic writing

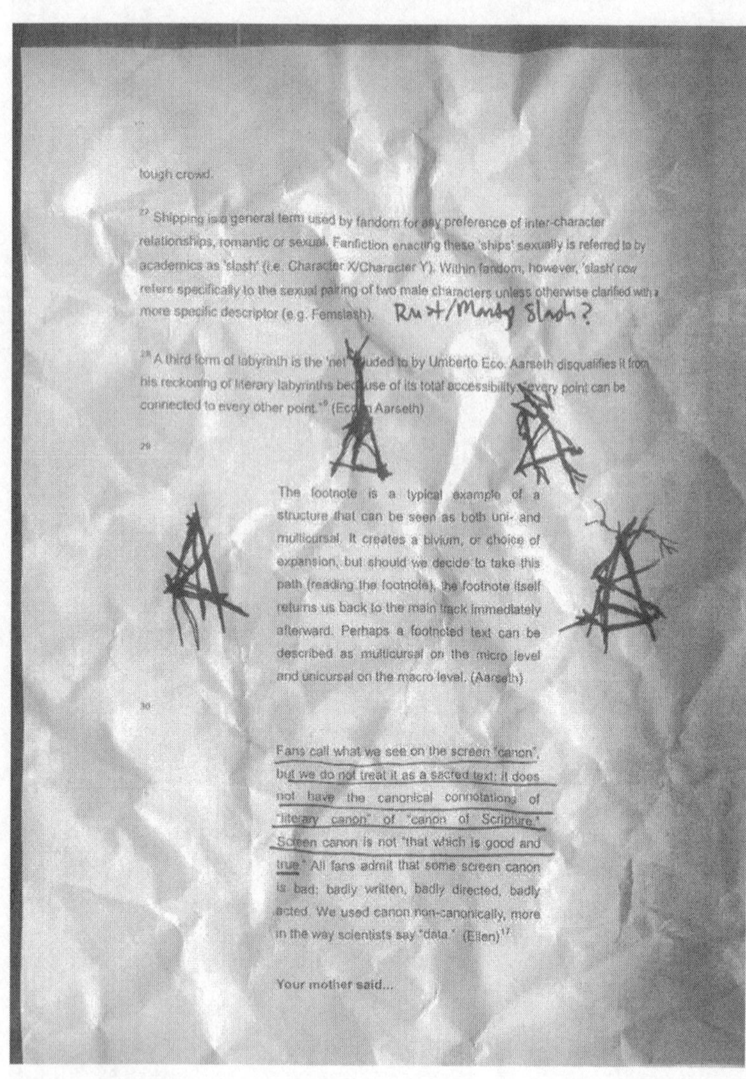

tough crowd.

[27] Shipping is a general term used by fandom for any preference of inter-character relationships, romantic or sexual. Fanfiction enacting these 'ships' sexually is referred to by academics as 'slash' (i.e. Character X/Character Y). Within fandom, however, 'slash' now refers specifically to the sexual pairing of two male characters unless otherwise clarified with a more specific descriptor (e.g. Femslash). Rust/Marty Slash?

[28] A third form of labyrinth is the 'net' alluded to by Umberto Eco. Aarseth disqualifies it from his reckoning of literary labyrinths because of its total accessibility: "every point can be connected to every other point."[9] (Eco in Aarseth)

29

> The footnote is a typical example of a structure that can be seen as both uni- and multicursal. It creates a bivium, or choice of expansion, but should we decide to take this path (reading the footnote), the footnote itself returns us back to the main track immediately afterward. Perhaps a footnoted text can be described as multicursal on the micro level and unicursal on the macro level. (Aarseth)

30

> Fans call what we see on the screen "canon", but we do not treat it as a sacred text: it does not have the canonical connotations of "literary canon" of "canon of Scripture." Screen canon is not "that which is good and true." All fans admit that some screen canon is bad: badly written, badly directed, badly acted. We used canon non-canonically, more in the way scientists say "data." (Ellen)[17]

Your mother said...

[Pessimist] [nihilist]

What a bunch of fucking ~~hipster~~ shit! Christ almighty. What is it with assholes having to build altars to every-fucking-thing? Falsers. All of you.

~~December 14, 2009 2:42 PM~~ (an online comment on announcement of ~~Black Metal Theory~~ symposium~~, presented as above in Hideous Gnosis)~~[35]

TRUE DETECTION

To do rigorous theology is to perforate the Divine's corpus with heresies. (Cyclonopedia, Negarestani)[3]

[31] "In terms of [Hidden Writing] the main plot is the map or the concentration blueprint of plot holes (the other plots). Every hole is a footprint left by at least one more plot, prowling underneath." Negarestani.[3] In *House of Leaves*, the initial layout of the house on Ash Tree Lane could be seen as: a blueprint for the 'labyrinthine void' it ultimately contains;[32] a site for the emergence of the other.[33]

Viewing the ~~map~~ house from (above) an extra-dimensional perspective

[32] It is a minuscule spatial discrepancy that first alerts Navidson to the strangeness of the house: the internal dimensions exceed the external by a quarter of an inch (echoed physically in the book cover, a quarter of an inch shorter than the pages). From this point on, unexpected architectural features of the house lead to passages the house's original dimensions cannot accommodate, and exploration only increases their incomprehensibility. The further Navidson intrudes into the depths of the house, the larger those depths seem to be.[34] He begins the film with the power of ownership, but sacrifices an almost-complete surface knowledge (save that quarter of an inch) of his house on the gamble that exploring it will lead to a knowledge of its entirety – or at least as complete a knowledge as *he*, Will Navidson, can ever claim.

The tensions at work in a cybertext, while not incompatible with those of narrative desire, are also something more: a struggle not merely for interpretative insight but also for narrative control: 'I want this text to tell my

I am so fucking important

story: the story that *could not be without me.'*
(Aarseth, emphasis her own)

[33] In his book *In the Dust of this Planet: Horror of Philosophy Vol. 1*, Eugene Thacker discusses the role of the 'magic circle' in literature as a place where the world(-in-itself) can reveal hidden aspects of itself – that is to say, reveal the hidden nature of things, without revealing their secrets and making them unhidden. Thacker is a Black Metal theorist,[11] and *In the Dust of this Planet* is a book that considers BMT with regard to the horror genre in literature and film.

y'know,
for kids

> Here the motif of the magic circle serves as a boundary between the natural and the supernatural, and the possible mediations between them that are made possible by the circle itself. Hence the magic circle is not only a boundary, but also a passage, a gateway, a portal, a flat circle, an endless loop

The magic circle can refer to an actual circle, or more specifically the summoning circle featured in so many horror films, but may also refer to any site where boundaries support the emergence of the other: "the screen, the tennis court, the court of justice, etc., all are in form and function play-grounds i.e. Forbidden spots, isolated, hedged round, hallowed, within which special rules obtain." T.V shows are magic/flat circles

[34] Themes of Black Metal Theory include, but are not limited to: rot, decay, darkness, oil, dust, ashes, the fly, the spider, night, subverted religious themes such as: Satanism, paganism, demons, the demonic, Baphomet, to name but a few. BMT has a certain amount of overlap with other philosophical themes and methods, including: geo-philosophy, accelerationism, pessimism, existentialism, medievalism, speculative realism etc. and various fictions

swarms
spirals

[35] Black Metal Theory (BMT) is charged by metalheads with the dual crimes of a) taking metal too seriously in assuming it has any value as theory and b) betraying an inherent trait of metal as a pure, pre-Theoretical entity. Most academics engaged in BMT writing, however, are metalheads themselves, their analysis a labour of love for their source material (you could call it 'fanalysis' but nobody does – yet). The BMT book *Hideous Gnosis* contains a section featuring online comments responding to the announcement of a BMT symposium. An exemplary exchange takes place between commenter Andreas Bauer and Nicola

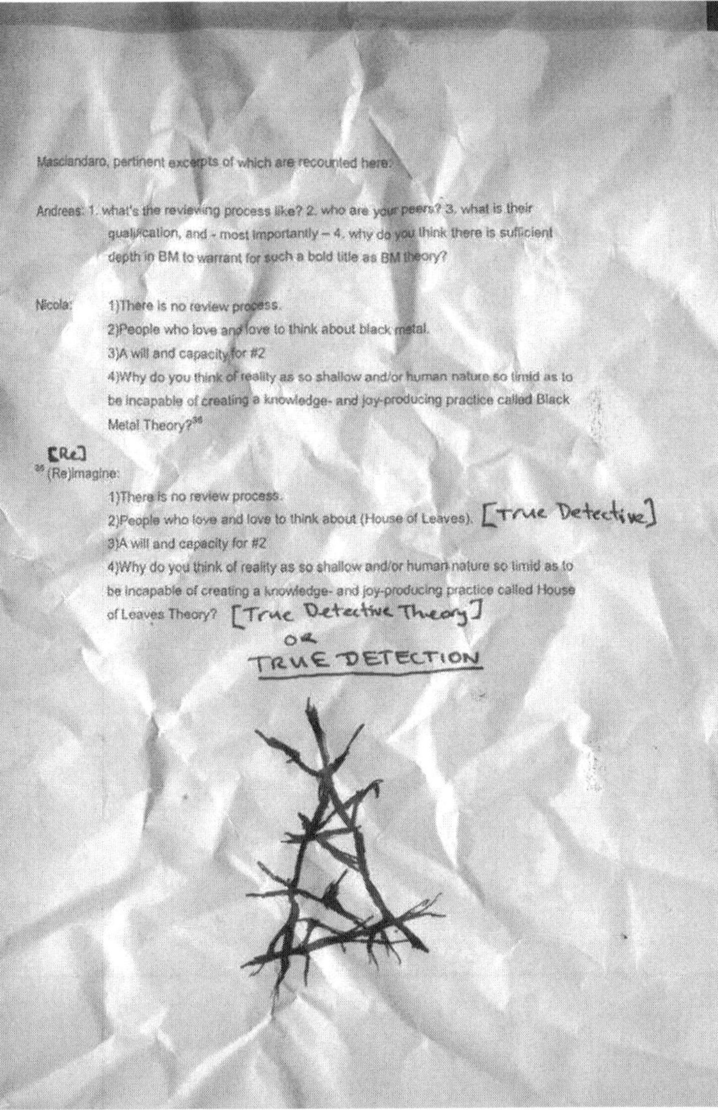
Masciandaro, pertinent excerpts of which are recounted here:

Andreas: 1. what's the reviewing process like? 2. who are your peers? 3. what is their qualification, and - most importantly – 4. why do you think there is sufficient depth in BM to warrant for such a bold title as BM theory?

Nicola: 1)There is no review process.
2)People who love and love to think about black metal.
3)A will and capacity for #2
4)Why do you think of reality as so shallow and/or human nature so timid as to be incapable of creating a knowledge- and joy-producing practice called Black Metal Theory?[35]

[Re]
[35] (Re)imagine:
1)There is no review process.
2)People who love and love to think about (House of Leaves). [True Detective]
3)A will and capacity for #2
4)Why do you think of reality as so shallow and/or human nature so timid as to be incapable of creating a knowledge- and joy-producing practice called House of Leaves Theory? [True Detective Theory]
OR
TRUE DETECTION

SCHISM

Printed in Great Britain
by Amazon.co.uk, Ltd.,
Marston Gate.